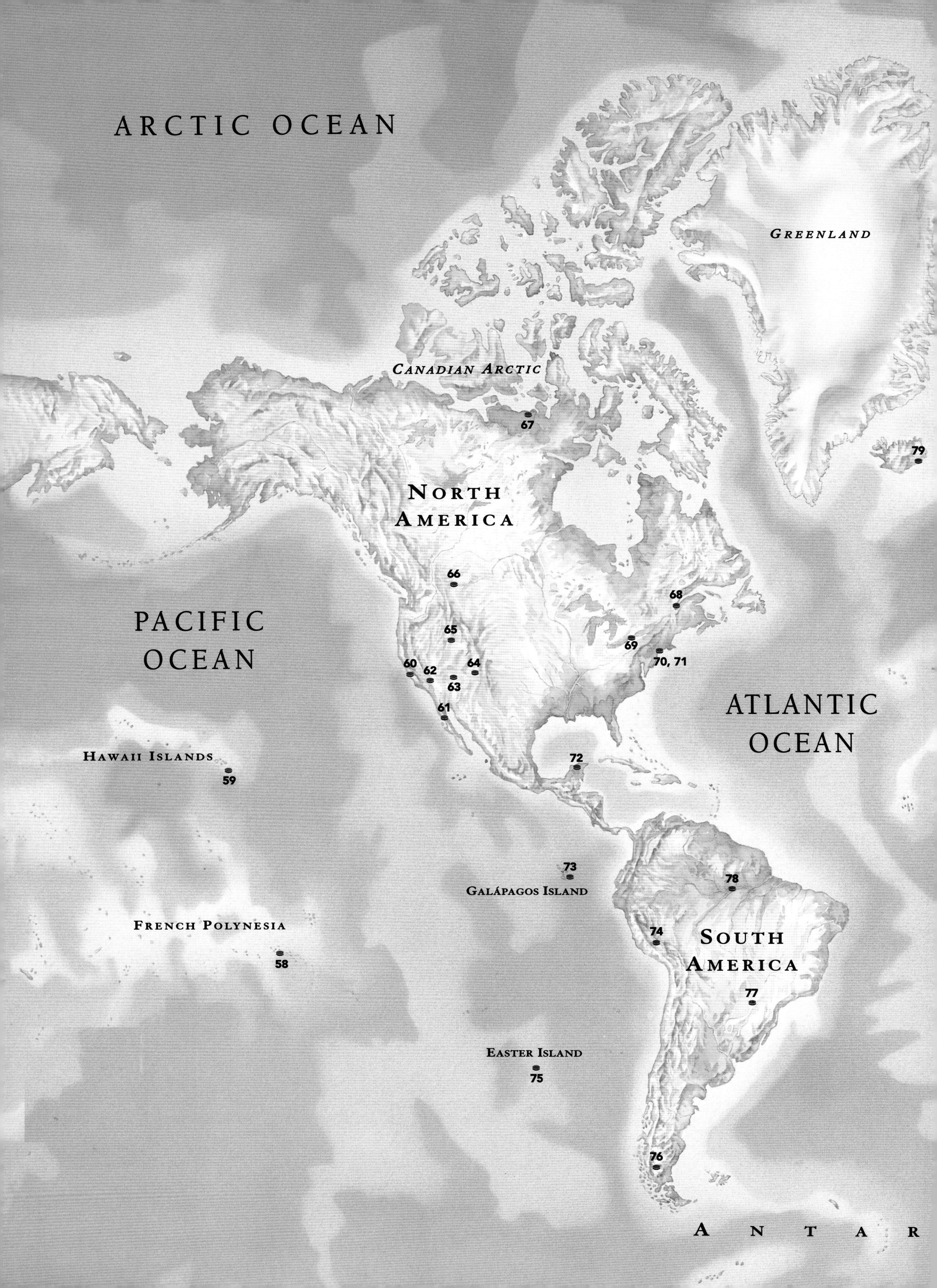

ARCTIC OCEAN

GREENLAND

CANADIAN ARCTIC

67

79

NORTH
AMERICA

66

68

PACIFIC
OCEAN

65

69

60   62   64

70, 71

63

61

ATLANTIC
OCEAN

72

HAWAII ISLANDS

59

73

GALÁPAGOS ISLAND

78

FRENCH POLYNESIA

74

SOUTH
AMERICA

58

77

EASTER ISLAND

75

76

A N T A R

ARCTIC OCEAN

N

ASIA

EUROPE

22

23

1

16

4-5-6   17   19

2   15   18

7   8   14

9   13

3   10

11-12   20   36   37

80   21   38

24   26   53

52   51

44   54

41   46

45   54

43

42   47

48   49

PACIFIC
OCEAN

28   39
29   40
25   35
27   50

AFRICA

33

34

INDIAN
OCEAN

32

30   31

AUSTRALIA

Great Barrier Reef

55   56

57

NEW
ZEALAND

C T I C

CONTENTS

PREFACE   PAGE   6

EUROPE

1. WESTMINSTER ABBEY -
   LONDON - UNITED KINGDOM   PAGE   8

2. MONT-SAINT-MICHEL - FRANCE   PAGE 12

3. SAGRADA FAMILIA CHURCH -
   BARCELONA - SPAIN   PAGE 14

4. NOTRE-DAME CATHEDRAL -
   PARIS - FRANCE   PAGE 18

5. EIFFEL TOWER - PARIS - FRANCE   PAGE 24

6. VERSAILLES - FRANCE   PAGE 26

7. CHAMBORD CHÂTEAU - FRANCE   PAGE 30

8. MONT BLANC - ITALY, FRANCE   PAGE 34

9. PORTOFINO - ITALY   PAGE 38

10. THE LEANING TOWER - PISA - ITALY   PAGE 40

11. THE COLOSSEUM - ROME - ITALY   PAGE 42

12. THE SISTINE CHAPEL - VATICAN CITY   PAGE 44

13. THE ST. FRANCIS BASILICA - ASSISI - ITALY   PAGE 48

14. ST. MARK'S BASILICA - VENICE - ITALY   PAGE 52

15. NEUSCHWANSTEIN - GERMANY   PAGE 58

16. UNTER DEN LINDEN - BERLIN - GERMANY   PAGE 62

17. STAROMESTSKÉ NÁMESTÍ - PRAGUE
    - CZECH REPUBLIC   PAGE 66

18. THE ROYAL CASTLE - BUDAPEST - HUNGARY   PAGE 68

19. THE OLD TOWN - KRAKÓW - POLAND   PAGE 70

20. THE PARTHENON - ATHENS - GREECE   PAGE 74

21. SANTORINI - GREECE   PAGE 76

22. THE HERMITAGE - ST. PETERSBURG - RUSSIA   PAGE 80

23. THE KREMLIN - MOSCOW - RUSSIA   PAGE 84

AFRICA

24. THE ROYAL PALACE, MOSQUE - FÈS - MOROCCO PAGE 90

25. SAHARA DESERT - LIBYA   PAGE 94

26. LEPTIS MAGNA - LIBYA   PAGE 98

27. ABU SIMBEL - EGYPT   PAGE 102

28. THE PYRAMIDS OF GIZA - CAIRO - EGYPT   PAGE 108

29. THE TEMPLE OF KARNAK - LUXOR - EGYPT   PAGE 112

30. THE SKELETON COAST - NAMIBIA   PAGE 116

31. OKAVANGO DELTA - BOTSWANA   PAGE 118

32. VICTORIA FALLS - ZIMBABWE, ZAMBIA   PAGE 122

33. NGORONGORO - TANZANIA   PAGE 124

34. KILIMANJARO - KENYA, TANZANIA   PAGE 128

35. RAS MOHAMMED - EGYPT   PAGE 130

ASIA

36. HAGHIA SOPHIA - ISTANBUL - TURKEY   PAGE 134

37. NEMRUD DAGH - TURKEY   PAGE 136

38. CAPPADOCIA - TURKEY   PAGE 138

39. THE DOME OF THE ROCK - JERUSALEM - ISRAEL PAGE 142

40. PETRA - JORDAN   PAGE 146

41. ISFAHAN - IRAN   PAGE 150

42. KHAJURAHO - INDIA   PAGE 152

TEXTS
CARLA SERRA
SILVIA BOMBELLI

GRAPHIC DESIGN
PATRIZIA BALOCCO LOVISETTI
PAOLA PIACCO

EDITORIAL DIRECTOR
VALERIA MANFERTO DE FABIANIS

EDITORIAL COORDINATION
ENRICO LAVAGNO
AMBRA PELLICCIA

43. THE TAJ MAHAL - AGRA - INDIA   PAGE 156

44. K2 - CHINA, PAKISTAN   PAGE 160

45. MOUNT EVEREST - NEPAL, CHINA   PAGE 162

46. THE POTALA - LHASA - AUTONOMOUS
REPUBLIC OF TIBET   PAGE 166

47. PAGAN - BURMA   PAGE 170

48. WAT PHRA KAEW - BANGKOK - THAILAND   PAGE 174

49. ANGKOR WAT - CAMBODIA   PAGE 178

50. BOROBODUR - JAVA - INDONESIA   PAGE 182

51. THE TERRACOTTA ARMY - XI'AN - CHINA   PAGE 186

52. THE FORBIDDEN CITY - BEIJING - CHINA   PAGE 192

53. THE GREAT WALL - CHINA   PAGE 198

54. THE GINZA DISTRICT - TOKYO - JAPAN   PAGE 200

OCEANIA

55. AYER'S ROCK AND THE OLGAS - AUSTRALIA   PAGE 204

56. GREAT BARRIER REEF - AUSTRALIA   PAGE 208

57. MOUNT COOK - NEW ZEALAND   PAGE 212

58. BORA-BORA - FRENCH POLYNESIA   PAGE 214

AMERICA

59. MT. KILAUEA - HAWAII - USA   PAGE 218

60. GOLDEN GATE BRIDGE - SAN FRANCISCO -
CALIFORNIA - USA   PAGE 222

61. BAJA CALIFORNIA - MEXICO   PAGE 226

62. LAS VEGAS - NEVADA - USA   PAGE 230

63. THE GRAND CANYON - ARIZONA - USA   PAGE 234

64. MONUMENT VALLEY - UTAH, ARIZONA - USA PAGE 238

65. THE YELLOWSTONE NATIONAL
PARK GEYSERS - WYOMING - USA   PAGE 242

66. BANFF AND JASPER NATIONAL PARKS -
CANADA   PAGE 248

67. THE CANADIAN ARCTIC - CANADA   PAGE 252

68. QUÉBEC CITY - CANADA   PAGE 256

69. NIAGARA FALLS - USA, CANADA   PAGE 260

70. MANHATTAN - NEW YORK CITY - USA   PAGE 262

71. THE STATUE OF LIBERTY -
NEW YORK CITY - USA   PAGE 268

72. CHICHÉN ITZÁ - MEXICO   PAGE 270

73. GALÁPAGOS ISLANDS - ECUADOR   PAGE 274

74. MACHU PICCHU - PERU   PAGE 278

75. EASTER ISLAND - CHILE   PAGE 280

76. CERRO FITZ ROY - ARGENTINA   PAGE 282

77. IGUASSÚ FALLS - ARGENTINA, BRAZIL   PAGE 284

78. THE AMAZON RIVER BASIN - BRAZIL   PAGE 288

EUROPE

79. THE VATNAJÖKULL GLACIER - ICELAND   PAGE 292

80. THE ALHAMBRA - GRANADA - SPAIN   PAGE 294

INDEX   PAGE 300

4 from left to right At dusk, the slender spire of fabled Mont-Saint-Michel abbey is mirrored in the ebb tide off the Normandy coast. The Sphinx was carved out of the Giza plateau during the reign of Khufu or Kafre (4th Dynasty, 2575-2476 B.C.), and was first restored by Merneptah (1213-1203 B.C.), a son of Ramesses II.

The Pagan valley, in Myanmar, is dotted with grandiose Buddhist shrines (stupas), which were built from 847 to 1298, before the Mongols invaded the country. The rounded Olga Hills, in Australia's Northern territory are a natural sanctuary for the Aborigines, who consider them to be the terrestrial manifestations of various mythical figures. When

completed in 1930, New York's Chrysler Building was the world's tallest (1048 ft/391 m), but was soon surpassed by the Empire State Building. The Vatnajökull glacier, Iceland's largest (3240 sq. mi/8100 sq. km. of ice) seen through North Atlantic fog. The glacier is linked to Hvannadalshnukur (6357 ft/2119 m). Iceland's highest peak.

PREFACE

Amazing Places is a quick trip to the most beautiful sights in the world, described and illustrated so that you can enjoy them while comfortably seated in your armchair.

This book is therefore a sort of proposal for armchair tourism *à la carte*: readers can choose what they want according to their taste and mood and give free rein to their imagination thanks to the elegant photographs and the brief but inspiring texts. Our aim here is not to describe the wonders in detail, but to stimulate you to search for more information about them.

The aim of this book is to call attention to at least some of the treasures considered indispensable for humanity (the UNESCO World Heritage List has over 700 of these), providing a sample of the inspiring beauty that surrounds us.

Our voyage begins in London, and then proceeds to the Royal Palace in Budapest, the Hermitage in St. Petersburg, the Prado in Madrid, the Leaning Tower of Pisa, the St. Francis Basilica in Assisi and the Colosseum in Rome, to mention only a few sights. We then head slowly toward the Orient to discover natural treasures such as Everest and K2, eternal temples such as the Taj Mahal in India and the Wat Phra Kaew in Bangkok, the Friday Mosque of Isfahan, and then go to Africa for the pyramids of Giza, the Sahara Desert and the Victoria Falls. In America you can stop at Yellowstone to admire the geysers, see the Golden Gate Bridge in San Francisco or visit the Canadian Arctic region. And lastly, there is Oceania, with Mt. Cook, Bora Bora and Ayer's Rock – far distant Pacific lands.

These are only some of the wonders that await you. All you need to do is turn the pages.

6 The curtain rises: five acts incorporating fifteen scenes present the around-the-world adventures of Phileas Fogg and Passepartout. In the late 19th century, Verne and the playwright Adolphe d'Ennery adapted the famous book for the stage. The poster's ocean liner, racing train, Oriental parade, and savages on the attack whetted the audience'appetite.

8-9 For a thousand years, Westminster Abbey, a former Benedictine abbey rebuilt in the Gothic style, has been the venue of great state religious and political occasions, including coronations.

8 bottom left The solid façade of the abbey was built in the 18th century; it has twin bell towers that soar over either side of the porch.

8 bottom right The exterior decoration displays the gilded crests of England's great aristocratic families. In the center is the royal coat of arms; the motto "Dieu et mon droit," is attributed to Henry VI (1422-61).

9 The left bell tower has a large enameled clock and decorative sculptures of saints and prophets.

WESTMINSTER ABBEY
LONDON, UNITED KINGDOM

The real name of this historic landmark is the Collegiate Church of St. Peter in Westminster, but for British subjects and tourists alike it is Westminster Abbey, or the western abbey, as distinct from St. Mary-of-the-Graces, which lies to the east and is hence Eastminster. The original Romanesque abbey was built for a community of Benedictine monks. Destroyed by the Danes and badly damaged by the fire of 1298, it was restored and rebuilt in French Gothic style. The Neo-Gothic façade with two bell towers (225 ft/68 m high) was added later, in the 18th century.

Westminster is synonymous with the royal family: since 1066, with the William the Conqueror, the coronation of almost all the English kings has been celebrated here. The exquisitely wrought throne dates from the early Middle Ages; the panels and props are decorated with architectural motifs (arches, quatrefoils, etc.) and richly embellished with many layers of gold leaf and other colors. Eighteen British rulers are buried in the abbey, as are scientists, writers and musicians such as Charles Darwin, Sir Isaac Newton, Ben Jonson, and Henry Purcell, as well as military leaders who demonstrated courage in colonial campaigns and in the defense of the nation. The entire transept, to the right and left of the high altar, is occupied by the memorials and tombs of great figures of English literature; the Poets' Corner has those of Lord Byron, Chaucer, Tennyson, Mary Shelley, Dickens, Kipling and T.S. Eliot.

Westminster Abbey is certainly large – 515 ft (156 m) long and 112 ft (34 m) wide – but its record-making feature is its Gothic nave, which is 112 ft (34 m) high and is the loftiest Gothic nave in the United Kingdom. Entering via the west portal, immediately to your right is St. George's Chapel, once a baptistery and is now a First World War memorial. Farther along, one is struck by the beautiful *Last Supper*, a glass mosaic by Antonio Salviati over the high altar. Just behind this are the Royal Chapels; the main one, with three aisles and magnificent fan vaulting, is dedicated to Henry VII.

But there are other surprises in store. By going along the south aisle and through the large cloister, you

10 top Almost all of these polychromed stained-glass windows in the Abbey's main façade have had to be replaced with modern stained glass. The panels illustrate the saints in Paradise.

10 center These royal tombs are situated in a side chapel. Besides nobles, the cathedral also has the tombs of 'common citizens,' mostly greats of English literature such as Geoffrey Chaucer, who lies in the Poets' Corner.

10 bottom The highly decorated half-wall dividing the nave from the choir is one of the most beautiful in the Abbey. On each side, the large niche contains a commemorative sculpture. Visible above are the pipes of the majestic organ.

10-11 The monks used the choir for their prayers, now the 44-member Abbey choir is seated there.

EUROPE

reach the Chapter House, an octagonal space known as the "cradle of free Parliaments" since the Great Council met here in 1257. From that time and up to the 17th century Parliament met here. The cloister also affords access to the Pyx Chapel, which has the oldest altar in the abbey and once housed a casket with the samples used to establish the weights and values of the British coins.

Another attraction worth a visit is the Norman Undercroft, or crypt, which, besides being the home of the Westminster Museum, boasts a bizarre collection of life-size wax statues that are realistic portraits of famous figures of the past that 'took part' in the funerals celebrated in the church. The statue of Edward III is on the other hand made of wood.

Going back into the abbey proper, you can admire the walls, which are made of numerous panes of glass that cover the area between the piers and the vault, which is supported by a single central pier. The entire surface, with interlace carving, conceals the supporting structure.

Due to a strange but intentional optical effect, the vault seems to plunge downward and then float upward again.

12-13 The islet off the Normandy coast was named for the Archangel Michael, to whom the sanctuary is dedicated. Mont-Saint-Michel is a famous pilgrimage site and was once the headquarters of the Knights of St. Michael.

12 bottom left Daily high tides isolate Mont-Saint-Michel from the mainland; low tides provide access across the wet sands

12 bottom right The green island is situated in the Gulf of Saint Malo. Rising in the center is the 12th-century Gothic-style La Merveille complex, built thanks to donations from King Philip Augustus.

13 The sanctuary and the cloister of Mont-Saint-Michel. Monks live year-round in the Abbey, which also accomodates people making retreats.

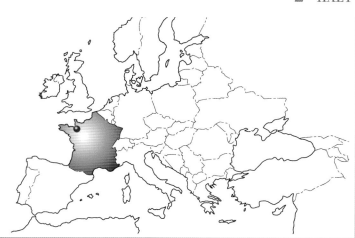

MONT-SAINT-MICHEL
FRANCE

Mont-Saint-Michel, which is accessible only via a single causeway, lies on a stretch of sand off Normandy and is isolated daily because of the tides, which rise with truly amazing speed. In fact, over the centuries, many pilgrims have been surprised by the currents and have lost their lives. According to legend, in the early 7th century, St. Aubert, bishop of Avranches, dreamed that the Archangel Michael had asked him to build an oratory on a cliff. He had the same dream again and, convinced, began the construction on an islet then known as Mont Tombe. This is modern-day Mont-Saint-Michel, a small island in southwest Normandy that every year draws tourists and pilgrims from all parts of the world. The village at the foot of the monastery was founded as a resting place for the pilgrims visiting the sanctuary and then expanded along the road that goes from the beach to the top of the islet.

Since the time the oratory was constructed there have been many sieges, and the buildings have collapsed and been rebuilt and enlarged many times. What has remained almost totally intact is the Grande Rue, the narrow cobblestoned street that runs from the beach to the island, lined with cafés, refreshment bars and souvenir shops – in some ways like the Middle Ages, when the pilgrims stopped for refreshment and collected stones, shells and cobblestones as souvenirs of their spiritual journey. Only in 1203, after a terrible fire had damaged the abbey's Romanesque church, did large-scale construction work begin, resulting in a complex on the north side of the hill, La Merveille (the marvel), consisting of two massive Gothic structures three stories high.

In the east wing, on the ground floor, is the Aumônerie, where the monks offered hospitality to the pilgrims and gave alms to the poor. On the first floor there was the Salle des Hôtes or guest quarters, and on the top floor was the monks' refectory, illuminated by the light that filtered through the tall ogee windows embedded in the walls. The west wing of La Merveille has a warehouse and the Salle des Chevaliers or Knights' Hall, which is divided into four aisles separated by rows of stone columns with capitals. Once the monks used this space as a scriptorium to study or to copy texts by hand (an "amanuensis" is the word for a person who hand-copies a document). Only around 1470 did this become the Hall of the Knights of Saint-Michel, an order established by King Louis XI. This was the period when a small army consisting of about 100 knights settled at the monastery to defend it from the English. This was also the time when the first ramparts were built to reinforce the defensive gates of the village. Lastly, above the Salle des Chevaliers is the monastery proper, where the absolute silence is pleasantly interrupted only by the sound of the waves of the sea, which often surge to a considerable height.

The entire Mont-Saint-Michel complex reminds one of a fairy tale because of the Gothic architecture, and because on foggy days it has something ethereal about it, and because viewed from the mainland it appears to be suspended between the water and the sky. The idea of a peaceful atmosphere is shattered somewhat if one thinks of the treacherous tides and the attacks Mont-Saint-Michel was subject to over the centuries – from the English during the Hundred Years' War to the Huguenot assaults in the late 1500s. During the French Revolution and up to 1863 the island was actually converted into a prison area. Only in the 1920s did Mont-Saint-Michel resume its religious role, even though very few monks have stayed there to animate the spiritual life of the abbey. However, the faithful are quite happy with a symbol, the gilded votive statue of the Archangel Michael that dominates the scene atop the campanile.

14 Detail of one of the façades of the Sagrada Familia, the church designed by Antoni Gaudí. This impressive structure, which is the symbol of Barcelona, was begun in 1882 - and was never finished because it was too costly. Work continues.

15 The original design of the Sagrada Familia was lost during the Spanish Civil War bombardments. The Nativity façade is the only one conceived and built by Gaudí.

SAGRADA FAMILIA CHURCH
BARCELONA, SPAIN

Although it is an unfinished work, the impressive cathedral that rises up in the north district is to all intents and purposes the symbol of Barcelona. The construction of the Sagrada Familia began in 1882 after a design by the brilliant architect Antoni Gaudí, who worked on it for more than 40 years, up to the time of his death. When the construction yard was opened Gaudí moved his studio there and then settled there. After his death in 1926 the work proceeded slowly and was interrupted on occasion, for example, during the Spanish Civil War. It resumed in 1952 under the supervision of another architect, who was obliged to modify the original project plans, which had been lost during one of the Fascist bombings of the city.

According to Gaudí's original design the cathedral, in Gothic style, was to be 363 ft (110 m) long and 148.50 ft (45 m) high, while the main dome was to reach a height of 528 ft (160 m). There were to have been three façades – representing Christ's Birth, Crucifixion, and Resurrection – seven aisles, and 18 towers symbolizing Jesus, the four Evangelists, the Virgin Mary and the Twelve Apostles. Today, however, the Sagrada Familia as conceived by Guadí comprises only two façades (Crucifixion and Nativity) and part of the left transept and apse. The only façade finished by Gaudí himself is the Nativity, with sculpture groups depicting the birth of Jesus and natural elements such as plants, clouds, flowers and stalactites, the fruit of his creative originality.

Inaugurated in 2000, the Crucifixion façade is the work of the architect Josep Maria Subirachs, who merged his own style (modern and more temperate) with Gaudí's extravagance. The reconstruction of the cathedral, resumed in recent years, mostly concerns the west portal (the Portal of the Passion), where new statues were placed, as well as a bas-relief of Christ wrapped in his shroud. An interesting detail in the latter work is that Jesus seems to be looking at the viewer.

The reconstruction work is in progress but is going slowly because of the high costs involved. Financial support comes mainly from donations from the state and from individuals, plus revenue from visitors.

According to experts, it will take fifty more years to finish the cathedral.

All the same, it is a must. The interior, which is like an enormous construction yard, is well organized and has amenities for visitors such as prefabricated elements that afford a close-up view of several architectural details. Going up the tower is a thrilling experience that must not be missed. A spiral staircase leads to the top of the right-hand portal towers (Portal of the Nativity), which offer a stupendous panorama of the city as well as a close-up look of interesting architectural elements on top of the Sagrada Familia.

From the exterior, observing the structure from bottom to top, you can admire the levels of construction, which begin from stone blocks that gradually form the Gothic spires characterized by Modernist decoration. Besides being harmonious, the exterior on the whole is based on rigorous mystical symbolism in which every decorative and architectural element has a precise meaning, which is explained in the notes on the large photographic reproduction of the west façade on exhibit in the crypt museum. Here we can see other material connected to the planning and realization of the cathedral, such as the plaster of Paris preparatory studies for the decoration and a large model of the church.

16 top The decoration on top of the pinnacles of the church are typical of Gaudí's style, which seems to be a sculptural rendition of corollas, pistils, berries and pine cones.

16 bottom and 16-17 The friezes on the exterior of the church, such as these representing the Holy Family and Christ crowning Mary, are framed by the classic motifs Gaudí liked so much: areas of rocks shaped by the wind.

17 bottom These two busts are on the Passion façade. The sad, intense faces are made even more dramatic by the way the stone is sculpted and the contrast in size between the heads and the bodies.

E U R O P E

where around you, and only by taking refuge in the house of God (the cathedral) will you be safe."

Atop Notre-Dame, at a height of about 495 ft (150 m), is an enormous cast iron lantern built in the 19th century to replace the original wooden one. The stained glass windows and tombs (the most famous is that of King Richard the Lion-Hearted of England, a great soldier and a leading exponent of the medieval code of chivalry), on the other hand, date from the 13th century, while Escalier des Libraires (a stairway) in the transept,

famous for its elegant wrought iron railing, dates from the 14th century. The overall vista of the interior is truly inspiring, when the large rose windows on the south and north façades with 80 scenes from the Old Testament are illuminated by the sunlight and seem to catch fire and come to life. There are also 23 noteworthy bas-reliefs (1319-51) depicting scenes from the life of Christ. These reliefs are painted and partly gilded, and are the work of Jean Ravy and his nephew Jean de Bouteiller.

22-23 *The central altar in the apse is surmounted by stained glass windows depicting the life of Jesus. They illuminate the austere interior in different ways, depending on the angle of the sunlight on the glass.*

23 top left *Massive, finely wrought columns with vertical decorative motifs lend a more towering quality to the nave, which is 130 meters long and 35 meters high.*

23 top right *This aisle has arcades and large double lancet windows. From here one can go to some of the radial chapels that house reliquaries and tombs, and to the entrance of the Treasury, which has a collection of miniatures, illuminated manuscripts and precious religious objects.*

23 bottom *The beautiful stained glass of the central rose window created by Viollet-le-Duc illustrates the vices, the virtues, the signs of the Zodiac and the months, with the Virgin Mary in the middle.*

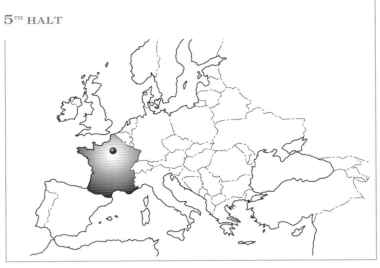

EIFFEL TOWER

PARIS, FRANCE

24 Detail of the base of the Eiffel Tower. Despite its complexity, the structure was built in a little over a year by a team of 250 workmen.

25 The colossal tower, which weighs almost 10,668 tons, was designed by Gustave Eiffel. Every year over 3 million people ascend it to enjoy panoramas of Paris.

The Eiffel Tower marked a fundamental stage in the architectural evolution of Paris and became the symbol of modernity that inspired many artists, poets, painters and photographers. And to this day, visitors to the city cannot but be struck by the majesty and lightness of this metal giant that in the evening is illuminated, transformed into a sort of terrestrial lighthouse for the French capital.

Curiously enough, the structure was conceived as a short-term project. The engineer Alexandre Gustave Eiffel designed it on occasion of the Paris exposition of 1889 in the Champ-de-Mars, and once this ended it was supposed to be dismantled. It took more than 6300 tons of iron to build this milestone of modern architecture. It is about 966 ft (293 m) high,

almost 1056 ft (320 m) if we count the modern television transmission antenna on its top. The tower rests on four arched masonry piers; these "legs" merge as a single shaft that supports the light, soaring iron framework structure. The tower becomes more slender toward the top and is interrupted by three observation platforms that can be reached either by stairs or an elevator. On the first level there is a restaurant with a panoramic view, while on the top are a meteorological station, a radio station and the above-mentioned antenna.

The top of the tower once housed the study of Eiffel, who was an expert builder of viaducts and iron bridges long before he designed this structure. But his favorite work, his precision instrument, as

it were, was the Eiffel Tower. The engineer made over 5000 drawings for his project, designing over 15,000 structural elements and 25 million holes for rivets. Besides its height, which remained a record up to 1930, when the Chrysler Building was constructed in New York City, the Eiffel Tower is extremely light, weighing in total only about 7224 tons, which makes it a sterling example of stability and ingenious designing technique. At the outset, the leading artists and literati in the city came out against the structure in a period of vociferous cultural protest, and in 1909 the tower even ran the risk of being demolished. It was saved only because it proved to be an ideal platform for the antennas needed for the new science of wireless transmission.

16 top The decoration on top of the pinnacles of the church are typical of Gaudí's style, which seems to be a sculptural rendition of corollas, pistils, berries and pine cones.

16 bottom and 16-17 The friezes on the exterior of the church, such as these representing the Holy Family and Christ crowning Mary, are framed by the classic motifs Gaudí liked so much: areas of rocks shaped by the wind.

17 bottom These two busts are on the Passion façade. The sad, intense faces are made even more dramatic by the way the stone is sculpted and the contrast in size between the heads and the bodies.

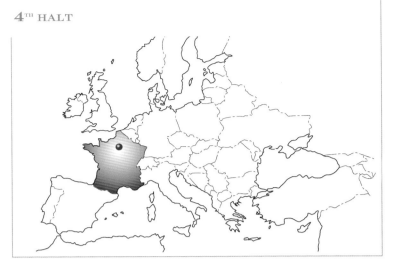

NOTRE-DAME CATHEDRAL
PARIS, FRANCE

This great world-famous cathedral was celebrated by Claude Monet, who painted it several times, and Victor Hugo, whose novel *Nôtre-Dame de Paris* is set in the Gothic church in medieval Paris. Over the centuries Notre-Dame has witnessed great historic events: the coronation of Henry IV of England was held in it; during the French Revolution it was christened the Temple of Reason, and Napoleon Bonaparte had himself proclaimed emperor there in 1804; and in August 1944, while German snipers were taking their parting shots, General de Gaulle celebrated the liberation of Paris from Nazi occupation there.

Those who see the cathedral for the first time are impressed by its grandeur, both as an architectural masterpiece and for its sheer size. In fact, it is 429 ft (130 m) long, 158 ft (48 m) wide and 115.5 ft (35 m) tall and can contain up to 9000 persons. Perhaps because of the influence of Hugo's dramatic story of Quasimodo and Esmeralda, Notre-Dame seems to transcend the barrier between reality and fiction. Already while going up onto the porch one has the sensation of an unreal atmosphere, as if time had stopped in the Middle Ages. Notre-Dame was built over the remains of a Romanesque church (whose crypt is still intact) at the behest of Louis VII and Bishop Maurice de Sully, who wanted to construct a church on the Île de la Cité (the island in the Seine that is Paris' historic center) that could vie with the Gothic abbey of Saint-Denis. Construction began in 1163 and continued for over 150 years, thus leaving us a clear picture of the evolution of the Gothic style. In particular, the choir, transepts and central nave belong to the classical period (1163-1200), while the main façade, some parts of the nave and of the choir are late Gothic (1200-1320).

On each side of the façade there is a tower, Saint-Romain (the oldest) and the tall Tour de Beurre (15th century), which houses a carillon with 56 bells. Going up to visit the towers one has a close-up view of another special feature that has made Notre-Dame famous: the gargoyles, water spouts in the form of grotesque medieval mythological creatures, humans and animals, sculpted in stone. Structurally they serve to drain rainwater from the roof gutters. Symbolically they represented the guardians of the cathedral, sentinels capable of keeping demons at bay. But another interpretation of the gargoyles is that they represent a rather explicit message to the faithful: "Evil is lying in ambush every-

18 The façade and the apse of the Paris cathedral, which was built along the Seine over the remains of a small Romanesque church that was also called Nôtre Dame.

18-19 This aerial view of the cathedral is like the one you can enjoy from the top of the south bell tower, with its 13-ton 17th-century bell. In the mid-foreground is the south transept with its two rose windows.

19 bottom left The sides and back of Nôtre Dame are characterized by a series of massive buttresses made lighter by sinuous lines that impart elegance and harmony to the whole.

19 bottom right These statues lie along the area where the nave and transept cross. There are twelve of them, depicting tutelary saints and the Madonna and Child.

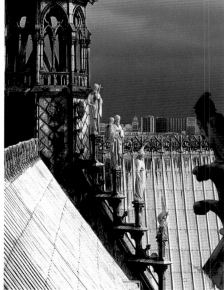

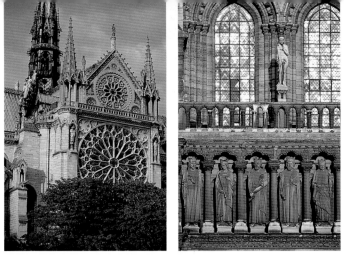

E U R O P E

where around you, and only by taking refuge in the house of God (the cathedral) will you be safe."

Atop Notre-Dame, at a height of about 495 ft (150 m), is an enormous cast iron lantern built in the 19th century to replace the original wooden one. The stained glass windows and tombs (the most famous is that of King Richard the Lion-Hearted of England, a great soldier and a leading exponent of the medieval code of chivalry), on the other hand, date from the 13th century, while Escalier des Libraires (a stairway) in the transept,

famous for its elegant wrought iron railing, dates from the 14th century. The overall vista of the interior is truly inspiring, when the large rose windows on the south and north façades with 80 scenes from the Old Testament are illuminated by the sunlight and seem to catch fire and come to life. There are also 23 noteworthy bas-reliefs (1319-51) depicting scenes from the life of Christ. These reliefs are painted and partly gilded, and are the work of Jean Ravy and his nephew Jean de Bouteiller.

22-23 The central altar in the apse is surmounted by stained glass windows depicting the life of Jesus. They illuminate the austere interior in different ways, depending on the angle of the sunlight on the glass.

23 top left Massive, finely wrought columns with vertical decorative motifs lend a more towering quality to the nave, which is 130 meters long and 35 meters high.

23 top right This aisle has arcades and large double lancet windows. From here one can go to some of the radial chapels that house reliquaries and tombs, and to the entrance of the Treasury, which has a collection of miniatures, illuminated manuscripts and precious religious objects.

23 bottom The beautiful stained glass of the central rose window created by Viollet-le-Duc illustrates the vices, the virtues, the signs of the Zodiac and the months, with the Virgin Mary in the middle.

EIFFEL TOWER
PARIS, FRANCE

24 Detail of the base of the Eiffel Tower. Despite its complexity, the structure was built in a little over a year by a team of 250 workmen.

25 The colossal tower, which weighs almost 10,668 tons, was designed by Gustave Eiffel. Every year over 3 million people ascend it to enjoy panoramas of Paris.

The Eiffel Tower marked a fundamental stage in the architectural evolution of Paris and became the symbol of modernity that inspired many artists, poets, painters and photographers. And to this day, visitors to the city cannot but be struck by the majesty and lightness of this metal giant that in the evening is illuminated, transformed into a sort of terrestrial lighthouse for the French capital.

Curiously enough, the structure was conceived as a short-term project. The engineer Alexandre Gustave Eiffel designed it on occasion of the Paris exposition of 1889 in the Champ-de-Mars, and once this ended it was supposed to be dismantled. It took more than 6300 tons of iron to build this milestone of modern architecture. It is about 966 ft (293 m) high,

almost 1056 ft (320 m) if we count the modern television transmission antenna on its top. The tower rests on four arched masonry piers; these "legs" merge as a single shaft that supports the light, soaring iron framework structure. The tower becomes more slender toward the top and is interrupted by three observation platforms that can be reached either by stairs or an elevator. On the first level there is a restaurant with a panoramic view, while on the top are a meteorological station, a radio station and the above-mentioned antenna.

The top of the tower once housed the study of Eiffel, who was an expert builder of viaducts and iron bridges long before he designed this structure. But his favorite work, his precision instrument, as

it were, was the Eiffel Tower. The engineer made over 5000 drawings for his project, designing over 15,000 structural elements and 25 million holes for rivets. Besides its height, which remained a record up to 1930, when the Chrysler Building was constructed in New York City, the Eiffel Tower is extremely light, weighing in total only about 7224 tons, which makes it a sterling example of stability and ingenious designing technique. At the outset, the leading artists and literati in the city came out against the structure in a period of vociferous cultural protest, and in 1909 the tower even ran the risk of being demolished. It was saved only because it proved to be an ideal platform for the antennas needed for the new science of wireless transmission.

26 top Built from 1632 on, the royal palace achieved its 'golden age' under the Sun King, Louis XIV.

26-27 The Versailles palace is reflected in the waters of the canal, a tributary of the Seine.

26 bottom left One of the palace's huge inner courtyards, which was once crossed by dozens of coaches that transported noblemen and politicians. It is estimated that the stables could accommodate up to 2500 horses.

26 bottom right Versailles is made even more lovely by its gardens, which are still considered among the most beautiful in the world. They were designed between 1664 and 1668 by the famous architect-landscaper André Le Nôtre.

27 left This sculpture of Bacchus is part of the decoration of the Versailles gardens.

27 right The pools were one of the special features of the Sun King's famous receptions. The most theatrical is the so-called Pool of Neptune.

VERSAILLES
FRANCE

In the early 17th century the area around the small village of Versailles was extremely marshy but quite suitable for hunting. This is the reason Louis XIII had a residence built there in 1630 that was later converted into a castle by the architect Philibert Le Roy. In 1661, during the reign of the Sun King, Louis XIV, Versailles was drastically rebuilt into a sumptuous palace to which he summoned the entire court, thus making it the virtual capital of the French kingdom. In 1789, with the outbreak of the French Revolution, the king and queen had to return to Paris and the palace was stripped of its treasures. Thanks to Louis Philippe, it was restored and transformed into the monument and museum we see today.

In front of the palace is the Place d'Armes or parade ground, an enormous semicircle in the middle of which are the royal stables, which could house 30,000 horses. Once past the gate of honor there are three large courtyards, the most famous of which is the Cour des Ministres, where the Montgolfier brothers experimented with their first balloons. From here one goes to the central edifice, which is the home of the History Museum, with its gallery of portraits of royalty, as well as the Opéra Royal, made of carved wood and decorated with sculptures, built on occasion of Louis XVI's marriage to Marie Antoinette.

But the oldest and most famous part of the palace is the king's large apartment: six drawing rooms in Italian Baroque style, richly decorated with marble, tapestries and stuccowork, that were used by the Sun King for audiences or for court entertainment. These are the Salon de Vénus, frescoed with mythological scenes; the Salon d'Abondance, with a bust of the Sun King by Bernini; the Salon de Diane and Salon de Mercure, given over to games, billiards, etc.; the Salon de Mars, the music hall, which boasts a fine painting by Domenichino of David. Lastly, there is the Salon d'Apollon, the throne room.

Farther on is the Galerie de Glaces (247 ft/75 m long and 40 ft/12 m high), a masterpiece by Charles Le Brun. This gallery is illuminated by 17 windows facing northwest that are reflected in the same number of large mirrors, while the ceiling is completely frescoed with scenes depicting the king's life. Other wonderful edifices are the Opera House and the king's small apartment with paintings by Guido Reni, Van Dyck and Lanfranco, which includes the famous Salon de l'Oeil de Boeuf, where the court dignitaries witnessed the Lever du Roi and Coucher du

28-29 and 28 bottom left The drawing rooms of Versailles have portraits of aristocrats and political figures. Note the abundance of austere polychrome marble, which enhances the brilliant gilded stuccowork.

28 bottom right The Gallery of Battles boasts the commemorative paintings of the major French military victories, including the famous canvas by Delacroix of the Battle of Taillebourg.

29 top left This drawing room is sumptuously decorated with frescoes and precious tapestries.

29 top right The royal chapel of Hardouin-Mansart was finished in 1710. The upper gallery was reserved for the women taking part in the services, while the men sat in the nave.

29 bottom The Gallery of Mirrors, the masterpiece of the French architects Le Vau and Le Brun, was the venue for the most important receptions. The Treaty of Versailles was signed here in 1919.

Roi ceremonies, when the king arose in the morning and went to bed at night. The Grands Appartements de la Reine (the Queen's Apartments) are no less stunning and precious, with their stucco molding, frescoes, and carved wood paneling: it took no less than 30 years to restore the queen's bedroom alone.

And then there are the gardens, which cover and area of 272 acres (110 hectares) and are an extraordinary example of the luxurious French-style garden. Richly decorated with theatrical elements, fountains and statues of Apollo that alternate with pools, woods and flower beds, the gardens were laid out by landscape architect André Le Nôtre, who worked on them for over thirty years with an army of 250 gardeners and 40,000 laborers. Here there are pools surrounded by bronze putti and nymphs; belvedere terraces with astounding perspective views such as the 'axis of the sun,' along which one can gaze across the entire park; tree-lined paths and avenues with fountains; and an amphitheater whose tiers are covered with shells. Furthermore, the gardens boast two canals for romantic boat rides, the large Orangerie, and the famous Petit Trianon and Grand Trianon pavilions that the Sun King used for his many amorous trysts.

30-31 The château, seen here from above, is surrounded by a 13,585 acres (5500 hectares) park that was once a hunting reserve and is now a national park. The Chambord complex is considered one of the best examples of French Renaissance architecture.

30 bottom left The double spiral Staircase of the Guards is ascribed to Leonardo da Vinci. It leads to the apartments of Francis I and Louis XIV, as well as to the Hunting Museum on the second floor.

30 bottom right Francis I, portrayed here on horseback and in lavish ceremonial dress, ordered the construction of the fabulous château in 1519.

31 The sumptuous château was a favorite with the kings of France from 1545 on, when it was finished. It is made of white tufa from the Loire area that at sunset takes on pinkish-orange hues.

CHAMBORD CHÂTEAU
FRANCE

Of the many lovely châteaux along the Loire River in France, originally built for defensive purposes but soon converted into elegant pleasure villas, the most celebrated and luxurious is Chambord, situated almost 10 miles (16 km) east of Blois. Construction began in 1519 for Francis I, who it is said wanted to have a fortress so magnificent that it would make his eternal rival Charles V envious. The design, which some have ascribed to Leonardo da Vinci, who lived in this region in the latter part of his life, is quite audacious and even called for the deviation of the Loire so that its waters would wash the walls of the château. But it was really the bed of the smaller Cosson River whose course was modified, and, as mentioned above, it must be said that not all scholars agree that it was the Tuscan genius who designed the manor, although two French archaeologists, Do-

minic Hofbauer and Jean-Slyvain Caillou, recently demonstrated that the ventilation system of the royal bedrooms is identical to the one found among Leonardo's sketches, as is the drawing of the famous double spiral staircase that enbled the noblemen and noblewomen to go to the upper floors without seeing one another. In any case, whoever designed the rest of the château must have had exquisite aesthetic taste, since he succeeded in transforming a basically medieval construction (a quadrilateral with four massive towers on the corners) into a refined edifice for sumptuous feasts and banquets with a 21 sq. miles (55 sq. km) hunting reserve around it.

The château itself is nothing less than huge, with 440 rooms, 84 stairways and 365 fireplaces! Not to speak of the luxuriant park, which is now the largest enclosed wooded reserve in Europe, popu-

lated with wild animals within walls that extend for 20 miles (32 km). Francis I, who died before the château was finished, spent only a few days of his long reign here, but for centuries afterwards Chambord was the venue of receptions, tournaments and military exercises whose extravagance can easily be imagined simply by walking through the drawing rooms or looking out from the terraces. Also known as 'the palace of frolicking and pleasure,' Chambord was built thanks to the exorbitant taxes imposed by Francis I on his subjects and the clergy alike in order to satisfy his every whim. And he chose to use this money to finance the construction work of the château (almost 2000 persons worked for 15 years to build it) and purchase furnishings, rather than to promote public works or to pay the ransom for his sons who were being kept prisoners in Spain.

32 top These two exceptional and precious Parisian tapestries were made at the end of the 16th century according to a design by Laurence Guyot.

32 bottom This Tournai tapestry was made around 1530 and is on display in the Chambord museum. It represents a wolf hunt and is an example of the lavish decoration that was once in the halls.

32-33 Detail of a tapestry by Bernard van Orley dating from the late 16th century; note the border decorated with birds and fruit.

MONT BLANC
ITALY-FRANCE

The highest mountain in western Europe at 4810 meters, Mont Blanc stands out in an area on the Italian-French border. The massif has about 25 miles (40 km) of thrilling peaks, from Col de la Seigne to Col du Gran Ferret. The border separating the three countries is marked by the irregular pyramid of Mt. Dolent (12,602 ft/3819 m), one of the loveliest and most grandiose mountains in the group. The range occupies 258 sq. miles (645 sq. km) and is made up of granite, mica-schist, gneiss and crystalline limestone, all minerals dating from before the Carboniferous period. This is a magnificent example of the forces of nature that is always spectacular and impressive, from the peaks that look like lace against the sky such as the Aiguille du Midi (Needle of the South) or the Dente del Gigante (Giant's Tooth), to the vast expanses of pure white glaciers and the green valleys with grazing land or covered with fir trees. On the south slope, in Italy, the massif plunges from the highest peaks onto the Veny and Ferret valleys, the starting point for the crossing of the Mer de Glace, the largest glacier. On the opposite side, in France, the massif consists of powerful, aligned rocky spires that descend along the softer slopes.

Two Frenchmen made the first successful ascent of Mont Blanc in 1786. Michel-Gabriel Paccard and Jacques Balmat went up from Chamonix along the so-called *ancien passage*. But the most famous climb was made in August of the following year by Horace-Bénédict De Saussure, after whom the botanical garden, established at an altitude of 7194 ft/2180 m), was named. It has about 600 different species of alpine flora from every part of the world that thrive in this terrain of morainic origin.

The botanical garden is the first stage in the Mont Blanc cableway, which starts from the Italian La Palud station and slowly goes up, offering one of the most thrilling spectacles in the world. Once past the Pavillion du Mont Fréti, it runs to the Punta Helbronner (11,484/3480 m), which offers a great panorama of the Italian, Swiss and French Alps. Another stage on the ride is over the Gigante glacier, and then over the Vallée Blanche to the Aiguille du Midi at an altitude of 12,678 ft (3842 m). This is the highest part of the route, with a splendid view of the north slope of the massif. Then a gallery leads to the station, and the route descends to Chamonix, the French ski resort connected to the Italian one, Courmayeur, via the highway tunnel. Inaugurated in 1965, the tunnel runs for 7.2 miles (11.6 km) into the very core of Mont Blanc, the giant of Europe.

34 Mont Blanc (15,983 ft/4810 m) is a truly striking peak. On the French side there are grandiose spurs with rocky spires that descend along the slopes where the glaciers lie.

34-35 The highest peak in Europe was conquered for the first time in 1786 by two French mountaineers. Nowadays, anyone start toward the summit by cableway, which goes up to the Aiguille du Midi (12,678 ft/3842 m).

35 bottom The Mont Blanc chain stretches for about forty kilometers from the Col de la Seigne to the Col Ferret, with breathtaking peaks such as the Giant's Tooth (left) that are difficult tests for international mountaineers.

36-37 The Giant's Tooth (13,169 ft/4014 m) and the colossal mass of the Grandes Jorasses (13,880 ft/4206 m) tower over the Val Ferret. The Italian valley is connected to Switzerland by the Col du Grand Ferret.

38-39 and 39 right The old houses with their tall, narrow façades painted in pastel colors follow the configuration of the small harbor, which is a natural bay protected from the wind where luxury yachts now dock.

38 bottom left Centuries-old olive trees and cluster pines frame the bay of Portofino, which is the same splendid crescent that the French author Guy de Maupassant described in 1889.

38 bottom right Villa Beatrice is one of the exclusive residences built on the promontory between the 19th and the 20th centuries by aristocrats from all over the world who were spellbound by the Pearl of the Tigullio Gulf.

39 left Between the famous small square that descends toward the sea and the 12th-century church of San Martino, is the oldest section of this former fishermen's village, which was already settled by the ancient Romans, who called it Portus Delphini.

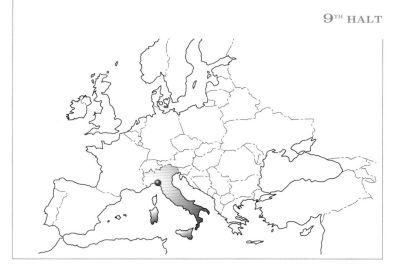

PORTOFINO
ITALY

" And behold, all of a sudden, we discover a hidden cove with olive and chestnut trees. A small village, Portofino, spreads out like a crescent around this calm basin." This is what Guy de Maupassant wrote in his *La Vie Errante* about his entrance in 1889 on a yacht into the splendid bay of Portofino. To this day we can experience the same emotion as the great French author, who was one of the first to describe the fascination of this Ligurian village. Before then, Portofino was known only to a small circle of English aristocrats, friends of the British consul Sir Montague Yeats-Brown, who in 1845 converted the 16th-century bastion into a splendid villa on top of the promontory. Over the years, the town became a pleasure ground for European royalty. And a German baroness saved it from the destruction ordered by the Nazi command-ers who were retreating from the Allies. Today, isolated among the cluster pines, Brown's castle offers visitors the very same panoramic view of the Tigullio Gulf, a small bay surrounded by the age-old village consisting of many small pastel-colored houses huddled together at the foot of San Martino Church, built in the 12th century in Lombard Romanesque style.

Portofino was a poverty-stricken village inhabited by fishermen who moored their boats in the small harbor that protected them from both wind and sea. But ancient Portus Delphini, described by Pliny the Elder and praised so highly by Petrarch, is now filled with luxury yachts. The small square that descends toward the sea has become the haunt of the international jet set. The houses, which until the 1950s were miserable hovels, are now worth their weight in gold and have been converted into boutiques and fashionable cafés. And yet, as if by some benign witchery, the picture postcard setting has remained the same. There must be something magical behind the fortune of the pearl of the Tigullio Gulf, framed by the green Monte di Portofino, an incredible hilly area protected as a nature reserve. Here, along the sea, there co-exist, in close contact, two contrasting atmospheres, Mediterranean and Central European, which correspond to two different types of vegetation: Aleppo and cluster pines, garigues and holm oaks on the slope facing the sea, and hornbeam, chestnut, oak and hazel trees on the north slope. This is one of the many strange local features. Another one is that in the small medieval church of San Giorgio the saint's remains were miraculously brought here from the Holy Land by the Crusaders.

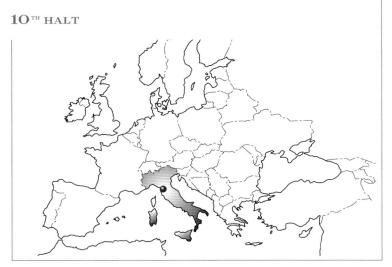

40 and 41 On the grass of the Campo dei Miracoli of Pisa, next to the Cathedral, stands the 181-ft (55-m) campanile better known as the Leaning Tower, which began to lean even during its construction, which was finished in 1350.

THE LEANING TOWER
PISA, ITALY

Will it fall or not? That is the question. For over 800 years the Pisans and the whole world have periodically wondered about the fate of the Leaning Tower of Pisa, but up to now, after an incredible number of debates, articles, fantastic proposals and unsuccessful remedies, it seems that the great monument is in no danger of collapsing. The campanile of the Romanesque cathedral of Pisa, commonly known as the Leaning Tower, is a superb example of how every cloud has a silver lining. If it were standing straight it would only be an architectural gem built in the elegant Pisan style that became widespread in so many other places. The tower stands in the marvelous Campo dei Miracoli, the square next to the Pisa Cathedral and the Baptistery. It is a beautiful white cylindrical structure almost 181 ft (55 m) high whose soaring effect is enhanced by six levels of open loggias on high blind arches, with a 294-step spiral staircase inside that leads to the belfry. The freestanding campanile is simple, elegant and functional, and is known throughout the world.

But the story does not end here. From the outset things began to go wrong, and the destiny of a city and a monument changed forever. According to tradition, a certain Gerardo di Gerardo began work on the tower in 1173 and the architect Bananno Pisano abandoned the construction a few years after the first stone was laid. At that stage the tower was between the third and fourth level when land subsidence caused it to lean. Since no one was willing to dare continue construction of the tower, it resumed only in 1257 and proved to be an arduous task, to say the least. Giovanni di Simone, a promising architect with a fine intellect, began to correct the inclination and continued to do so till his death at the battle of Meloria. Another Pisano, Tommaso, then completed the tower in the mid-14th century.

Already in the late 13th century there was a problem: an inclination of 36 inches (90 cm) that seemed to be unstoppable. Over the years, the 14,453 tons of marble concentrated within only 3050 sq. ft (285 sq. m) standing on alluvial terrain brought the inclination to almost 9.9 ft (3 m). While in the 18th century this phenomenon was considered charming, in the 19th century people began to wonder how long the tower would remain standing. Then in the 1900s, experts decided that something had to be done to remedy the situation. From 1990 on, 17 different teams of experts came up with many fantastic solutions, some of which proved to be downright harmful. The 18th team seemed to be one with the right proposal: the press and TV did coverage of the laying of 600 tons of lead that would counterbalance the tower. But soon afterwards the land began to subside democratically, as it were, that is, on both sides. The following year it was the turn of the experimenters, the exponents of liquid nitrogen that was supposed to freeze the terrain. In 1997 the 'simplifiers' came forward to propose anchoring the top of the Leaning Tower to horizontal steel tension rods set in blocks of concrete, like a sort of tug of war. Finally, in the late 1990s the most efficacious idea was put into action: earth was removed from the northern part to compensate for the subsidence on the southern side, and in 2001, once the terrain had consolidated, the infiltrations had been reduced and what could be restored had been restored, the tower straightened up and now has an inclination of only 15.8 inches (39.6 cm). The monument and the myth are finally safe and sound.

42 *The largest amphitheater in Rome was built in AD 75 next to the Roman Forum under Emperor Vespasian, the founder of the Flavian dynasty. In order to entertain the citizens, the Colosseum became the venue of mortal combats between gladiators and bloody spectacles with wild animals that emerged from the underground section of the arena, an infernal labyrinth of corridors and trapdoors.*

43 *The Flavian Amphitheater is an elegant as well as rational structure. The 80 entrance arches gave access to the tiers, which had a seating capacity of 50,000. The inner corridors and stairs allowed this huge crowd of people to get to their seats. During the Renaissance, stones were taken from the façade of the Colosseum to be used as building material for palazzi and part of St Peter' Basilica.*

THE COLOSSEUM
ROME, ITALY

Although it belongs to an architectural type that was rather common in the ancient Roman world, and despite the fact that it is not the best preserved of its kind, the Flavian Amphitheater is so famous that its common name was used to designate all the monuments in this category - 'colosseum.' This appellation is of medieval origin and referred to the colossal statue of the Emperor Nero, which he himself had placed in his Domus Aurea (The Golden House). When the latter was destroyed, the Flavian Amphitheater was built it in its place, probably over the site of the artificial lake that Nero had laid out. Commissioned in A.D. 75 by Emperor Vespasian, the edifice was finished in A.D. 80, under his son, Emperor Titus. There were 100 days of festivities to celebrate the inauguration.

As many as 50,000 Roman citizens went to the Colosseum, filling its 235,400 sq. ft (22,000 sq. m), to watch the spectacles; they entered the amphitheater with a special ticket, a terracotta tablet or *tessera* that indicated the number of the gate and tier. Every row of seats was reserved for some particular category of person, from the sen-

ators and members of the imperial court – whose decorated seating tiers were made of marble and were located in the middle of either long side of the oval structure – down to the *clientes* or commoners.

The overall size of the oval structure is 555 by 515 ft (185 by 156 m), and it is the largest monument of its kind, with an arena that measures 250 by 138 ft (76 by 46 m), large enough to contain a spectacle reproducing naval battles. Actually, although not all scholars agree on this point, most of the spectacles held both in the Colosseum and in the other amphitheaters throughout the Roman Empire were violent. The gladiatorial contests or *munera,* and the bloody hunts of wild animals brought from Africa, known as *venationes,* were the most popular and numerous of these, but there was also large-scale martyrization.

The spectators, who were protected from the sun by a series of canvas awnings *(velaria)* set over the amphitheater, shuddered with fear when a panther seemed to emerge from the earth itself and attacked a family of Christians. In reality, in the underground areas there were windlasses that took the animals directly to the arena

hatches, as well as tunnels, storehouses, rooms where the 'props' were kept, the gladiators' lodgings, and prisons. The complex structures in the section that was occupied by the arena belonged to this labyrinth of chambers and corridors, which was roofed with robust wooden planks.

The Colosseum continued to host public spectacles, even though there were periods when the emperors prohibited violent spectacles, only to reinstate them once again. Finally, in A.D. 404 Emperor Honorius declared the *munera* and martyrizations illegal; this left only the *venationes*, the last of which took place in A.D. 523.

For most of the Middle Ages the Colosseum was a used as castle by the Frangipane family, but when it no longer served this purpose it was abandoned. As occurred with all the monuments in Rome, it was then used as an open-air ready source of both stone and metal, the latter being taken from the metal hooks used to fasten and anchor the blocks of stone. However, various popes did attempt to preserve the monument, and in 1820 Pope Pius VII ordered the construction of the structures that reinforced the amphitheater's outer ring.

44-45 *The vault of the Sistine Chapel in the Vatican was frescoed by Michelangelo between 1508 and 1512. Without any assistants the great artist painted the 33 scenes from the Old Testament, with the famous Creation of Adam in the middle.*

THE SISTINE CHAPEL
VATICAN CITY

From the time of its construction (1475-81), ordered by Pope Sixtus IV (after whom it was named), the Sistine Chapel posed several problems. First of all, the vault had to be lowered, and then the pope, who was a connoisseur, began to choose from among the host of fine artists of the time for the decoration of the chapel. He first commissioned masters to do both the marble screen that divides the rectangular space in two and the choir balustrade. Then he had to think about the fresco decoration, for which he chose the leading artists of the time, including Botticelli, Perugino, Ghirlandaio, and Pinturicchio, who frescoed the sidewalls and the one facing the altar.

But the real difficulties arose during the papacy of Julius II, who decided to ask Michelangelo to work in the Sistine Chapel. Someone in the Vatican called him the "Torment and the Ecstasy" in person, an artist who painted like an angel but had a devilish character. This comment may have been due to the fact that Michelangelo was really ugly, at least according to Vasari, who was by the way his dear friend: short, almost malformed, probably suffering from syphilis, certain dirty, eccentric and irascible. Nevertheless, through his works he was able to transform his horrible attributes into sublime beauty. At first, in 1506, Michelangelo was commissioned

to paint the ceiling, but he wanted nothing to do with this because he considered himself a sculptor and nothing else but a sculptor, an opinion shared by Bramante, who recommended Raphael (who in any case had executed some of the tapestries) for this work. But Pope Julius II was adamant and from 1508 to 1512 Michelangelo produced, in three registers, nine episodes from *Genesis*, with the world-famous *Creation of Adam* that stands out so brilliantly in the middle section. All alone – he had driven away almost all the assistants he had summoned – virtually without sleeping, forced to paint in the weirdest positions on the scaffolding and arguing continu-

46 *The majestic figure of Christ is the focal point of the Last Judgment behind the main altar, which was painted by Michelangelo in 1536-41. This work reflects to the full the religious torment of the artist.*

47 *The fresco depicts the souls of the dead about to be judged by God. There are 314 figures, including the self-portrait of Michelangelo on a skin held by St. Bartholomew, at the foot of Christ.*

EUROPE

ously and vehemently with the pope, Michelangelo succeeded in creating the nude figures of prophets and sibyls, biblical episodes and the ancestors of Christ, a masterpiece the astonished with world and filled the pope with pride.

But the story did not end there. As the proverb says, beauty engenders beauty. Pope Clement VII asked the master to do another fresco, this time of the Resurrection, on the back wall behind the altar. The pope died before work began, and Michelangelo hoped that the contract would be rescinded. But the new pope, Paul III, did not let him off the hook, as it were. He forced the artist to paint the *Last Judgment*, which he did from 1536 to 1541. As had occurred with the other works, the painting work was marked by a series of fits of anger, arguments, doubts about his skill as a painter, sleepless nights, accidents (he fell from the scaffolding and broke a

leg, and the healing process was long and difficult). In the end, after 450 working days, there came to life, on 2418 sq. ft (226 sq. m) of the wall, 314 figures destined to stun the world for centuries. Enormous, vibrating with passion, hardly dressed or nude (in 1564 the nudes were covered at the behest of Pope Pius IV, who thought they were scandalous), these figures transcend both the canons of perspective and the ideals of the Renaissance.

All told, Michelangelo painted 10,700 sq. ft (1000 sq. m) of power, pity and terror in the Sistine Chapel, ironically inserting a self-portrait in the guise of St. Bartholomew, not far from Jesus in the *Last Judgment*. Naturally, time damaged the frescoes, and in 1980 restoration work began that took fourteen years and stirred a lot of controversy. Let us hope that the restored originals we see today will last forever.

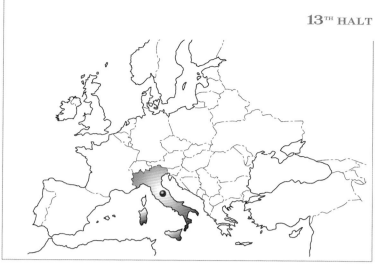

THE ST. FRANCIS BASILICA
ASSISI, ITALY

48 The top section of the nave of the Upper Church is decorated with a cycle of 34 frescoes with scenes from the Old Testament and from the life of Christ. Beneath this, Giotto painted 28 episodes from the life of St. Francis of Assisi.

49 left The basilica really consists of two churches set one above the other in a single body. The upper one is Gothic, while the lower one, which houses the tomb of St. Francis in the crypt, is Romanesque.

49 center and right St. Francis preaching to the birds and driving away the demons from Arezzo. In this cycle Giotto marked the transition from the rather static formalism of Byzantine painting to a dynamic style of pictorial narration.

Friar Elias was not without sin; on the contrary, the other friars often criticized his behavior, but it was St. Francis himself who named him his successor. Consequently, when the saint died and his remains were left in the Porziuncola chapel, Elias was so inspired by a grandiose plan that nothing and no one managed to dissuade him. Taking shape in his mind was the idea of a grand basilica to be built on Monte Subasio in Assisi in the shape of a tau cross. This symbol, which people believed warded off diseases, was a favorite with St. Francis, who used it as an emblem. The saint loved this mark because it reminded of the love of the Crucifix and the words in the Old Testament: "Go through the midst of the city, through the midst of Jerusalem, and set a mark upon the foreheads of the men that sigh and that cry,

for all the abominations that be done in the midst thereof."

Now all this had to be an integral part of the eternal dwelling place of the saint and become the tangible proof of the benediction bestowed upon all the pilgrims who would go there. Therefore, Elias chose the site of the so-called Inferno Hill, one of the most infamous parts of town, which he renamed Paradise Hill. He was so enterprising that in 1228 he managed to get permission from Pope Gregory IX, the patron of the Franciscan order, to build the longed-for basilica on this plot of land, which was donated by Simone di Pucciarello. In order to promote private financing of the project the pope issued the *Recolentes qualiter* papal bull, which offered indulgences for those who offered money for the construction of the St. Francis Basilica.

Now not all the members of the Franciscan order liked the project. For example, Friar Leo, one of those enamored of the tau cross, did not approve of it, which called for two splendidly decorated churches, one over the other, above the saint's tomb. St. Francis had preached poverty and humility, and now the idea of placing his remains in such a lavish setting seemed almost sacrilegious. But Elias did not give in; he transformed the urban landscape of Assisi and also revitalized the Italian painting of the time.

In 1230 he had the venerated relics of the saint taken to what was called the Lower Church. This edifice was built in the Umbrian Romanesque style and imparts an intimate atmosphere thanks to the massive side piers and the curved ribs that descend to the floor. The Lower Church is somewhat mysterious and

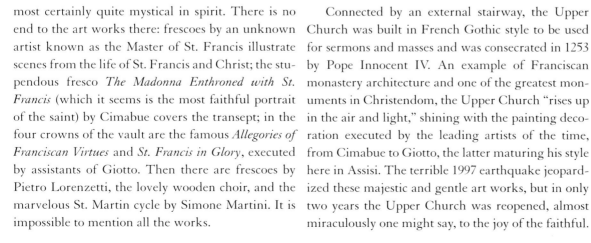

most certainly quite mystical in spirit. There is no end to the art works there: frescoes by an unknown artist known as the Master of St. Francis illustrate scenes from the life of St. Francis and Christ; the stupendous fresco *The Madonna Enthroned with St. Francis* (which it seems is the most faithful portrait of the saint) by Cimabue covers the transept; in the four crowns of the vault are the famous *Allegories of Franciscan Virtues* and *St. Francis in Glory*, executed by assistants of Giotto. Then there are frescoes by Pietro Lorenzetti, the lovely wooden choir, and the marvelous St. Martin cycle by Simone Martini. It is impossible to mention all the works.

Connected by an external stairway, the Upper Church was built in French Gothic style to be used for sermons and masses and was consecrated in 1253 by Pope Innocent IV. An example of Franciscan monastery architecture and one of the greatest monuments in Christendom, the Upper Church "rises up in the air and light," shining with the painting decoration executed by the leading artists of the time, from Cimabue to Giotto, the latter maturing his style here in Assisi. The terrible 1997 earthquake jeopardized these majestic and gentle art works, but in only two years the Upper Church was reopened, almost miraculously one might say, to the joy of the faithful.

50 *The Allegory of Poverty (above), one of the three frescoes that celebrate the Franciscan virtues, and Mary Magdalene at the port of Marseilles (bottom) decorate the vault and the chapel of the Lower Church.*

50-51 *The first stone of the church was laid in 1228, two years after St. Francis died. The Lower Church has a single nave divided into five bays whose walls and vaults are covered with frescoes.*

51 bottom left *The painted decoration is the work of the leading artists of 13th-14th century Italy. Among these are the brothers Pietro and Ambrogio Lorenzetti, the authors of the Last Supper in the Lower Church.*

51 bottom right *The link between Christ and St. Francis is underscored by the cycles of frescoes in the Lower Church concerning their lives. The Crucifixion is attributed to Giotto's school.*

ST. MARK'S BASILICA
VENICE, ITALY

This basilica is an Eastern temple in the heart of the Western world. For that matter, the Republic of Venice had always claimed it was the legitimate heir of the Byzantine Empire. St. Mark's Basilica epitomizes and exalts the pride of the Most Serene Republic; it is a sort of dazzling showcase created with the aim of astonishing visitors to Venice. In fact, it played host to the most important and formal public ceremonies: it was here that the newly elected doge was presented to the citizens, and this was where popes, princes, and ambassadors were received. Again, navigators went to the basilica to ask for divine protection before embarking on their long voyages. Only in 1807 did it become the cathedral of Venice, replacing San Pietro al Castello. Before that time St. Mark's was constantly being remodeled and beautified.

The imposing basilica with a Greek cross plan and five huge domes was the third church erected next to the Doge's Palace. The first was built in the 9th century to house the relics of the Evangelist St. Mark, but it was destroyed by fire. The second church was demolished to make room for an edifice more in keeping with the burgeoning political and maritime power that Venice represented. The new church was consecrated in 1094, but every year additions were made in a mixture of lavish, extravagant Eastern and Western influences. The complexity and richness of the decoration grew apace with the growing power of the Republic. The first mosaics on St. Mark's date from the 11th century and on both sides of the main entrance they depict saints. These were the work of Byzantine artists, whose technique was inherited by the Venetians. The latter soon showed great skill and real passion in the execution of brilliant gilded mosaics, and covered the domes, walls and floor of the basilica with mosaics that occupied an area of 42,800 sq. ft (4000 sq. m). In the 16th century there were even mosaic reproductions of works by such great artists as Titian, Veronese and Tintoretto. Among the most beautiful mosaics are the 12th-century ones in the nave representing the Pentecost. A century later the Ascension was depicted on the central dome, while the lunettes and vaults in the atrium were decorated with scenes from the Old Testament (the Dome of Genesis, with the Creation in the shape of concentric circles, is simply splendid). The passion for mosaic art can also be seen in the floors, which are made up of fragments of marble, por-

52 *The Orientalizing style of the architecture and the Lion of St. Mark, which is holding the Gospels under its paw, are the symbols of the Venetian Republic, the queen of the eastern Mediterranean.*

52-53 *St. Mark's Basilica, with a Greek cross plan and five impressive domes, was the third church to be built next to the Doges' Palace. The more the power of the Venetian Republic increased, the more the basilica was enlarged and decorated.*

53 *bottom left* *On the tympanum of the main arcade is the winged Lion of St. Mark. In the early 15th century, the statue of the saint, surrounded by a series of angels, was placed on the pendentive of the cusp.*

53 *bottom right* *This porphyry sculpture group, executed in the 4th century AD, depicts Diocletian and three other emperors. The four, known as the Tetrarchs, were supposed to work together to ensure good government for the Roman Empire.*

54 The nave with the high altar was the venue of the most important ceremonies of the Venetian Republic. This is where the newly elected doge was presented to the citizens and where popes, princes and ambassadors were received.

55 top The interior of the Basilica was decorated over the centuries with bright mosaics, marble pavements, porphyry and glass inlay, statues and other treasures, many brought from Constantinople as war booty.

55 bottom Although it was sacked after the fall of the Republic, the Treasury still boasts rare Byzantine icons, including the famous Pala d'Oro, created in the 10th century and consisting of 250 panels studded with precious stones.

56-57 The five domes are dressed with mosaics illustrating episodes from the Bible. The technique used, as well as the iconographic program, reveal the Republic's close ties with Byzantine tradition.

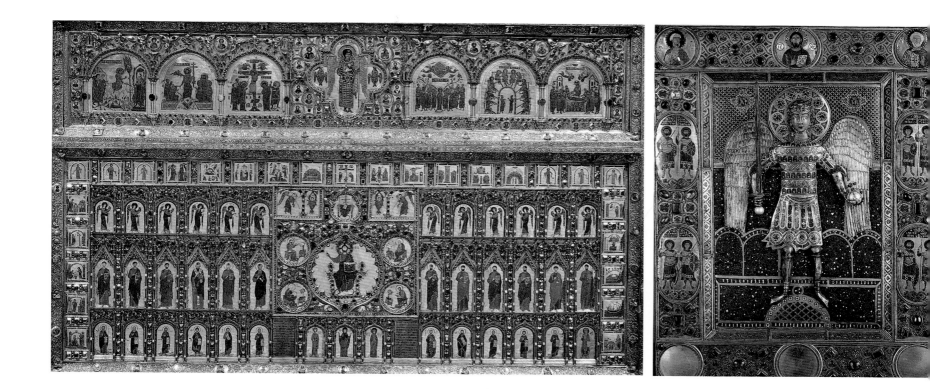

phyry and glass arranged so as to create geometric patterns and allegorical scenes with animals.

The art treasures the Venetians had taken from Constantinople in 1204 as war booty were also added to·the basilica. These included the famous gilded bronze horses, whose origin is still being debated. They may have been executed during Constantine's age (4th century A.D.), or may be early Roman or even Hellenistic works. What is certain is that these stupendous horses were taken to Venice, after the conquest of Constantinople during the Fourth Crusade. In 1798 Napoleon took them to Paris, and they were given back to the Venetians in 1815. The horses were recently restored and are now in the St.

Mark's Museum, while copies stand on the façade terrace. An idea of the rich array of artworks in St. Mark's can be got by visiting the Treasury, which although sacked after the fall of the Venetian Republic, still boasts a precious collection of Byzantine masterpieces, including icons, gilded reliquaries and other exquisite objects. The same fate awaited the famous Pala d'Oro, the icon behind the high altar, a staggering assembly of 250 Byzantine enameled panels from the 10th to the 12th century, all studded with precious jewels. Napoleon took some of the stones back to France with him, but with all those dazzling pearls, rubies, sapphires and amethysts that remain no one notices the difference.

58 *The fairy tale castle was commissioned by King Louis II of Bavaria and finished in 1869. Enamored of German mythology and the music of Richard Wagner, the king was a veritable expert of the Lohengrin saga.*

59 *Despite the bizarre mixture of architectural styles ranging from Gothic to Baroque, the castle, viewed here from the front, boasts a heating and plumbing system that was very modern for its time.*

NEUSCHWANSTEIN
GERMANY

It looks like a castle in a fairy tale, and in a certain sense it is, since Walt Disney used Neuschwanstein as a model for the setting of his *Sleeping Beauty*. But it is first of all one of the universal symbols of Germany during the Romantic period. The castle rises in southern Bavaria, almost on the Austrian border, dominating the surrounding countryside from 3185 ft (965 m) above sea level. King Ludwig II of Bavaria had it built here in 1869, on a tall rocky spur above the Pöllath rapids, after a design by the stage designer Christian Jank. As the king confided to his friend Richard Wagner, it was the realization of his childhood dream: a castle like the one of Lohengrin, the Knight of the Holy Grail, as depicted in many frescoes.

Though embodying a combination of various architectural styles, overall Neuschwanstein looks like an enchanted castle. On the exterior the five stories are dotted with small towers and pinnacles that are either flanking or set one above the other. The interior is a blaze of precious fabrics, frescoes, carved wood and marble. But above all it appears to be a tribute to the chivalric sagas and operas of Wagner, who drew inspiration from German epic poems for his compositions. For example, the throne room, in Byzantine style, with a mosaic floor made of over two million tesserae, and almost completely dressed in marble, was inaugurated as the Hall of the Holy Grail of Parsifal. Here there is a painting of St. George and Dragon, with the Falkenstein Castle (the fourth castle the king had planned to build but never did) in the background.

Once past the small winter garden, one arrives at the royal apartments, where columns separate the main hall and a smaller hall known as 'the swans' Corner.' The motif on the walls is from the legend of Lohengrin and the miracle of the Holy Grail, while the doors of the library are decorated with frescoes illustrating the story of Tristan and Isolde and Siegfried. The paintings in the Cantors' Hall once again refer to the legend of Parsifal. But King Ludwig's real obsession was the bedrooms, which were to be lavishly decorated, to an exaggerated degree. Thus, he hired fourteen woodcarvers who for three years carved, in oak wood, the baldachin, the central column, the washbasin (with running water) and the chair he used for reading. Furthermore, the fretwork at the base of the feet of the bed depicts the Resurrection of Christ, an allusion to the symbolic relationship between sleep and death. The bedcovers, tapestries and curtains are embroidered with the Bavarian coat of arms, with the swan and lion of the Wittelsbachs, the dynasty that Ludwig came from.

Despite its luxuriousness, the entire castle exudes an air of incompleteness (to this day there are still rooms, not open to the public, with unplastered bricks). This is due to the fact that the works were interrupted after Ludwig II was arrested and confined. A romantic dreamer who had little political competence, this monarch used all his wealth to build castles one after the other, and in some cases at the same time. Considered an insane visionary unfit to govern Bavaria, he was exiled to his château on Lake Starnberg, where he died.

60-61 *This reception hall in the Neuschwanstein castle contains a combination of Moorish decoration, Renaissance carved wood paneling, medieval chandeliers and classicizing paintings.*

60 bottom *This gallery of the palace (left) was used for receptions, while at right is the throne room, in which the gilded friezes and decorated double colonnade are enhanced by the light from the huge candelabra with an Oriental-like shape.*

61 top *The two paintings by Christian Jank were executed for King Louis. They depict a scene in the Castle of the Holy Grail and Parsifal's meeting with the king of Cumberland. They are in the Cantors' Hall, built for performances of Wagner's music.*

61 bottom *This photo of the throne room highlights the elegant mosaic floors in Byzantine style. However, King Ludwig did not enjoy all this luxury very long, because he was declared insane and died before the castle was finished.*

EUROPE _____

62 top This view of the Unter den Linden avenue includes the statue of Frederick the Great, the University, the Deutsche National Museum, the cathedral and large radio-TV antenna that has an observation tower with a splendid view of the city.

62 center Humboldt University was opened in 1810, and Einstein and Hegel were among the professors who taught there.

62 bottom left The Brandenburg Gate connects the Unter den Linden and 17 Juni Street. The large area was the venue of important events, political rallies and military parades.

62 bottom right The Berliner Dom is a large Neo-Baroque structure standing in the middle of the Island of Museums; it was the royal church of the Hohenzoller family and contains the sarcophagi of Frederick I and his wife.

63 The new wing of the Deutsche National Museum was designed by Ieoh Ming Pei.

UNTER DEN LINDEN
BERLIN, GERMANY

The town planners who designed the Champs-Elysées in Paris and the Mall in Washington DC drew inspiration from this avenue. Unter den Linden was named after the tall linden trees planted in the heart of Berlin in 1647 by Frederick William II of Prussia in order to connect the elector's palace with gates of Berlin via a large, elegant and pleasant avenue for horses and coaches. It enjoyed an immediate success, so much so that only fifty years later Frederick the Great (1740-86) decided to widen and beautify the street even more, transforming it into the city's main artery, which ran from east to west as an ideal link between Moscow and Paris and, more concretely, the royal castle with the former Tiergarten hunting area. The symbol of this noble avenue is the Brandenburg Gate, now the only remaining one of the

fourteen that once afforded access to the city. It consists of six Doric columns 86 ft (26 m) high, modeled after the Propylaea on the Acropolis of Athens, which support the majestic bronze statue of the chariot pulled by four horses and driven by the Winged Victory goddess that Napoleon took as war booty and exhibited in Paris until 1814, when the Prussians defeated the French.

Since then the Brandenburg Gate area has been the venue of many historic moments: the most famous diplomatic visits to Berlin, including those of the Czar Nicholas I and Mussolini; the infamous 1933 fire at Bebel Platz, where the Nazis burned books by Marx, Engels, Lenin, Brecht, Heine, Mann and Gorky, among others; historic parades such as that of the Red Army, which in 1945 hoisted the Soviet flag over the gate, and

those of the German government. After reunification in 1989, the Gate, designed by the Neo-Classic architect Karl Friedrich Schinkel, became symbol *par excellence* of Germany, with the Prussian eagle and the Iron Cross atop the pole held by the Winged Victory.

Leaving aside historic events, over the centuries Unter den Linden changed appearance many a time, beginning with the layout of the trees themselves, which originally were planted in six rows, then in four and finally uprooted in 1935 so that troops and parades could pass by more easily. Today it is an elegant street, shaded by new, much smaller linden trees, and is regaining its former allure thanks to the restoration work being done on the large aristocratic residences damaged during the Second World War and only partly rebuilt afterwards. After

E U R O P E

the fall of the Berlin Wall and the unification of Germany, what had been the hub of the German Democratic Republic (East Germany), that is, the Unter den Linden district, is once again the heart of the entire city, and for almost a mile (1.5 km) this avenue, which is now 198 ft (60 m) wide, reveals four centuries of history and culture.

In fact, the street was the home of such famous personalities as Bettina von Arnim, the great poet Henirich Heine, the sculptor Gottfried Schadow (who executed the chariot on Brandenburg Gate), and the humanist Wilhelm von Humboldt. The university on Unter den Linden is named after Humboldt. Among its faculties is the lovely Altes Palais pavilion, the Kommode and the former royal library, and some of its most famous professors were the Grimm brothers, Hegel, Feuerbach, Einstein and Robert Koch, the physician. Then, strolling along the avenue we see the Staatsbibliotek, one of the most important libraries in Europe, with 7 million volumes, incunabula, maps and manuscripts, and a notable architectural work as well, a Neo-Baroque gem designed by Ernst von Inhe and built in the early 1900s. Then there is the Staatsoper, the famous opera house rebuilt after the World War II bombardments and reopened in 1955 with a production of a Wagner opera, and the Opern Café, with an abundance of staircases and purple velvet drapery, which also features contemporary art shows.

66-67 *The Gothic spires and the gilded statue of the Madonna on the Tyn Cathedral tower over the Old Town square. The church, construction of which began in 1365, soon became the center of the Bohemian religious reform movement.*

66 bottom *The square has always been the focal point of the capital. As long ago as 1091 it hosted a lively marketplace. Elegant buildings soon rose up around it and in 1338 the Town Hall (right) was constructed here.*

67 left *The Town Hall tower has a 15th-century astronomical clock. When every hour strikes, a fantastic procession of statues of the Apostles and other figures emerges from the clock.*

67 center and right *The square is like a guide to the history of Prague architecture: from the frescoed Romanesque houses to the Gothic arcades, the Rococo buildings and the Art Nouveau façades.*

STAROMESTSKÉ NÁMESTÍ
PRAGUE, CZECH REPUBLIC

Staromestaské Námestí is the liveliest, most elegant square in Prague as well as the main one. The buildings constructed there in the last thousand years have made it the worthy venue for all the major city events. The most important pages of the nation's history have been written here: from the election of George of Podiebrad as king of Bohemia in 1458 to the execution of 27 Bohemian patriots who led the revolt against Hapsburg rule in 1621. The old Town Hall (Staromestská Radnice), built in the late 1300s-early 1400s, is the hub of the square. Now it looks like a sequence of Gothic and Renaissance edifices with different colors, decorated with mosaics and richly carved portals. The Town Hall tower has the famous astronomical clock, a 15th-century mechanism that offers a spectacle after each hour has been struck: two small windows on the face open wide and the polychrome statues of the Twelve Apostles come out, and their procession is accompanied by the statues of Death, the Miser, the Turk and the Dandy, after which a trumpet fanfare announces that the show is over. On the light blue clock face, which is divided into 24 sections, some spheres indicate the hour and the position of the sun and moon, while in the lower part there is a calendar with the signs of the Zodiac. The top of the 229.5-ft (69.5-m) tower of-

fers the best panoramic view of Prague. The square's north side is dominated by the St. Nicholas Church, finished in 1735 to a design by the architect Kilian Ignaz Dientzenhofer. The façade, decorated with many statues, is a masterpiece of the Prague Baroque style. The splendid dome is frescoed with episodes from the life of St. Nicholas and St. Benedict, the work of Kosmas Damian Asam. On the east side of the square are the spires and towers of the Tyn Cathedral, dedicated to St. Mary. Founded in 1365, it soon became the center of the Bohemian reform movement: up to 1620 it was the main Hussite church in Prague.

John Huss, the founder of this movement, is celebrated with the monument in the square, inaugurated in 1915. This Czech religious reformer and hero was condemned for heresy and burned at the stake in 1415. The interior of the Tyn Cathedral, with a nave and two aisles, contains the Gothic sculpture group of Calvary, a pulpit with a stone baldachin dating from the late 15th century, and fine paintings by Karel Skréta, a noted 17th-century Czech painter. The

church also houses the oldest font in the city (1414) and the tomb of the great astronomer and astrologer Tycho Brahe. The courtyard of the church is surrounded by buildings with different architectural styles. Outside the church there are many fine sights: the medieval house of the 'stone bell,' which was restored in its original Gothic style; the Renaissance residence of the Granovsky family with its marvelous loggia; and the Baroque porticoes of the Stepanovsky Palace. In Staromestská Námestí Square our survey of the history of Prague art continues with a series of buildings that were originally Romanesque that have pastel colors and are decorated with particular signs, such as 'The House of the Stone Ram,' named after a 16th-century bas-relief of a ram with only one horn. Then there are the Tyn School, characterized by its porticoes with 14th-century Gothic vaults; the Neo-Renaissance Storch house, which is decorated with a late-19th century painting of St. Wenceslaus on horseback; and the rococo splendor of the Kinsky Palace, whose façade is ornated with statues and stuccowork representing the four elements. Franz Kafka studied in last-mentioned building from 1893 to 1901. The great Prague author was born and lived next to the square, where he frequented the literary club in the House of the Golden Unicorn.

THE ROYAL CASTLE
BUDAPEST, HUNGARY

The imposing Royal Castle dominates the old citadel of Buda. Despite raids, invasions and bombardments, it still stands out like a sentinel. For centuries the palace has been one of the symbols of Budapest, which really consists of two cities, Buda and Pest, which are separated not only by the majestic Danube River but also by history, tradition and art. Pest is in a lower position, is flat, and is a commercial center with Art Nouveau buildings. Buda, on the other hand, rises up on the top of a hill and is the most ancient and noblest part of the capital of Hungary. The first king to live there was Béla IV, who after the Tartar invasion of 1241 decided to utilize the natural defense offered by the rocky bluff on the right-hand bank of the river. He thus began construction of the Oregtoronyo, the old tower. In the 14th century, under the Angevin rulers, the fortress became the royal residence, surrounded by a small village, which was the original old town of Buda. The second period of construction and enlargement of the palace took place in the 15th century, under King Sigismund of Luxemburg, who had French and Italian architects build a new wing facing the Danube. The Friss Palot or Cool Palace overlooked the city with a large tower placed on the bastions and a chapel. King Matthias Corvi-

nus had the famous library built next to this and also added Renaissance gardens to the complex. Under his reign the royal palace became the center of power and culture, where science and the arts were especially appreciated.

But this golden age was short-lived. The year 1541 marked the beginning of Turkish occupation of the city, which ended only in 1686. The palace was abandoned and the pashas preferred to reside in an old Franciscan convent rather then inside the city walls. During the Austrian siege of Budapest, the Christian League and Ottoman army exchanged cannon shots for months. A powder magazine exploded and left the palace in ruins. In the 18th century the third reconstruction of the palace was begun by the architects Jean-Nicolas Jardot and Franz Anton Hildebrandt: in 1770 the royal palace of Maria Theresa had over 200 rooms. However, it was first used as convent and then as the seat of the university, and only in 1791 did it become the residence of a branch of the Hapsburg dynasty.

The fourth phase in the life of the palace began in 1890, when the architects Miklos Ybl and Alajos Hauszmann designed a new wing, dominated by a massive dome and the Baroque façade with its symmetrical columns. Emperor Franz Josef and his wife Elizabeth spent long holidays in the new 1003-ft (304-m) long complex. The castle once again became the seat of power during the regency of Admiral Nicholas Horthy in the 20th century. But in 1945 it was totally destroyed by fire: only the walls were left, while all the elegant furnishings were lost forever.

Once again, however, the Royal Palace has regained its original appearance, thanks to long and careful restoration work. Today the fortress houses the collections of some local history museums and a beautiful collection of Hungarian art that ranges from the Middle Ages to the works of local Impressionists such as Pál Szinnyei-Merse, as well as contemporary art works of the Nagybàny and Szolnok schools. The tumultuous history of the palace is narrated by means of models, original documents and exceptional finds, such as the 62 Gothic sculpture pieces found in 1974 under a heap of ruins. They had been thrown there and then buried during one of the many rebuilding phases.

68 and 69 bottom *The Royal Palace, which is 304 meters long, is a citadel of power on top of the Buda hill, dominating the Danube and the more modern and commercial Pest district.*

68-69 *The impressive dome and Baroque façade studded with columns are highlights of this construction, which was rebuilt several times from the 14th century on. This is the last wing, which was added in 1890.*

70-71 Rynek Główny is one of the largest medieval squares in Europe. In the background is the Gothic-Renaissance Sukienice, the 14th-century textiles market.

70 bottom Kraków's two main churches flank the square: St. Adalbert (left) and the Gothic-style Our Lady of the Assumption (right), with its two bell towers. On the taller one (268 ft/81 m), every hour a trumpeter plays a hymn that is interrupted, in memory of the sacrifice of the sentinel killed by the Tartars while he was sounding the alarm.

71 In the Old Town, the luxurious buildings decorated with statues testify to the importance of Kraków in the past, thanks to its strategic position on the so-called Amber Road leading to the Baltic Sea.

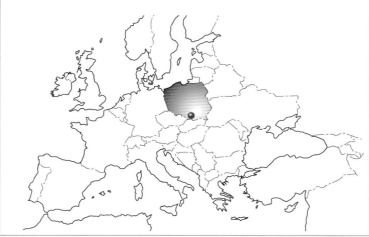

THE OLD TOWN
KRAKÓW, POLAND

For 560 years, up to the end of the 16th century, Kraków was the capital of Poland. Its Jagellonian University, the oldest center of learning in the country, had such famous students as Copernicus and Lenin, Nobel Prize winners for literature (Czeslaw Milosz, 1980, and Wyslaza Szynborska, 1996), some saints, and a pope, Karol Wojtyla (John Paul II). The university is located in 15th- and 16th-century buildings, such as the Collegium Maius, which houses the Golden Globe (1510), the first cartographic document showing the American continent. Another leading cultural institution is the synagogue in Kazimierz, the Jewish quarter. Founded in the 15th century, the temple has a Renaissance cemetery.

The Athens of Poland lies in a basin along the Vistula River. It has always been a bastion of Western Europe and Christianity. The Old Town, Stare Miasto, bears witness to the historic importance of Kraków, with its sumptuous palazzi that are the vestiges of the wealth and prestige of the city due to its position on the so-called Amber Road toward the Baltic. The first historic landmark on the Wawel Hill is the royal castle or Zamek, built in Romanesque-Gothic style and then rebuilt and enlarged in the 16th century with the contribution of Italian architects. Its halls are decorated with splendid tapestries made in Brussels, caisson ceilings, collections of weapons and armor, and the Crown Treasury. Next to the castle is the St. Wenceslaus Cathedral, a Gothic masterpiece constructed in 1320 with the incorporation of parts of several earlier churches. Eighteen side chapels were added later. The most precious of these is the one dedicated to Sigismund I the Elder; with its grandiose gilded dome it is considered one of the most beautiful Renaissance chapels north of the Alps. The cathedral also houses the royal tombs and that of the patron saint St. Stanislaus. For the Polish people, another pilgrimage site on the Wawel Hill is the Grotto of the Dragon, the monster slain by King Krak. According to legend, in order to free himself of the seven-headed monster, the astute ruler offered it a sheep filled with sulfur. The greedy dragon gobbled it up and then became so thirsty he dove into the river and drank so

72-73 *The Romanesque-Gothic Royal Castle stands on the Wawel Hill overlooking the Vistola River, the Zamek. This fortress now houses a collection of tapestries and the Crown Treasury.*

72 *bottom left* Plus ratio quam vis *is the motto of the city: reason is worth more than force. Here we see the oldest university in Poland (left), where famous figures such as Copernicus and Pope John Paul II* studied. *The university is located in old buildings such as the Collegium Maius, which houses the Golden Globe (1510), the first cartographic document that shows the American continent.*

72 bottom right and 73 Gold,
marble, inlaid wood, statues and
paintings: rich decoration is a feature
of many churches in Kraków. The
former capital of Poland boasts about
a hundred churches, and naturally
was a bastion of Western, Christian

Europe. In fact, the advance of the
Tartars was checked right under the
city walls in 1241, and in 1683 the
Catholic king John III Sobieski passed
through the city gates on his way to
Vienna to drive away the Turks, who
had almost reached the latter city.

EUROPE

much water that he burst. Thus, Krak was free to found his city on the hill – Kraków.

In order to reach the heart of the old town from the hill you have to take the old Royal Street, lined with monuments and historic buildings such as the house of the 20th-century painter Jan Matejko. The Rynek Główny, the market square, is one of the largest medieval squares in Europe. The oldest building in Kraków is the Gothic City Tower, the only remaining part of the complex demolished in 1818. In the middle of the square is the Sukienice, the 14th-century indoor fabrics market consisting of workshops with carved wooden façades dating from the 1300s, old railings, and enormous chandeliers hanging from the ceiling, which is decorated

with the crests of the Polish cities. The northeast corner of the square is dominated by the Gothic church of Our Lady of the Assumption, with its perfectly preserved original stained glass windows, as is its high altar, one of the largest in the world, sculpted in 1477-89 by Veit Stoss. Two towers crown the façade; the taller one is embellished with a cluster of eight small towers surmounted by a gilded dome. Every day, from this point, a trumpeter plays the notes of the hymn to the Virgin Mary and then suddenly interrupts his execution. This is a ritual commemorating the Tartar siege: according to legend, a sentinel managed to warn the citizens of the arrival of their enemies, but the sound of his trumpet was cut short by a deadly arrow.

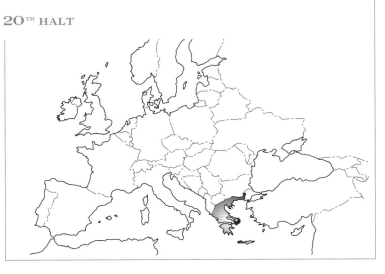

THE PARTHENON
ATHENS, GREECE

The Parthenon is one of most thrilling and fascinating temples in the world. It is the symbol of Athens and of its great civilization, which contrasted with the symbol of physical power represented by Sparta. The temple was erected on the Acropolis in honor of the goddess Athena Parthenos in the 5th century B.C. (between 447 and 438 B.C., to be exact); the architects were Ictinus and Callicrates, who were commissioned to do the work by Pericles. The Acropolis is the highest part of the hill that dominates the city. Already inhabited in the Neolithic period, it was gradually transformed into a sacred precinct with the construction of various temples, the main one being the Parthenon of the virgin goddess, the protectress of Athens.

The Parthenon, with 17 columns on the long sides and 8 on the short sides, is an admirable example of Doric art. The great sculptor Phidias supervised the sculptural decoration of the temple; this included the huge Athena Parthenos statue, which no longer exists. The fact that Phidias also took part in the architectural design is clearly revealed, and not only by historical sources. In fact, the edifice was built with a sculptor's sensibility. There are several figurative parts that betray the influence of his style and of the aesthetic vision that prevailed in Athens during its artistic golden age. Nothing was impossible for this master sculptor. His skill lies precisely in his capacity to render everything he represents and models in the most naturalistic manner. The light that suffuses a statue creates many chiaroscuro effects that lend a pictorial as well as plastic quality to the work. This in fact was Phidias' greatest innovation: he used light to 'paint' the statues. This is clearly visible in the fragment of the three goddesses Hestia, Dione, and Aphrodite witnessing the birth of Athena from the head of Zeus. In addition there is the superb rendering of the drapery, which adheres perfectly to the figures and is arranged in myriad folds, thus creating subtle and carefully gauged chiaroscuro effects, so that the sculptures are 'painted' with light and shadow.

Over and above its notable artistic features, through the centuries the Parthenon served different purposes. It was first converted into a Christian church and afterwards into a mosque when the Ottomans conquered Greece. The Turks then used the temple as a powder and weapons magazine. In 1687, during the Venetian siege of Athens, mortar shots from a ship hit the temple, practically destroying it. Later on, the remaining parts were used for the partial reconstruction of the temple that, however, did not include many sculptures; these had been purchased in the early 19th century by Lord Elgin and transported to London, later becoming part of the British Museum collection.

There has been a dispute between the Greek and British governments over the restitution of the so-called Elgin Marbles to Greece. According to the British, the Parthenon sculptures are one of the greatest artistic treasures in the world, and the fact that they represent the aesthetic vision and genius of antiquity, a model for so many later cultures, justifies their being kept in the British Museum. The dispute is still going on, but even without its sculptures the Parthenon is an astounding masterpiece.

76-77 The churches in Santorini are also whitewashed and have no friezes, but the roofs are painted the same color as the sea.

76 bottom and 78-79 Two views of Thera, perched on the craggy cliffs. The vertical configuration of the island is due to its volcanic origin. Recent studies have confirmed the date of the last eruption: 1500 BC.

77 left A view of Santorini, the island of panoramic views. Its strategic position attracted the Minoans and Dorians, as well as the Ptolemies of Egypt, who occupied it in order to control the Aegaen Sea.

77 right A panoramic view of the citadel-town of Thera that embraces a stretch of small houses in white tufa and goes as far as the lava stone beaches.

SANTORINI
GREECE

Callisti is its real name – 'the most beautiful.' Indeed, Santorini is especially fascinating and stands out among the splendid islands in the Cycladic archipelago for its original configuration, which makes it truly unique.

According to the geomorphologic reconstructions of the land, Santorini is presumably the result of an extremely violent volcanic eruption; it is what remains of the lower part of a volcano that exploded during its last eruption, creating two other nearby islands, Aspronissi and Terrasia.

With its 43 miles (69 km) of coastline, Santorini offers an impressive gamut of scenery. The west coast is marked by precipitous cliffs that plunge into the sea, while the east side descends softly, forming a very fertile plain and some lovely inlets towered over by the Profitis Ilias massif. But it is not the natural scenery alone that makes the island so fascinating. It is very interesting from an archaeological standpoint as well; rather recent digs have brought to light the remains of prehistoric settlements that were completely forgotten and 'buried' by the volcanic detritus that spread everywhere after the volcano exploded around 1500 B.C.

From that time on the island began its second life, as it were, coveted for its strategic position by the Spartans and Athenians, and later occupied by the Byzantines and Turks. Not far from the pink beach of Akrotiri, one of the loveliest and most famous on the island, are the ruins of Thera. This is a prehistoric city that is a sort of small Pompeii, the place where the local population was concentrated when the volcano unexpectedly exploded. Among the buried ruins, archaeologists found pottery, stone and bronze tools, jewels and small works of art. Furthermore, there are remains of frescoes of high artistic quality that have led some scholars to state that Thera was the mythical land of Atlantis, the cradle of an incredibly evolved civilization that was destroyed by a tidal wave and buried under water and ashes. But the locals seem to give little credence to this theory, as they are more concerned with preserving their traditions and heritage, as can be seen along the narrow marble streets of Oia, an enchanting village with cream-colored rock-hewn houses with blue domes that exudes a genuine island spirit.

80 top The czars wanted a showcase worthy of their power, and the Italian architects skillfully fulfilled their wish through elegant Baroque architecture with a profusion of statues, columns and arches.

80-81 The Winter Palace, a dazzling Baroque masterpiece rich in gold decoration, was built mainly by the architect Francesco Bartolomeo Rastrelli, who in 1731 was summoned to the court of the Czarina Elisabeth, the daughter of Peter the Great.

80 bottom The Column of Alexander, 155 ft (47 m) high, rises up in the middle of the Palace Square, the heart of the city. It was here that the October Revolution began.

81 Only by observing the Hermitage from above does one understand the ambitious scope of the czars' project: to give Russia a capital that could vie with the other European ones in beauty and refinement.

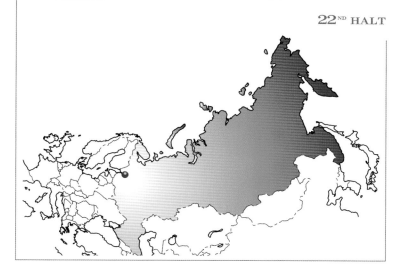

THE HERMITAGE
ST. PETERSBURG, RUSSIA

St. Petersburg is the creature of Peter the Great (1689-1725). But in order to build the new palace, his successors did not hesitate to tear down the one built by founder of the capital city. Over the years, the Hermitage, constructed as the Winter Palace and czars' residence, has become one of largest and most important museums in the world, admired not only for its architecture and the furnishings in its 1004 rooms, but also for its magnificent collection of artworks. Facing one of the largest and most majestic squares in Europe, the museum immediately strikes one with its fantastic white and green Baroque appearance. Many people contributed to its grandeur and fascination. In 1703 Peter the Great decided to create a new city in the wolf- and bear-infested steppe. He wanted "to open a window of Russia onto the Baltic," as Pushkin wrote; but above all

he sought to check the influence of Sweden in northern Russia. While waiting for the finishing touches to be put to the fortress, the czar lived in a modest Dutch-style house on the Neva River. But his daughter Elizabeth entertained even more grandiose ideas. In 1731 she commissioned the architect Francesco Bartolomeo Rastrelli to design the new Winter Palace in Baroque style, with the aim of overshadowing the beauty of the great European royal residences. The construction work lasted eight years, between the last phase of Elizabeth's reign and the brief rule of Peter III, thanks to the efforts of more than 4000 persons. However, Rastrelli was unable to finish the work. He had arrived at St. Petersburg at the age of sixteen and, after having designed and built some of the loveliest buildings in the city, he was fired by Catherine the Great (1762-1796 merely

because he had served Czarina Elizabeth too well. The new empress, a Teutonic autocrat, wanted an absolutely luxurious, opulent palace as huge as her empire – in other words, unequalled. After ascending the throne, Catherine the Great ordered the construction of the Small and Great Hermitage and of the theater in the Neo-Classical style, her favorite. And her love of art was responsible for the creation of one of the foremost and most popular museums in the world, which houses 3 million exceptional works of art. In fact, it was she who in 1794 purchased her first art collection, in Berlin. The czarina decorated the family apartments with the most precious furnishings and objects she could find in Russia and abroad. These included works by Italian, Flemish, Dutch, and French painters such as Giorgione, Guido Reni, Rubens, Rembrandt, and Poussin. And

her successors to the throne of Russia added to the Hermitage collection.

Walking through the lavish rooms is like losing your way among the riches and beauty of the history of European painting, with masterpieces by such greats as Botticelli, Caravaggio, Titian, Tiepolo and Leonardo da Vinci and on, up to Monet, Van Gogh, Degas, Picasso and Matisse. The rooms themselves are masterpieces, with an abundance of marble, gold leaf and stuccowork. Exquisite examples are the Emperors' Staircase designed by Rastrelli, the Field Marshals' Hall by the architect Montferrand, the Hall of Peter the Great designed by Stasov, and the Military Gallery, featuring 322 portraits of the heroes of the 1812 war against Napoleon. Among the rarities kept

in the Hermitage, there are Paleolithic era finds, figures made of stone and bones depicting women and birds that were found at Irkutsk, in Russia's far eastern region. Then there are gems of Greek and Roman art, weapons and armor, precious goldsmith work, porcelain, and fabrics. Mention must also be made of the collection of 300,000 icons, handmade objects, and treasures that afford a picture of more than 1000 years of Russian history. The Hermitage collections travel through time and space, from one continent to another, from ancient Egypt to India, from the Far East to the Ural Mts., and from prehistoric times to the present. This is a spellbinding itinerary that must be followed slowly, letting oneself be inspired by the astonishing objects on display.

82 top The splendid statue of Cupid and Psyche by Antonio Canova is displayed to great effect in the Hermitage Museum, together with about 3,000,000 other works of art of all ages collected throughout the world.

82 bottom The 1004 rooms in the Winter Palace are in themselves a masterpiece of 17th-century architecture. A complete visit is a marathon: it covers13.5 miles (22 km) of splendid inlaid wooden floors.

82-83 The Emperors' Staircase was designed by the architect Rastrelli with an abundance of marble, gold leaf and stuccowork. The Winter Palace was finished in the 19th century by another Italian architect, Carlo Rossi.

83 bottom In 1764 Catherine the Great began to purchase works of art to decorate the palace. Thus began the collection of thousands of masterpieces that make the Hermitage one of the leading museums in the world.

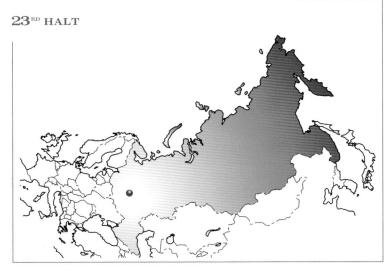

THE KREMLIN
MOSCOW, RUSSIA

The stars on the Tower of the Redeemer twirl in the wind and gleam in the sunlight. The five stars made of ruby-colored glass were the last symbolic addition (1937) made on the Kremlin, which is already rich in symbols. The Marquis de Custine called the Moscow citadel "the Mont Blanc of fortresses." It has been called almost everything under the sun: prison, sanctuary, bastion against invaders and Bastille against the people, the refuge of despots and the last home of the defenders of the fatherland. Certainly, the Kremlin, from the Russian word for citadel, *kreml*, is the symbol of Russian sovereignty, the center of power first of the czars' empire up to the October Revolution in 1917, and then of the Soviet regime and its state administration until the demise of communism.

Facing Red Square, the Kremlin is an architectural complex that has become unique because of enlargement and rebuilding effected in different periods.

Although the most ancient settlements in the Moscow area date from the Bronze Age, the city was first recorded historically in 1147. Construction of the Kremlin began during the rule of Yuri Dolgoruky, the prince of Kiev. The layout we see today dates to 1367-68, when Prince Dimitry Donskoi built a large fortification whose white walls gave Moscow the appellation of White City. The enclosure perimeter extends for about 1.5 miles (2.4 km) and has twenty towers. The height of the walls, which have forked crenellation, ranges from 16.5 to 63 ft (5 to 19 m), while the tower with the spires added in the 17th century reach a height of 234 ft (71 m).

Originally the walls were protected by sloping wooden roofs and were designed and built by Italian engineers and architects, including Antonio and Alevisio Friazins and Pietro Antonio Solari, a member of the family of architects that contributed to the construction of the Duomo in Milan. The erection of the Taynitskaya Tower in 1485 marked the beginning of the creation of an innovative system of fortifications in Russia. With an arched entrance and a passageway with loopholes that connected it to the nearby stone bridge, the tower hid two secrets: the well and the tunnel that led to the bank of the river, which was vital for providing water in case of a siege.

In the second half of the 15th century Russian architects and sculptors also contributed to the construction, but they proved to be incompetent; in fact, one of the walls actually collapsed. So in 1475

84 left Since its foundation in 1147, the Kremlin has been the political-administrative seat of Moscow. Construction began with the fortress, enclosed by a crenellated perimeter wall over 1.25 miles (2 km) long.

84 right Of the twenty towers we see today, all surmounted by tall spires, the most famous is the Tower of the Redeemer. It was built in the 1400s and completed in 1625 with a clock and bells.

84-85 The massive complex stands along the Moscow River, which traverses the capital. The Kremlin is a veritable fortified city that contains various buildings, churches and gardens.

85 bottom The Grand Palace, which was damaged during the French occupation, was rebuilt in 1839-49 in an eclectic style that ranges from Gothic to Neo-Classical. For decades it was the seat of power in the Soviet Union.

86-87 *The Annunciation Cathedral was built right in front of the Grand Palace in 1484-89. It was originally intended to be the czars' private chapel.*

86 bottom *The style of the religious monuments, which were erected in the Kremlin in the 16th century, was typically Russian-Byzantine, but the Italian architects used building techniques that were innovative for that time.*

87 *Two symbols of czarist Moscow: the Assumption Cathedral (above), where the czars were crowned, and the Czar Bell (below), whose tower is 267 ft (81 m) high and was never damaged by fire or bombardments.*

EUROPE

another Italian, Aristotele Fioravanti, was commissioned to create the large central dome surrounded by four smaller domes. The style employed was the typical Russian Byzantine one, but the technique was quite innovative. In the same period the citadel witnessed the construction of small Orthodox churches, and in 1505 work began on the Arkhangelski Cathedral dedicated to the Archangel Michael, a successful blend of Venetian Renaissance motifs and Byzantine domes decorated with hundreds of frescoes and icons. At the same time the foundations were laid for the 267-ft (81-m) bell tower of Ivan the Great, the symbol of czarist Moscow and of the Kremlin's solidity, since it was never touched either by fires or bombardments. In order to improve the defensive system, in 1508-16 a wide and deep trench was dug on the east side of the walls; it was later filled with water and in the early 1800s was filled with earth. Drawbridges were added to the Spasskaya and Nikolskay towers around which important commercial activity developed.

In the 1600s new work was begun on the Kremlin. The most important addition was the Twelve Apostles Church. In 1625-85, spires were added to all the towers except the Nikolskaya in order to lend them a more soaring and powerful aspect. These seem to herald the arrival of Peter the Great and his successors, who spent huge sums of money to erect luxurious Neo-Classic buildings, such as the Senate built for Catherine the Great, another ruler who loved to think and act on a grand scale.

88 top When designing the Kremlin buildings, the Italian architects had no qualms whatsoever about mixing Venetian Renaissance motifs, Byzantine, decoration, stained glass windows, stuccowork and finely carved columns.

88 bottom Monumental entrances, marble and a great deal of gold leaf characterize the large salon in the Faceted Palace. This building was constructed in 1487-91, but the frescoes date from 1668.

88-89 Red, the color of power, dominates in the throne room of the Terem Palace. However, the floral decoration creates an intimate, warm atmosphere. 'Terem,' in fact, means 'private home.'

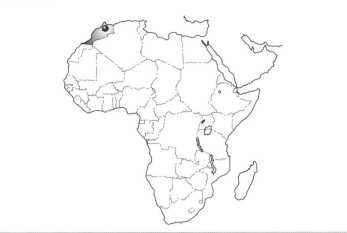

THE ROYAL PALACE, MOSQUE
FÈS, MOROCCO

Fès, the most ancient and fascinating of the four imperial cities in Morocco, is the realization of the medieval Arab dream. The date of its foundation is still wrapped in mystery. What is certain is that in the year 807 the sultan Mulay Idriss founded a settlement that later became the city of Fès, which remained the capital of the country until 1912. The city is a mirage mirrored in the water of the man-made basin opposite, shining brilliantly with its precious white, gold and green ceramic tiles, set against a sky so blue that it seems to be painted. Behind the splendid filigreed bronze portals lies the Royal Palace, Dar el-Makhzen, which truly seems to be emerging from a legend nar-

rated in the desert at night. Situated in Place des Alaouites, the palace was built in the 13th century together with the new city, Fès al-Jedid, which lies right next to the original old city, Fès al-Bali. The royal complex, a veritable citadel, extends for 200 acres (81 hectares), comprising the mosque, parade ground, gardens with fountains, refined buildings and the madrasa, the Islamic theological school with lodgings for the students that was founded in the first half of the 14th century by the sultan Abu Said Othman.

The Royal Palace was used both for the sultan's garrisons and as his residence, but it has always "jealously closed its portals, with the ivory façade and Saracen

tiles of that pine green color that Muhammad said was as beneficial as the face of a woman," as Slimane Zeghidour writes. There is even a harem, so much in fashion in these parts, as well as the domed tomb (*koubba*) of a *marabout*, a monk warrior particularly venerated by the people. The interiors are an exercise in luxury, an endless flow of geometric decoration that paradoxically stems from a prohibition. In fact, Allah forbids the representation of men and animals, and this divine imposition gave rise to an art that plays with geometric and floral motifs, breaking them up, interweaving them, and multiplying them ad infinitum. Circles, stars, flowers, and vines are repeated on the capitals, in

90 The elegant colors of the mosaics create abstract geometric patterns and arabesques that frame the splendid filigree bronze portals of the Royal Palace, built in the 13th century.

90-91 and 91 bottom The Royal Palace is a citadel. Its surface area of 200 acres (81 hectares) contains richly decorated buildings, the madrasa or Koranic theological school, and gardens with fountains.

91 top Some halls are open only on special occasions, such as the Festival of the Throne.

the niches, on the domes, façades and fountains and even the pavements.

A classic example of this decoration is to be seen in the inner courtyard of the best-known monument in Fès, the al-Qarawiyin mosque. According to tradition it was a woman, Lalla Fatma Bent Muhammad al-Fehi, who had it built in 857 with the inheritance from her wealthy father, a refugee from Kairouan. But only in 1135 did the sultan Ali ben Youssek make it the splendid edifice we see today. This was the home of the most ancient religious school of the Maghreb, as well as one of the most important in all Islam. Entrance is forbidden to non-Muslims, but you can see something through the open doors. The two lovely kiosks in the courtyard are strikingly similar to the Court of the Lions in the Granada Alhambra; one

dates from the 16th century, and both are decorated with slender marble columns surmounted by delicate interlace work carved out of the same stone. Only Muslims can admire the fabulous 13th-century chandelier, the most ancient hourglass in the world, a prayer rostrum that was brought from Cordoba, as well as delicate stucco decoration restored to its former splendor in the 1950s. The oratory is a veritable forest of 270 columns divided into sixteen aisles. The huge library was founded in the 10th century and rebuilt in the 14th century. The wisest and most cultured Islamic scholars of every age came to this library to study some of the 30,000 volumes, 10,000 of which are manuscripts. The precious collection includes rarities such as the 9th-century gazelle-hide Koran and a manuscript by the Muslim scholar Averroës, who lived in the 14th century.

94-95 and 94 bottom The Acacus massif extends 95 miles (150 km). The sand has peaks that rise 1980 to 4290 ft (600 to 1300 m). On the bed of sand dunes are bizarre rock formations sculpted by

the ghibli (the desert wind) and water: a labyrinth of spires, solitary monoliths, castle-like masses, and arches. The area also has a host of tracks hidden among the dunes and rocks.

95 The desert appears to be uninhabited, but is actually the domain of the legendary 'blue people,' the Tuareg, who for centuries were guides for the camel caravans along the tracks that seem to vanish in the horizon. This

a magical landscape, an overpowering attraction for dozens of Europeans who in the 19th century attempted to follow the tracks of the German traveler Friedrich Hornemann, the first person to penetrate the Libyan Desert (1798).

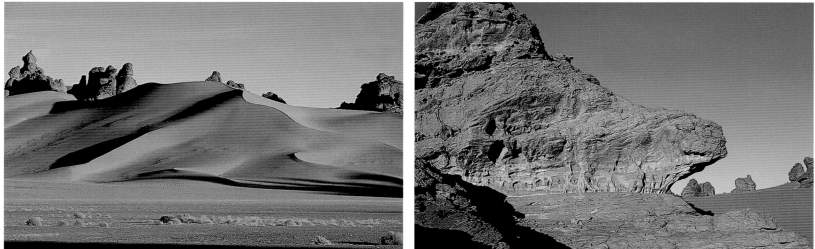

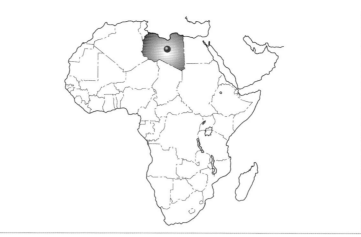

SAHARA DESERT
LIBYA

In the heart of this boundless sea of sand dunes the tracks seem to lead nowhere. But on the contrary for millennia they have served almost as motorways for the camel caravans led by the legendary blue men, the Tuareg, formerly caravaners and invincible raiders and still the lords of the Sahara Desert. The Tuareg are the only people to know the jealously guarded secrets and mysteries of this huge rectangle of sand and rock that occupies the region of the African continent ranging from the Atlantic Ocean to the Red Sea. The landscape of sand dunes is interrupted by mountain reliefs and sedimentary plateaus delimited by long rock cliffs. The largest desert in the world was once a fertile area covered with woods and prairies and traversed by rivers that allowed the local populations to live by hunting and fishing. Proof of this Saharan lifestyle in ancient times is afforded by the re-

mains of human settlements and by rock paintings and carvings. Their discovery excited and still excites the many Europeans enamored of the Sahara who followed the footsteps of the German Friedrich Hornemann, the first person to penetrate the Libyan Desert (1798). And the adventure continues. The Acacus Massif, in fact, is a recent discovery. It dates from 1955, when the Italian paleethnologist Fabrizio Mori revealed to the world this gallery of prehistoric paintings and graffiti. He had found a gigantic open-air picture gallery of rock paintings that in 1985 UNESCO declared a World Heritage Site. Running from north to south for 93 miles (150 km) and 28 miles (45 km) wide, the massif reaches an altitude of 4265 ft (1300 m). The rocks lying on a bed of golden sand have been forged into the most curious shapes by the *ghibli*, the hot,

dusty desert wind: pointed towers, massive castles, solitary monoliths, rock faces decorated like lace, triumphal arches such as the grandiose Fozzigiaren, one of the largest formations of its kind in the Sahara Desert. There are over one hundred rock-painting sites, but it takes the eye of the Tuareg to find the way through seemingly inaccessible valleys. After which you are face to face with dancers 12,000 years old, hunters, rhinoceroses and mouflons. Carved in the stone is the history of the legendary Garamantes population mentioned by Herodotus – caught up in their daily activities, plowing the fields, breeding long-horned oxen, engaged in hunting on chariots pulled by four horses. And here we see them on official occasions, while they are in battle and then making peace, which is marked by an exchange of gifts: a lesson in diplomacy 8000 years old.

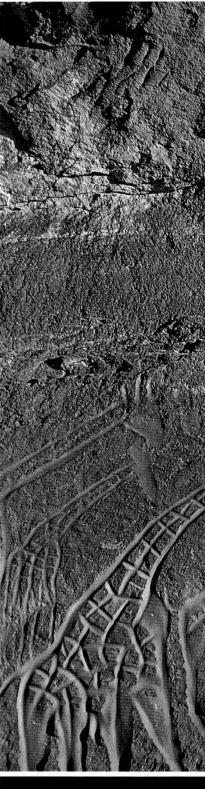

AFRICA

96 and 97 In 1955, the Italian ethnologist Fabrizio Mori discovered extraordinary prehistoric rock paintings and graffiti, a veritable open-air gallery 12,000 years old. Included in the carvings are rhinoceroses and mouflons, men plowing the fields, breeding long-horned oxen, and hunting on horse-drawn chariots. These prehistoric people lived here when the area that is now a desert was filled with rivers and forests.

98-99 and 98 bottom left Leptis Magna boasted one of the liveliest marketplaces in the Roman Empire. Founded by the Phoenicians on the coast of Libya, the city enjoyed its golden age in the 2nd-3rd century AD.

98 bottom right The Roman Emperor Septimius Severus, who was born in Leptis Magna, transformed the city into a miniature Rome that was filled with lovely cipolin marble columns.

99 left A short tunnel leads to the theater with its perfect acoustics. This is one of the most ancient brick Roman theaters.

99 right The Arch of Trajan, together with those of Septimius Severus and Tiberius, stands along the wide *decumanus* that led to the harbor.

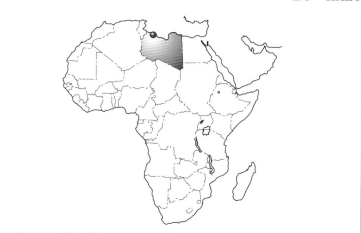

LEPTIS MAGNA
LIBYA

Grandiose is the appropriate word: an overwhelming display of statues, women's faces carved in sandstone, arches and columns standing out against the deep blue sky. With its typical scent of salt and desert mixed together, Leptis Magna – situated in Tripolitania, the area in Libya halfway between Alexandria and Carthage – enjoyed its golden age under Emperor Septimius Severus, who ruled the Roman Empire from A.D. 193 to 211. Founded by the Phoenicians in the 7th to 6th centuries B.C., Leptis was in the center of a region particularly suitable for trade, the only natural harbor in the extremely dangerous Gulf of Sidra, where the sand of the Sahara Desert penetrated the waves, creating treacherous sand bars. The small settlement near the Lebda River therefore became the port of call for those who wanted to go into the interior, sail on to other Mediterranean harbors, or merely stock up on water. With the arrival of the Roman conquerors in the 1st century B.C. and the subsequent period of peace, Leptis Magna became more beautiful and cultivated. The rich merchants who lived there competed in the construction of monumental works in keeping with a town plan that was rigorously schematic yet conceived to astonish visitors entering the city. The citizens' cosmopolitan character was legendary, as they were curious about and interested in the customs of other people. In fact, in the 1st century B.C. the local art patrons announced a competition to beautify the city; it was won by the Tapapi family, which left to posterity a long list of works, such as the large marketplace, one the most striking in the world, where the stands were carefully conceived from both an aesthetic and practical standpoint. Another famous monument was the theater, with perfect acoustics and a temple dedicated to Ceres made of the best cipolin marble available.

Septimius Severus, who was severe both in name and character, was born here in this sun-drenched land. In order to lend glory and prestige to his birthplace, he made it magnificent and powerful. His triumphal arch was built at the intersection of the two principal city streets, the *cardo* and *decumanus*, and it was almost entirely decorated with elaborate marble bas-reliefs and friezes. The forum had a huge basilica whose central hall was over 99 ft (30 m) high. However, with time the port began to silt up and Leptis declined with the end of the rule of the house of Severus. Then new rulers arrived: the Vandals, Byzantines, and Arabs. And, in the end, there remained only the wind whispering among the ruins steeped in mystery.

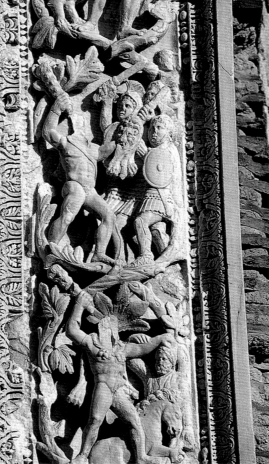

100 top The head of Medusa, dozens of copies of which were sculpted, still keeps watch over the Forum of the House of Severus.

100 bottom The columns of the Severan basilica are dressed with friezes and bas-reliefs representing mythological figures, gods and historic events.

100-101 The Severan basilica has a Byzantine nave 100 ft (30 m) high that is decorated with splendid sculpted columns.

101 bottom The arcades and portals of the Forum built by the Severan emperors vied in elegance with the monumental works that the rich city merchants had built to outshine one another.

102-103 and 102 bottom left The Pharaoh Ramesses II had two monumental temples built in the desert region of the upper Nile Valley, Roman Nubia: one dedicated to himself and the other to his beloved queen, Nefertari.

102 bottom right On the wall of the forecourt there are very detailed relief sculptures of the pharaoh's major military victories, including the famous Battle of Qadesh against the Hittites. Here we see some prisoners at the temple entrance.

103 Ramesses II (left) is depicted with the double crown, the symbol of the unification of Upper and Lower Egypt. At his feet are smaller statues of the princes and princesses (right).

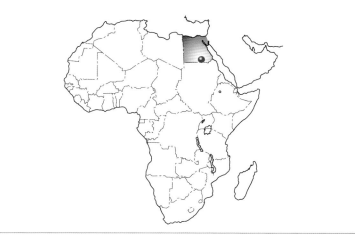

ABU SIMBEL

EGYPT

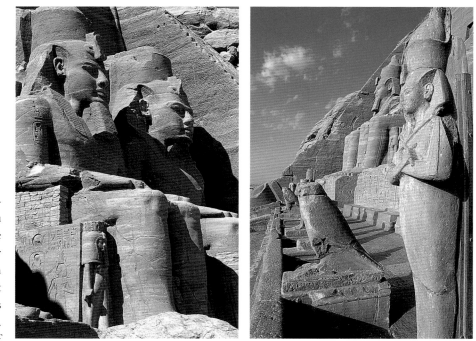

The two temples of Abu Simbel, which lie almost at the border between southern Egypt and ancient Nubia, far surpass our expectations. The hundreds of photographs we have seen in newspapers and books, the dozens of documentary films on TV, are nothing in comparison with the actual site, where the powerful and majestic combination of nature and human ingenuity are overwhelming. There are moments when one can take in this beauty almost in solitude, savoring the emotional impact of the sacred site above and beyond its touristic value. And it is an unforgettable experience. The Great Temple is the more spectacular of the two: the four colossi of Ramesses II wearing the double crown on his head are seated against the mountain, scrutinizing infinity from a height of 66 feet (20 m). At the foot of this rock relief are the blue waters of Lake Nasser. The statues exude such might that one can easily understand why

they were placed in this spot. They are a silent warning to enemies not to dare think of harming the Kingdoms of Upper and Lower Egypt, because the pharaoh is there, keeping watch over them. The façade, which is 109 ft (33 m) high and 119 ft (36 m) wide, has little need of decoration because of the presence of the imposing statues. The other members of the royal family are depicted standing and are small compared to the sovereign, while the defeated populations are sculpted on either side of the thrones. In the middle, above the entrance, is a large high relief of the god Ra in the guise of a falcon.

But if the façade is awe-inspiring, the interior surpasses it for the refined carving and the supernatural spirit that pervades it. In the forecourt Ramesses takes on the

appearance and essence of the god Osiris. The eight pillars that support the ceiling are decorated with the same number of stone images of the pharaoh with the appearance and attributes of the god of the afterlife. Beyond these, on the walls are scenes of the famous Battle of Qadesh, during which the Hittites suffered a sensational defeat at the hands of Ramesses II, at least according to Egyptian propaganda. Here the hooves of the horses rearing up over the vanquished, the vibrant tension of the bows in the pharaoh's hands, the tragic details of the limbs mangled during the battle, create both a poetic and brutal effect that is at once realistic and symbolic.

The farther one penetrates into the temple the smaller the chambers become, because in Egyptian temples the god that dwelt in the sanctuary had to be able to see the worshippers, who were not allowed to see him, hidden in the penumbra of a small chamber. Thus one arrives at the

104 top Scenes of ceremonies and battles decorate the interiors of the two temples. The refinement of the sculptures creates an effect that is both poetic and tragic.

104 bottom left In the last chamber there are four rock-hewn statues. Three of them are illuminated by sunlight during the equinox.

104 bottom right This bas-relief in the Great Temple of Ramesses II portrays the pharaoh leading an attack on his chariot.

105 In the forecourt of the Great Temple the eight pillars supporting the ceiling are decorated with portraits of the pharaoh in the guise of the god Osiris.

AFRICA

heart of the temple, in the back chapel. Here, twice a year, sunlight strikes the four disturbing rock-hewn statues of Harmakhis, the deified Ramesses, Amon-Ra and Ptah.

The nearby Temple of Hathor, which was really dedicated to Nerfertari, the Great Wife of Ramesses, is much more intimate in character. Here the prevailing feature is harmony, with delicate, colorful relief sculpture, stupendous scenes of offerings to the goddess, and portraits of the deified queen. These masterpieces survived the ravages of time, but in the early 1960s temples ran the risk of being submerged by the waters of the lake that would be created by the construction of the Aswan High Dam. A UNESCO project was then put into effect: the monuments were dismantled and cut into 1036 blocks, each with its own number and weighing 30 tons, which were then reassembled 660 ft (200 m) away on a level 211 ft (64 m) higher. The task took five years, until 1968, becoming the largest and most successful salvage operation of an archaeological monument. Thanks to this project, we can enjoy the beauty of this site, which has been declared one of the seven wonders of modern times.

106-107 The façade of the Temple of Nefertari has six statues 33 ft (10 m) high depicting the pharaoh and his consort.

106 bottom Dedicated to the goddess Hathor, the temple is richly decorated with scenes of the royal couple (below).

107 Delicacy and harmony are the principal features of the sculptures (above) and decoration in the smaller temple. In the hypostyle hall (below), which is divided into three aisles, are the portraits of the goddess Hathor and the deified queen Nefertari.

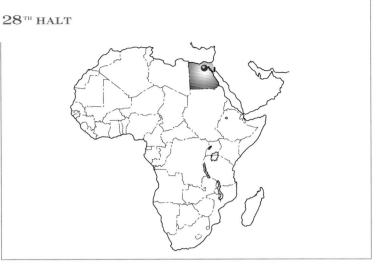

THE PYRAMIDS OF GIZA
CAIRO, EGYPT

It is almost as if they are making fun of human beings. They have been there for almost 5000 years with their perfect pointed structure, towering over the plain of Giza, without revealing very much of their secrets. The three grandiose pyramids have always been the symbol of a challenge. Having abandoned the old theories about slaves whipped to death and unspeakable torture, today we know that the pyramids were built by teams of expert laborers supervised by engineers, architects and master builders who used and combined their great skill, serious mathematical calculations and primitive but precise tools. In exchange laborers received food for themselves and their families, the right to a tomb and hence to immortality, and the privilege of being part of a unique enterprise. In fact, the construction of the eternal dwelling place of the pharaoh was not mere building; it was an exploit that united the various tribes, the peoples scattered throughout ancient Egypt, into a common aim: merge the human and divine by means of the resurrection of the king, who would then take care of his successor and his people. At least this is what was prescribed by the *ma'at*, the Egyptians' model and spiritual ideal – justice, ethical behavior, peace, and harmony – and the basis of religious and political order in the country. In this ingeniously simple manner the Egyptians had enough to live on, the economy progressed, the monuments would duly impress visitors, and a nationalistic spirit was created that united everyone against possible foreigner invaders. In short, stable domestic peace was guaranteed.

The pyramids of Giza were erected during the Fourth Dynasty of the Old Kingdom (2686-2181 B.C.) and house the tombs of the pharaohs Khufu (Cheops), Khafre (Khephren), Menkaure (Mycinerus). For a long time, even in antiquity, there was much speculation about them. The Greek historian Herodotus (5th century B.C.), for example, wrote that 100,000 laborers worked for twenty years to build the first pyramid. It was Napoleon who during his expedition of Egypt shouted the following to his troops: "Men, from the heights of these pyramids, forty centuries look down on us!" and his men wrested the pyramids from millennia of oblivion, generating the Egyptology craze. In 1818, Belzoni, an Italian from Padua and former circus strong man turned explorer and archaeologist, finally managed to find the entrance to the

108 The top of the Pyramid of Khafre, built on a hillock and 136.5 meters high, still has its top and part of the original casing. The entrance was discovered in 1818 by the Italian explorer Belzoni.

108-109 The metropolis of Cairo in the background seems to be laying siege to Giza and the pyramids of Khufu, Khephren and Mycerinus (the smallest), which have become the symbol of Egypt.

109 bottom left The Pyramid of Cheops, 452 ft (137 m) high, is the most impressive. It was built with 2,500,000 blocks of stone weighing three tons each.

109 bottom right The monuments, built to house the remains of the three pharaohs, date from the Fourth Dynasty of the Ancient Kingdom (2575-2465 BC).

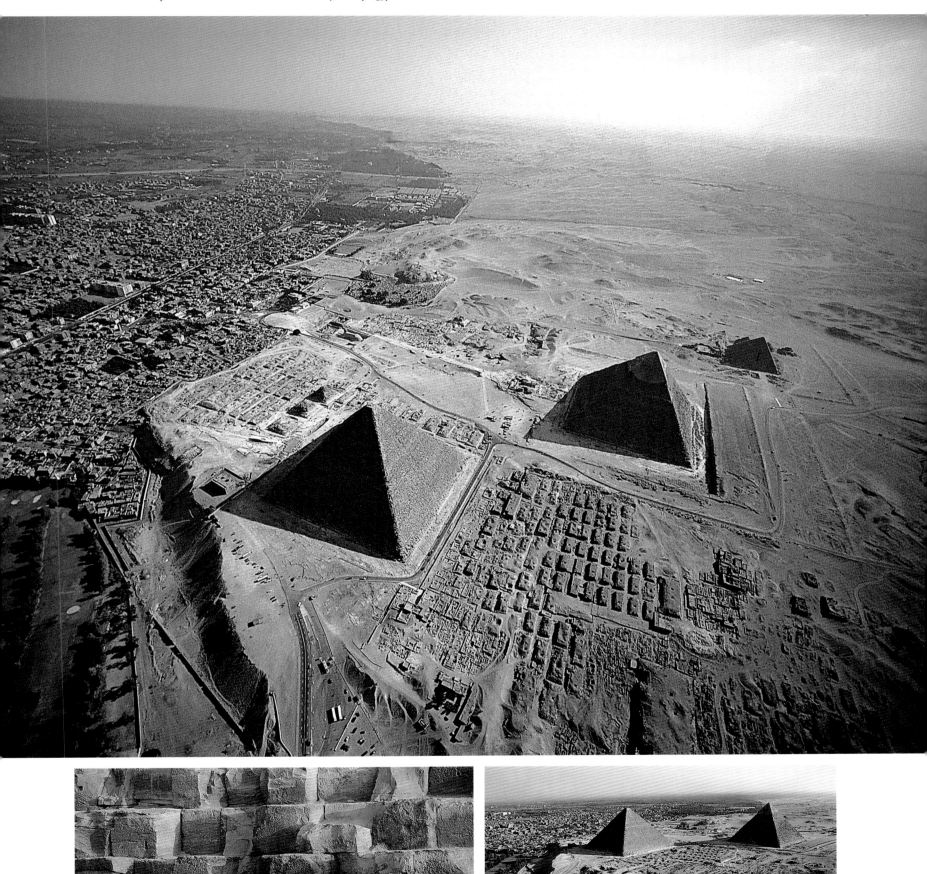

AFRICA

Pyramid of Khafre and, incidentally, could not resist the temptation of carving his name on those ancient stones. A short time later, the Genoan Giovanni Battista Caviglia (1772-1845) penetrated the Pyramid of Khufu – and Giza was invaded by scholars thereafter.

A great deal of progress has been made, but many questions concerning these majestic monuments are still awaiting an answer. The most recent mystery dates from a couple of years ago, when a camera mounted on a tiny robot penetrated the Great Pyramid of Khufu and found, in a vent, a small square door about 8 inches (20 cm) per side with two small bronze handles. Its presence there is inexplicable for the moment, and we do not know what it conceals. For that matter, we don't even know why the pharaoh's burial chamber has no artwork, inscriptions or grave goods. It is bare except for the monolithic red granite sarcophagus, which is empty and mute. What is known for certain is that the pyramids were the representation in stone of the sun's rays spreading over the Earth.

In most ancient Egyptian paintings and relief sculptures the sun sends shafts of light from its globe onto our planet that irradiate it, a cone on the surface. Hence the idea of a structure that would allow the divine rays to concentrate on its tip and then slide down to the ground, forming a pyramid of light and energy created by a ratio between height and perimeter that corresponds to the sacred number. Perhaps some day archaeologists will come up with definitive explanations. But for the time being, the Sphinx is keeping watch next to the pyramids.

*112 top The first pylon, with the
avenue of ram-headed sphinxes.*

*112-113 The monumental complex of
Karnak extends for almost 2 miles (3
km) in the city of Luxor and comprises
a series of buildings, columns, temples
and enclosure walls. The main
sanctuary was dedicated to the god
Amon-Ra.*

*112 bottom In this bas-relief,
Ramesses II pays homage to the god
Amon-Ra.*

*113 The obelisk of Queen
Hatshepsut, which is 99 ft (30 m)
high, is decorated with scenes from the
life of the only woman pharaoh of the
Two Kingdoms.*

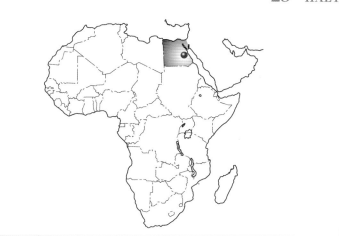

THE TEMPLE OF KARNAK
LUXOR, EGYPT

One of the most varied temple complexes in the ancient world is impressive but also rather confusing, in a permanent state of reconstruction, both oppressive and intriguing. The temples of Karnak – because the complex really comprises several temples located in the same enclosure – lie in the modern city of Luxor, on the east side of ancient Thebes, the capital of Egypt during the Middle and New Kingdom. The main one, the Great Temple, was dedicated to Amon-Ra, the sun god and leading Theban divinity, usually portrayed with a ram's head. Constructed in 1900 B.C., the temple continued to be enlarged until the 4th century A.D., since every pharaoh wanted to leave his mark there.

The first impression one has upon entering is one of striking grandiosity, despite the fact that few of the sphinxes that once lined the 2-mile (ca. 3-km) avenue that linked the Karnak and Luxor temples, have survived. The pylons are simply immense and, next to the one at right one can still see the inclined ramp, the ancestor of hoists or cranes. In fact, the Egyptian architects utilized unfired brick ramps to set the stone blocks at high levels.

The courtyard is the largest in ancient Egypt, 330 by 264 ft (100 x 80 m), comprising other rows of sphinxes on the sides, the Temple of Seti I at left and the Temple of Ramesses III at right. This latter edifice is particularly interesting for the colossi of the pharaoh at the entrance and in the inner portico, as well as for a small hypostyle hall (compared to the others) and gloomy shrine. Just before the second pylon in the large courtyard there is also an isolated statue of a proud Ramesses II, 49.5 ft (15 m) high and made of pink granite, which is accompanied by the small statue of his daughter Bent-Anta at his feet.

But the pride and joy of "the most venerated of places" is right before the second entrance: the sensational hypostyle hall, a veritable labyrinth, immortalized by movies. This consists of a forest of 134 columns, the twelve central ones of which have open papyrus bud capitals while the re-

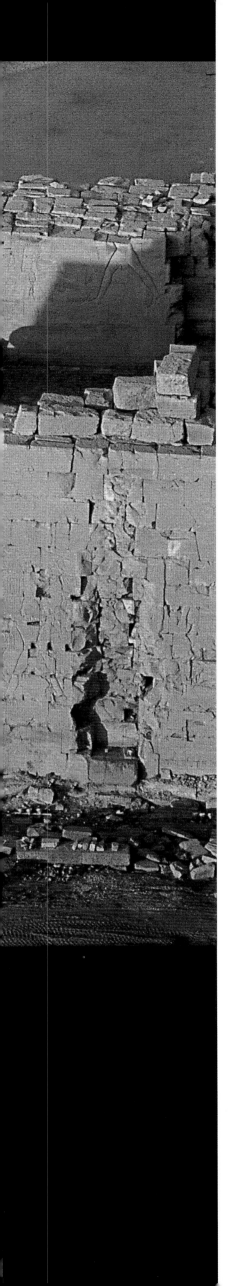

114-115 Near the sacred lake is the hypostyle hall, whose courtyard is filled with statues.

115 top Seti I left images of his exploits carved on the columns and walls of the large hypostyle atrium.

114 bottom The sanctuary was built in 1900 BC, but continued to expand up to the 4th century AD, since every sovereign wanted to leave his imprint there. Near the river is the pylon of Ramesses II.

115 bottom An overhead view of the courtyard and magnificent labyrinth of columns in the Great Temple of Amon.

maining 122 are of the bundled papyrus type. Here one is simply overwhelmed. Visitors and the guards with their light blue clothing materialize and disappear in a flash amid the tall architectural elements, while the play of light and shadow creates strange effects on the huge reliefs and brilliant paintings. One has the impression of being enclosed in something alien, and wavers between curiosity about the host of incomprehensible illustrations and a sense of disorientation.

But one need only exit via the former central avenue to regain the sense of the somewhat chaotic complex of ruins and temples that over the centuries have almost been piled up against one another. Set between relief sculptures and blocks of construction is the pointed obelisk of Hatshepsut, about 99 ft (30 m) of solid pink granite with scenes from the life of the only female ruler

of the Two Kingdoms. To the right is another monument mentioned by every guide and known by every tourist: the sacred scarab beetle, one of the most ancient symbols of Ra, who promises to fulfill the wishes of those who go round it three times counterclockwise. Next to this is the sacred lake where the ritual navigation once took place. Now its banks are the venue of the Sound and Light spectacle held for visitors.

All this is surrounded by a myriad of ruins of buildings, the priests' houses (20,000 priests once officiated here), storehouses for offerings, the temples dedicated to Ptah, Mut, Khonsu and Montu and their walled enclosures, colossi and reliefs. When it is restored to its former splendor, the Karnak complex will once again stun the world with its complexity, magnificence and beauty.

116-117 The Skeleton Coast extends for 310 miles (500 km) along the Atlantic Ocean. The macabre name refers to the many shipwrecks there caused by the strong ocean currents.

116 bottom left There are still hundreds of wrecked ships along the beaches. The sea here is one of the best regions for fishing on the West African coastline.

116 bottom right The water is extremely clean and the coast is by no means inhospitable. A colony of over 100,000 seals lives at Cape Cross, near Swakopmund.

117 The dune of the Namib Desert are spectacular mountains of sand up to 300 meters high that seem to plunge into the Atlantic Ocean. This is the point of origin of the precious fog that makes life possible in this region.

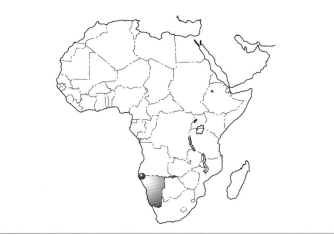

THE SKELETON COAST
NAMIBIA

This macabre name derives from the many ships lying there that capsized because of the strong Atlantic currents. And the land itself is not much more friendly. Those who managed to escape from the freezing waters of the Atlantic Ocean and the sharks, often ended up dying of hunger and thirst next to the wreckage of the ships and the carcasses of whales. Then, in a few weeks' time, the fine sand of the Namib Desert covered everything, humans and objects, with a thin light veil, transforming the fiery beaches into an open-air museum, which is now a national park. This reserve extends for about 310 miles (500 km) along the sea from the border with Angola.

This is a desert region that despite its name is truly spectacular. The sand dunes reach a height of 990 ft (300 m) and plunge into the dark water. The cold and stormy ocean is so clean and uncontaminated that is the ideal habitat for seals as well as for many fish such as huge salmon, tuna, and groupers. It would seem that no form of life could exist on the Skeleton Coast . But this is only a first impression, because plants and animals do live here … and they feed on the fog. In normal conditions, the masses of hot, humid air that form over the Atlantic should disappear with the torrid temperature of the desert. But just before arriving at the coast they meet the icy Benguela current, which comes directly from the Antarctic. The humid air thus cools, condenses, and becomes fog.

In the early morning one can watch the spectacle of this humid ghost that extends into the interior for over 25 miles (40 km). At dawn the entire coastline is buzzing.

Every organism has invented some system to make the best use of those drops of life. There is the tenebrinoid beetle, a Coleopteron (*Onymacris unguicularis*) that runs to the top of a dune and like an acrobat stands on its head and straightens out its back legs. Exactly as occurs on the outer surface of a glass containing a very cold beverage, the fog condenses along its body and drips down toward its mouth. Even more ingenious is the system adopted by the *Lepidochora* Coleoptera. These insects build trenches over a 3.5 ft (over 1 m) long. The water condenses on the high walls and then falls into this 'cistern.' Even the plants here have adapted. The tall grass on the dunes has short roots, but they extend for as much as 33 ft (10 m) in order to absorb the humidity of the sand. When the fog arrives, the half-dry lichens become a bright green and as long as there is a drop of water left they continue with this process of photosynthesis. Then they allow themselves to be transported by the wind into the 'living desert,' as the Namib is so aptly called.

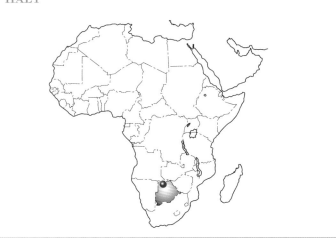

OKAVANGO DELTA
BOTSWANA

A sea of earth, a land of water: this is what the local Tswana population calls the luxuriant oasis of reed and papyrus, canals and islets created by the Okavango Delta in northern Botswana. This phenomenon is unique. Thousands of years ago, the unusual river somehow lost its bearings on the way to the ocean. The cold, clear waters of the Okavango River begin in the forests of Angola, 620 miles (1000 km) upstream. It then flows south, losing its way in the Kalahari Desert. Before fading away in the sand, the river branches off, creating a gigantic labyrinth of water and land, an area that ranges from 6400 to 8000 sq. miles (16,000 to 20,000 sq. km), depending on the intensity of the rainfall, and forms the largest internal delta in the world. Even more important, it creates, almost miraculously, the most uncontaminated natural paradise in Africa. The scenery of this marshland changes with every flood.

Every rainy season redraws the map of the river, forging a new network of canals, sandy islands, lagoons, stretches of savanna and new forests of mopane with its butterfly shaped leaves that elephants love to chew on. There are about 60,000 of these pachyderms in the area, so it is easy to see them bathing in the river or grazing in the meadows. There are also large numbers of giraffes, lions, lycaons, leopards, impalas, zebras, buffaloes, baboons, and curious and impertinent guenon monkeys. The Okavango Delta is the home and refuge of 164 types of mammals and 38 species of amphibians, and 550 species of birds nest there. The flora is also abundant, numbering about 3000 species of plants, from the baobab to the sycamore fig, the very useful fan palm and the unique sausage tree (*Kigelia africana*), so named because the fruit, which can weigh up to 9 lbs (ca. 4 kg), has the shape of a sausage. The so-called

rain tree (*Lonchocarpus capassa*) has trunks used to make the traditional *mokoro* dugout canoes, which are indispensable for moving about in this jungle of water amid the carpet of water-lilies, papyrus and rush, where birds of every shape and color play hide-and-seek: black coromants, bright green starlings, cranes with the long red- and black-striped beaks, yellow and red *Alcedo cristata* kingfishers, the tiny African jaçana, which hunts for insects in the water-lily flowers, and eagles with pitch-black plumage that make spectacular dives to catch fish. Other less peaceful creatures hide in the water: crocodiles and hippopotamuses, the latter defending their territory with loud trumpeting. This is also the domain of the timid sitatunga or marshbuck (*Tragelaphus spekei*), a rare water antelope with very long hooves that allow it to walk in the mud without sinking; in fact, it seems to float rather than walk on this immense lagoon.

118 From an airplane the Okavango Delta looks like a huge labyrinth of canals and islets. The river begins in Angola and ends in the arid Kalahari Desert, never reaching the sea.

118-119 Before ending its course in the desert, the Okavango River opens out in a fan-like pattern in northern Botswana, creating an unpolluted area of greenery that is a veritable paradise.

119 bottom   This immense oasis is the home of 38 species of amphibians and 164 species of mammals, including a great many lions. There are also a great number of birds–550 species, to be exact.

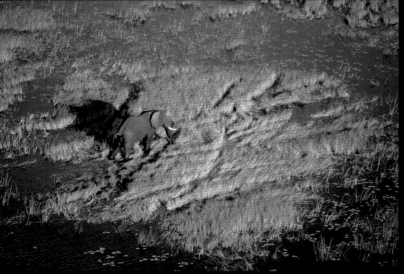

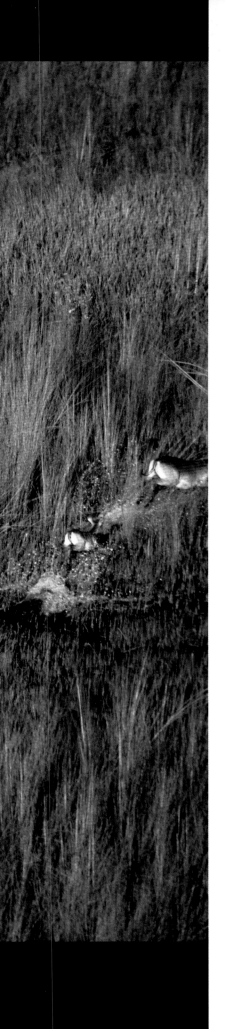

120-121 A herd of impalas crosses one of the lakes created by the largest interior delta in the world.

120 bottom left Elephants are particularly numerous here, since there is an abundance of mopane with the butterfly-shaped leaves these animals relish.

120 bottom right These zebras were photographed in the Moremi Reserve, at the northeastern tip.

121 Many hippopotami hide in the delta waters, emerging around evening to feed on the rich vegetation surrounding the marshes.

122-123 *Victoria Falls are shaped by the Zambesi River about halfway along its course, when the water falls 360 ft (108 m) along a front of almost 1 mile (ca. 1.6 km).*

The longest waterfall in the world was discovered 1855 by the Scottish explorer David Livingstone, who named it after his queen.

123 left *The local populations called the falls "thundering smoke." The mist created by the plummeting waters can be seen at a distance of 20 to 25 miles (ca. 30 to 40 km).*

123 right *Rainbows are continuously formed by the mist resulting from the enormous mass of water, which during the flood season has a discharge of 310 million gallons (500 million liters) per minute.*

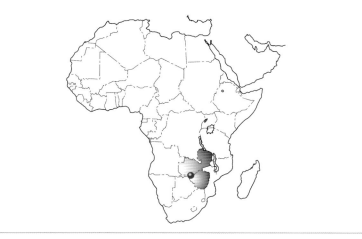

VICTORIA FALLS
ZIMBABWE, ZAMBIA

"**C**rawling terrorized at the tip of the island, I saw below me an huge gorge between one bank and the other of the Zambesi River; a mass of water thousands of feet wide was falling from a height of 110 ft (33 m) and became clogged up in an opening from 66 to 165 ft (20 to 50 m) wide. To the right of the island nothing could be seen except a thick white cloud, much like locomotive smoke." David Livingstone wrote this description on 15 November 1855, the day he discovered Victoria Falls, named in honor of his queen. The roughly estimated measurements made by the Scottish explorer and missionary were better for breadth than for height. The mass of water extends in width over 9/10ths of a mile (ca. 1.5 km) and plunges into the chasm from a height of 360 ft (108 m), creating the longest veil of water in the world.

The falls are shaped by the Zambesi River about halfway along its 1615-miles (2600-km) course. The mass of water is impressive indeed. During the flood season in February and March it has a discharge of 310 million gallons (500 million liters) of water per minute that plummets into the gorge with a deafening roar, creating a thick veil of mist that can be seen from 20 to 25 miles (ca. 30 to 40 km) away. It is no accident that the Kololo people called it *Musi-oa-tunya*, or thundering smoke. But it seems that in ancient times an even more poetic name was given to the falls: *seongo*, 'home of the rainbow.' Rainbows, in fact, are continuously created on the mist rising from the huge mass of water, even on moonlit nights. And the foam itself has generated a particular system of rain forest along the banks of the Zambesi, a labyrinth of liana that would have delighted Tarzan himself, with wild figs, primitive species of ferns, orchids, and ebony trees populated by the ubiquitous monkeys and small hummingbirds with brilliantly colored plumage.

Archaeologists have found prehistoric tools in the two national parks that protect 34 sq. miles (89 sq. km) of the environment along the falls, and it is no exaggeration to say that the Victoria Falls were here already 10,000 years ago. Since that time the river has eroded 1.5 miles (ca. 2.5 km) of basalt, causing an equivalent recession of the rapids. For about 150 years Victoria Falls have been an irresistible attraction. The first European tourist began to arrive there in May 1904, after the inauguration of the railway line from Cairo. Since then the flow has never stopped.

124-125 The largest crater in the world is covered with luxuriant vegetation that provides food for a large population of Burchell zebras, gnus and various species of antelopes.

124 bottom left The Lerai forest is rich in Acacia xanthopholea *and* Rauwfolia caffra *plants.*

124 bottom right The land becomes arid and barren only after long periods of drought.

125 The cone of Ngorongoro was gutted by a huge explosion. The area is a paradise rich in water for animals. In fact, large herds of gnus migrate to the banks of Lake Magadi to take advantage of this precious resource.

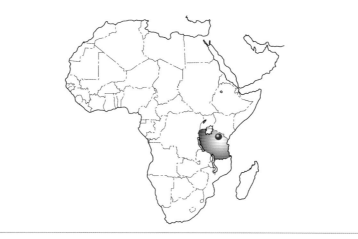

NGORONGORO
TANZANIA

The largest unflooded volcanic caldera in the world is like Noah's Ark, since the gigantic basin comprises a veritable Garden of Eden. Furthermore, it contains the world's most important concentration of large mammals that live in the wild: about 30,000 creatures representing about 40 species. Of the mammals that usually live in East Africa, the only ones lacking are the impala, the bastard hartebeest and the giraffe, because the plants they feed on are scarce in the crater. Ngorongoro lies in north Tanzania, near the Rift Valley, the huge trough that cuts through the Earth's crust from the Middle East to Mozambique. It has a surface area of 166 sq. miles (265 sq. km) and lies in the middle of the Ngorongoro Conservation Area, which is much larger, extending for 3315 sq. miles (8288 sq. km) to the plains of the Serengeti National Park.

Until 2.5 million years ago, the crater was a volcano about 19,800 feet (6000 m) high. Then a tremendous explosion literally gutted the cone. Only the sides of the mountain remained intact; they still enclose a round caldera 11.75 miles (19 km) in diameter, the largest in the world. The locals named it Ngorongoro, which means 'large hole.' With time, animals began to live there, since the new environment provided the ideal conditions for the needs of a large number of species. All the mammals can penetrate and leave the area freely by passing over the 1980 ft (600 m) or so that separate the base of the crater from the surrounding territory, but very few do so. And when they do, they return at once, because there is no reason in the world to abandon an oasis so rich in water in the middle of land made barren by the scorching sun. To the north of the Lerai Forest is the large, shallow Lake Magadi, which is the home of vast colonies of pink flamin-

gos. The chicks spend the entire day in this asylum under the watchful eye of an adult. At sunset thousands of pink forms return in search of their young, calling them one by one for supper. Sunset is the best time here, the ideal moment to observe, in the pools to the north, the gigantic hippopotami, which live in company with the other 'big five,' the five largest creatures in this ecosystem: the elephant, the Cape buffalo, lion, leopard and rhinoceros. At dawn, on the other hand, you can observe the lions hunting Burchell zebras, which abound in the crater, as do gazelles, antelopes, gnus and buffaloes. The lions move forward carefully and silently, remaining immobile until the right moment comes for them to attack their prey in elegant bounds. However, the result is by no means a foregone conclusion; in fact, statistics tell us that in 88% of the attacks the zebras manage to escape. The lions often profit from the

126 top *The animals at Ngorongoro have only one enemy - poachers. Because of its horn, which is considered aphrodisiacal, the black rhinoceros is the most highly prized creature.*

126 center *The other forty or so species of mammals live here peacefully, as can be seen by this litter of lion cubs.*

126 bottom *The hippopotami stay by themselves, keeping a certain distance, in the northern pools.*

127 *Until a few years ago, elephants were also hunted for their tusks. These creatures love to feed on the tree leaves in the Lerai forest.*

'work' done by the African hunting dogs, which always hunt in groups and are exceptional predators. At the end of their long chases, nine out of ten of these ancestors of dogs with long, pointed, bat-like ears succeed in catching gnus and gazelles. But just when they are about to feast on their prey, the king of the savanna or a pack of hyenas arrive.

However, this is all part of the natural balance, which only Man manages to upset. Indeed, the animals in the Ngorongoro crater have only one real enemy – poachers. Among the most sought-after animals are the elephant with its long ivory tusks and the black rhinoceros, highly prized for its horn, which people erroneously think is aphrodisiacal – a property it simply does not have, since like human fingernails it consists of creatine. However, the sexual prowess of these massive creatures is indeed real: they copulate for 30 minutes or more, compared to the few seconds of the other mammals. But this is certainly no reason to massacre them!

128 *A world of ice only a short distance from the Equator: perennial snow blankets the crater of Kilimanjaro. Renamed Uhuru–'liberty' in Swahili–this mountain is the highest peak in Africa (5895 meters).*

129 *The solitary volcanic mountain towers majestically over the savanna. At its feet, the Kilimanjaro National Park boasts five different botanical ecosystems with a surface area of 75,000 hectares.*

KILIMANJARO
KENYA, TANZANIA

Impossible, it's only a mirage. This was the reaction of the Royal Geographical Society of London to the tale told by the missionary Johann Rebmann in 1848. Such a high mountain, covered with perpetual snow as well as glaciers, simply could not exist on the Equator. But, Kilimanjaro was not a mirage, but had risen up 750,000 years earlier from a crevice that opened in the Rift Valley. This large volcano consisted of three craters, Kibo, Mawenzi and Shira. The last one to remain active was Kibo, which 100,000 years ago created the present-day caldera and the so-called Ash Well. It took a relatively short time for the lava to become an icy terrain. Kilimanjaro is the highest mountain in Africa (19,453 ft/ 5895 m), and for the natives, mountain climbers and explorers it is mythical. The

Wachagga people called it *Kilima-ndajaro*, or cold peak; for the Masai nomads it was the brilliant mountain because of the snow on the top. But it was named Kaiser Wilhelm in honor of Emperor William II of Germany, since the German geographer Hans Mayer and the Austrian Ludwig Purtscheller were to the first to climb the peak, which they did in 1889. Since 1962 the top has been called Uhuru, which means 'liberty' in Swahili, an apt name for this African symbol, which is so accessible. In fact, one need be only a good walker to go up from the entrance of the national park, established in 1973, to the summit at Uhuru Peak. From here the view ranges over the savanna, extending as far as the Indian Ocean. While ascending, climbers cross over different zones of vegetation and

rock formations. The climb begins in the tropical forest, among gigantic *Albizzia schimperiana* trees inhabited by colonies of guereza and other monkeys. The next belt is moorland, and from an altitude of 9900 ft (3000 m), the path winds upward through heather up to 10 ft (3 m) high, broom, and lobelia. Farther up there are only lichens scattered among the lava fragments, and then the bare, dark rock. The snow and ice cover the Kibo crater (15,520 ft/4703 m) up to the top. Large seracs crush the blocks of ice inside what was once an exceptional volcanic vent. This is an extraordinary alpine landscape that, according to scientists, is endangered because of the greenhouse effect. The snows of Kilimanjaro, which Ernest Hemingway made famous, may soon melt.

130-131 The southernmost tip of the Sinai Peninsula is surrounded by the Red Sea and the gulfs of Suez and Aqaba, which thus constitute a sort of natural *barrier. Unlike other tropical seas, it is an enclosed basin that is the home of unique species of fish that are protected in the Ras Mohammed National Park.* *130 bottom The Green Expanse, as the Arabs call this immense aquarium, separates Africa and Asia.* *131 The Ras Mohammed Park also comprises a long stretch of desert coastline.*

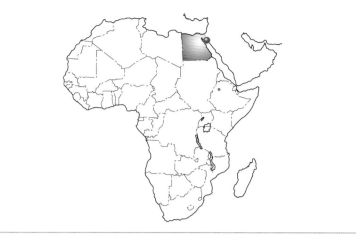

RAS MOHAMMED
EGYPT

This is the loveliest aquarium in the world, which may seem a rather limited definition of the largest national maritime park in Egypt. The Ras Mohammed Park lies on the southern tip of the Sinai Peninsula. The coast is barren, but if you dive into the crystal-clear sea you will find yourself in another world. With a mask and fins you are immediately in the virtual reality of a film by Jacques Cousteau. Thanks to its position and depth of over 2400 ft (800 m), the sea here offers all kinds of encounters. In the open sea you meet up with large deep-sea fish, tuna, curious Napoleon fish, large schools of barracuda and carangids, and sharks that are not very aggressive. Near the coast there are schools of multicolored fish darting here and there among the forests of gorgonians and coral, making circles and brushing against divers as if they were on display in a glass aquarium – an immense aquarium that separates Africa from Asia.

The Arabs called it *wadi-oirit*, or the green expanse. Westerners have renamed it the Red Sea because of an alga, *Trichodesmium erythreaum*, which lends a reddish hue to the water when the temperature is low. This exceptional bridge between Africa and Asia is closed off between the natural barrier at north of the Suez and Aqaba gulfs, and to the south by the Bad el-Mandeb straits. In short, this is an immense basin, which explains the presence of such unique fauna – over a thousand species of fish, one-fifth of them endemic. But this is not all. The madrepore reef of the Red Sea boasts over 400 species of coral. The water's temperature, even at a depth of 66 ft (20 m), is always above 20°C. The coral polyps could not live at a lower temperature. They are the meticulous, patient artisans who built the splendid coral reef here: millions of madrepores, consisting of a soft and live part and a calcareous part called corallite or skeleton.

These creatures are indefatigable builders. They can create isolated branches or massive formations that develop into fan-like forms, gigantic towers, extended flat configurations, pointed pinnacles, large loaf or leafy bush shapes. Next to them are other colonial organisms such as gorgonians and alcyonarians, also called soft corals because they have no skeleton, while the gorgonians have a hard and elastic skeleton and grow into spectacular flowery gardens. What these microorganisms have in common is their fiery, intense colors, from red to purple.

Coral reefs grow about half an inch a

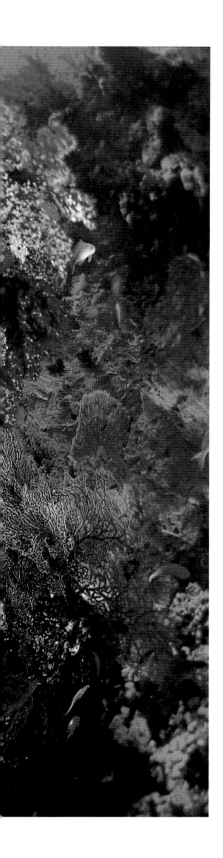

132 top Sharks that are not very
aggressive swim in the open sea near the
Ras Mohammed National Park.

132-133 Near the coast, just under the
surface of the sea, there is the lively and
multicolored world of splendid coral
gardens.

132 bottom The coral reef has 400 species
of corals, and over one thousand species of

fish, one-fifth of which are endemic, live
in the transparent and warm water.

133 top In the park diving is allowed in
about thirty spots on a rotation basis in
order not to disturb curious fish such as
the Napoleon fish (right).

133 bottom The most beautiful
gorgonian forests lie opposite Ras
Mohammed.

year in ideal conditions, which Ras Mohammed offers. Besides the mild water temperature, the park
has exceptional light, no rivers, hardly any rainfall,
transparent water, and a high evaporation level
with an appreciable percentage of salinity. Thus,
the Ras Mohammed Park boasts an underwater
Baroque city protected from predators, from
tourists in search of free souvenirs, and from the
anchors of boats with rather irresponsible owners.
In fact, only a small part of the park is open to the
public, which is the best guarantee for the survival
of the coral reef, which with its jagged shape provides a great many ideal habitats for different
species. The sedentary fish use it as a shelter to find
food, to reproduce and to hunt, and are in turn
hunted by migratory fish. Among the fine lace-
work of the madrepores and the tentacles of the
anenomes are the recognizable colored shapes of
the clown-fish, the striking 'beaks' of the parrot-
fish, the military chevrons of the butterfly fish, and
the splendid colors of the emperor angelfish, which
is the most beautiful in the area.

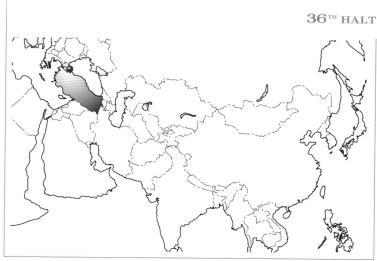

HAGHIA SOPHIA
ISTANBUL, TURKEY

134 In this view of the Golden Horn we can see the heart of Istanbul, whose focal point is the Haghia Sophia complex. The basilica was built at the behest of the Emperor Justinian in the first half of the 6th century AD.

135 left The Basilica of Haghia Sophia was originally Catholic, and then became a Greek Orthodox church and later a Muslim mosque, as can be seen by the furnishings and decoration.

135 right In 1935, Haghia Sophia was converted into a museum that houses precious works of religious art such as this mosaic. The domes are covered with mosaics that shine in the sunlight.

Haghia Sophia or St. Sophia lies near the famous Hippodrome in Istanbul, formerly Constantinople, right in the middle of the Golden Horn, the narrow inlet that houses the most beautiful monuments in the city, including the Topkapi Palace, the residence of the Ottoman sultans. The church, dedicated to Divine Wisdom (its name in Greek), was built by Emperor Justinian in A.D. 532-37 after a violent popular insurrection had caused a fire that destroyed the preceding basilica. It was the largest Christian church in the world until 1453, when Constantinople fell to the Ottoman Turks and it was converted into a mosque, complete with minarets and the furnishings typical of the Islamic religion.

Upon entering the church one is struck by the magnificent mosaics that decorate the half domes around the majestic central vault. The walls, on the other hand, are covered with frescoes and small, multicolored tesserae representing stylized flowers and geometric motifs that produce a kaleidoscopic effect. Indeed, the decoration of the interior of Haghia Sophia seems to prefigure the later prohibition of illustrations of human figures during the iconoclastic period, as the geometric patterns alternate only with the recurrent monogram of the emperor. On the sides, elegant Arabic script celebrates the names of Allah and Muhammad on four enormous oilcloth medallions. The central dome is 181 ft (55 m) high and has a 106-ft (32-m) diameter, an exceptional result if we stop to think that this basilica was constructed in the 6th century.

Haghia Sofia, now the Ayasofya Museum, is considered one of the most important monuments in the world, the symbol of the golden age of the Byzantine Empire and of the syncretism of Christianity and Islam in the area that is the cultural hinge between the two faiths. The square central space with its alternating sinuous and square niches is dominated by the main dome, crowned by forty windows that create an almost surreal play of light. Along this area there are large side aisles and monumental galleries. At the entrance are the large narthex and atrium with massive iron doors and vast porticoes used by the penitents and catechumens.

The overall effect of the edifice is spectacular, and to this day the elaborate carving of the capitals, the dazzling colors of the mosaics, the contrasts of the smooth marble, opalescent porphyry and precious stones that breaks up the light into a thousand shafts – all make for an unforgettable, thrilling experience.

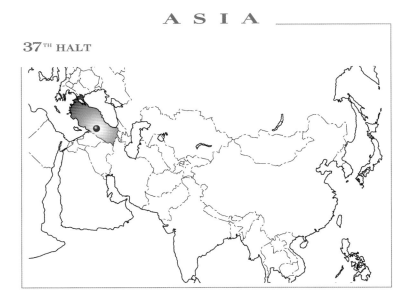

NEMRUD DAGH

TURKEY

The dreamlike land in southern Anatolia populated by enormous figures that emerge from the rock is towered over by the peaks of Mt. Nemrud, the most popular natural history site in Turkey. This mountain of the Taurus range is over 7095 ft (2150 m) high and also boasts the tomb of the great Antiochus I of Commagene, who is buried under a conical mound of stones that is so large (495 ft/150 m wide, 198 ft/60 m high) that it can be seen from a distance of 62 miles (100 km). Antiochus was a great king of the dynasty founded by Mithridates (1st century B.C. – A.D. 72) and was most certainly a megalomaniac, given the size of the open-air mausoleum that he had built to his eternal memory. Situated on the top of the mountain and discovered a little over a century ago, the Nemrud Dagh site has been examined by a team of experts from all over the world, who utilized very sophisticated instruments. And yet, the remains of the king have never been found under the grand rock portal that affords access to the tomb. On the other hand, the ornamental statues that line the path to the ancient sanctuary are perfectly visible and continue to communicate, with the eloquence of ancient times, the sacredness of the site and the ephemeral nature of worldly things.

The first statues are those of the lion and eagle that welcomed visitors at the enclosure entrance, while the last are five wise men seated along the rock-cut path who evoke divine grandiosity with their impressive size (almost 30 ft/9 m) and seem to warn people to assume a respectful attitude of prayer. Among the huge sculptures are the figures of Apollo, Zeus, the goddess of fortune Tyche, the Persian god Verathragna, icons of Iranian gods, and the portrait of Antiochus, who in greeting the other statues with his hand places himself on their level.

Nemrud Dagh is an interesting and unique example of the combination of Hellenic, Persian and Anatolian cultures and also offers various stone carvings that have something alchemic about them. There is even a finely decorated astrological tablet with the stars placed around the signs in such precise fashion that experts have been able to calculate the date it refers to, which is presumably that of the foundation of the sanctuary: 7 July 62 B.C. And this is not all. Some scholars say that these statues were aligned in keeping with the alignment of the planets on 16 July 98 B.C., the day Antiochus I was born.

136 left and 136-137 In the foreground are the colossal heads that belong to the statues (in the background) of Antiochus I, Apollo, Herakles and Zeus which, together with the sculptures of eagles and lions, keep watch over the tomb.

136 right The Nemrud Dagh complex boasts the tomb of the Greek-Persian king Antiochus I, who governed Commagene in the 1st century BC.

137 bottom left The burial area was laid out when Antiochus I was still alive, and it was brought to light only in 1881, when a German engineer discovered the enormous mound.

137 bottom right Antiochus I is probably buried under this heap of stones. Besides the statues, there are decorated stone slabs that represent portraits of the king and his family, as well as an astrological tablet.

138-139 This view of the Görëme Valley in Cappadocia shows the configuration of the terrain that was forged by centuries of water and wind erosion and that looks like a fairy-tale architectural complex.

138 bottom An example of the sculptural geological configuration created by rain erosion, behind which are hidden the many famous rock-cut churches in this semi-desert region.

139 left The pinnacles were shaped by the torrential rain, which liquefied and removed the soil around the dark, square rocks on the top, leaving only the 'shafts,' so that they look like natural umbrellas.

139 right The rock-hewn dwellings date from 4000 BC. Over the centuries, hermits and entire populations found refuge here. Some archaeological digs have brought to light entire underground cities.

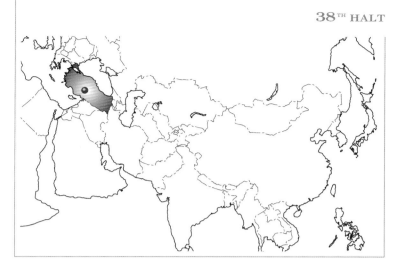

CAPPADOCIA
TURKEY

Magical scenery awaits those passing through the Cappadocian area, the fabulous region in central Turkey surrounding the cities of Nevsehir, Avanos and Ürgüp: a labyrinth of natural towers, crevices, ravines, pinnacles and rock castles. But the most spectacular landscape is in the valley of Görëme, famous for its beautifully frescoed churches; it is said that, of the nearly 3000 churches in Cappadocia, 365 are in this valley alone. Here the time-eroded rocks, including the bizarre cones and pinnacles nicknamed the Fairies' Chimneys, constitute a sort of open-air museum with an incredible complex of rock-cut monastery churches and chapels that make the trip to this region of Turkey a unique, unforgettable experience. Most of the chapels date from the 10th-13th century, the Byzantine and Seljuk periods, and consist of structures in the shape of a cross whose central dome is supported by four columns, all cut out of the rock concretions of volcanic origin. The side aisles of many of these churches also have many tombs for visitors to see. In fact, a trip to this area is like an obstacle course in a labyrinth of religious edifices, all of which are different. One goes from the Almali church, the most recent and smallest of the group, to the Yilanli church with its dramatic frescoes depicting the damned among coiled serpents, and the churches of St. Barbara and Carikli, this latter covered with ocher-colored decoration that reflects the hues of the surrounding countryside. A short distance away from this central group is the Tokali church, or so-called Church of the Buckle, known for its fascinating frescoed episodes from the New Testament. But this is not all. Here, century after century, the local populations, in order to escape from persecution and pillaging, carved entire underground cities out of the rock, complete with air vents and sleeping areas, refectories, grain storerooms, storehouses, stables, and communal kitchens and halls. The builders of the underground cities of Cappadocia made use of the folds in the terrain, the result of millions of years of activity on the part of the now dormant volcanoes. Initially the refuge of Christian anchorites and hermits, they became the home of entire populations; indeed, there are remains of settlements that date back to 4000 BC.

140 top The rock-cut churches are small constructions, at times mere votive chapels, that were often smoothed with such precision that they seem to be made of traditional masonry.

140 bottom The frescoes that cover all the walls of the churches in the Göréme Valley, which depict beautifully executed angels, saints and biblical scenes, have preserved their bright colors.

140-141 The classical structure of the church interiors can be seen here. Dating from the 10th-13th century, these structures have a Greek cross plan and wide niches framed by columns, four of which also support the central dome.

141 bottom This slightly deteriorated fresco is a classic example of Byzantine painting, both in the placement of the figures, which are all in the foreground, and because of the colors and the shape of the elegant and well-executed clothing.

39TH **HALT**

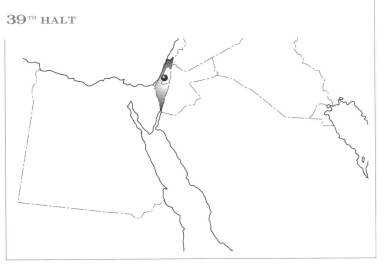

THE DOME OF THE ROCK
JERUSALEM, ISRAEL

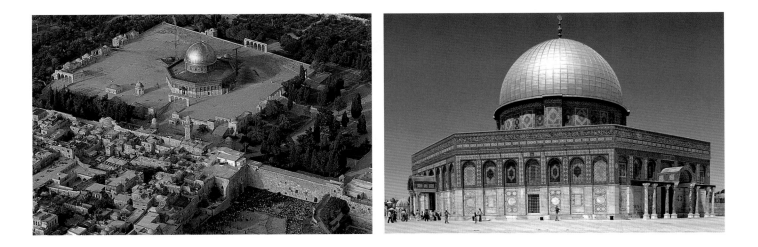

Jerusalem is the Holy City for Jews, Muslims and Christians alike and is rigorously divided into three zones reserved for these three religions. However, the spiritual and cultural hub of the city lies in its most ancient section, which boasts the monument that has become its symbol: the Dome of the Rock, also known as Omar's Mosque. This is the oldest existing monument of Islamic architecture, built during the Umayyad period (A.D. 661-750). For Muslims the marvelous dome of this holy edifice is not only a finely wrought example of artistic beauty, but also the living symbol of their faith. Built at the behest of the Caliph Abd al-Malik, it is located right over the holy rock that according to Judaic legend was the site of Abraham's sacrifice as well as the axis of the world,

while Islamic tradition considers it the site where the Prophet began his mystic ascent to the sky. It is said that right under this dome Muhammad led in prayer 124,000 prophets who had preceded him and from here ascended to the heavens in what is called Lailatul Miraj or Night Journey. The rock itself is a natural, irregularly shaped crag in the middle of the holy esplanade of Jerusalem.

During the reign of Abd al-Malik the Dome of the Rock had an octagonal plan of 85.8 ft (20.6 m) per side and was 31.35 ft (9.5 m) high, while the walls were covered by a wooden dome over 66 ft (20 m) in diameter that stood on a tall drum with sixteen windows supported by four pillars and twelve columns. The four portals that give access to the external ambulatory are

preceded by a vaulted portico oriented to the four cardinal points.

The influence of Syrian art is quite evident, especially in the system of triangles that serve as the link between the outer and inner circles of the mosque. As to the symbolic meaning of the dome itself, the fact that it converges and ends in one point is a sign of the believers' quest for divine unity. But the beauty of this monument transcends any purely religious belief, and in fact thousands of tourists from all over the world go to admire this magnificent construction. The walls of the interior are completely covered with marble slabs, while the dome is covered with pure gold leaf, so that it shines brilliantly all hours of the day and night, like a beacon of hope in the desert.

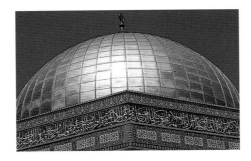

144 top The dome has a diameter of 66 ft (20 m) and is 112 ft (34 m) high.

144 center The decoration of the Dome of the Rock and the use of circular arcades betray the influence of Byzantine art and architecture.

144 bottom This ornamental motif combines the geometry of the linked circles and the poetic effect of the flowers, petals and shoots. White, blue and azure are the characteristic colors of the mosque.

145 The huge dome is completely decorated and houses the sacred rock that marks the exact point from which Muhammad began his ascent to the heavens. A passageway under the arcades gives access to the rock.

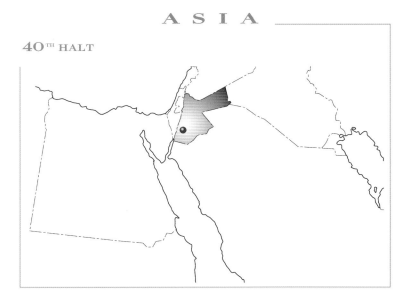

PETRA

JORDAN

On his way from Damascus to Cairo in 1812, the Swiss traveler and Orientalist Johann Ludwig Burckhardt heard of an ancient city called Petra in the marvelous country of Jordan, tucked in between impenetrable mountains. After days of traveling in search of the mysterious city, he spotted the city's first and most sensational monument, the Khazna or Treasury, a magnificent Nabataean construction cut out of the pink rock that to this day stands out among the colors of the wild countryside. Despite all the research and studies on the part of scholars, the Khazna is still very much a mystery.

Was this monument a temple, tomb or a hiding place for immense riches? It may have been all three, although the original name in Arabic derives from a legend concerning the treasure of an Egyptian pharaoh kept in the urn at the top of the edifice. For a long time, until the custom was prohibited, the local Bedouin used to shoot at the building with their rifles in the hope of breaking it open and finding the riches. The Khazna was probably used as a tomb, since Petra abounds in funerary architecture. Many tombs lie in the valley and on the surrounding plateaus: the royal Tomb of the Urn hewn out of the side of a cliff, the sepulchers with splendid façades that look like palaces, the public burial chambers set into the cult niches in the walls, and the frightening shaft tombs into which criminals were cast and left to die.

A particularly fascinating monument is the Castle of the Pharaoh's Daughter, which is rich in decoration modeled after the friezes in the valley temples on the Nile, which the Nabataeans were acquainted with because of the trade relations with Alexandria. Lawrence of Arabia also wrote about Petra, describing it as the most beautiful place on Earth, not because of its ruins, but for the colors of the red and black rocks with green and light blue stripes that look like small corrugations or folds, for the shape of its rocks and pinnacles, and for its fantastic gorge with spring water.

Archaeological digs have revealed that the Edomites, the future enemies of the Israelites, had settled there way back

146 The Treasury is the first monument one sees upon entering the fabulous city of Petra. It was discovered in the early 1800s by a Swiss traveler who for years had been searching for the legendary buried city.

146-147 Since they were skillfully cut out of the rock on sites that could not be spotted from a distance, the Nabataean constructions in Petra were hidden for centuries. Here we see the Treasury.

147 bottom left An aerial view of the area characterized by craggy rocks. The minerals in the soil create the marvelous colors of the Nabataean monuments, which range from ocher to bright pink and ruby.

147 bottom right From an architectural standpoint the structures in Petra are a mixture of Assyrian, Egyptian, Nabataean and classical styles. This photograph shows the al-Dair 'Monastery.'

148-149 The monumental complex in Petra includes two well-known tombs: the so-called Palace Tomb and Corinthian Tomb, which lie near the Roman theater and mark the necropolis area at the foot of the Monastery.

148 bottom left The Tomb of the Roman Soldier, who is portrayed in the central niche of the façade, is probably one of the most famous sepulchers in Petra.

148 bottom right This tomb lies near a rock face and consists of an impressive and highly decorated entrance that leads to the burial chamber proper cut out of the rock.

149 The Tomb of the Obelisks has an Egyptian-Nabataean shape and is crowned by broad pinnacles that look like tapered pyramids. The structure has an overall shape that tends to be stouter toward the bottom than the earlier 'classical' tombs.

A S I A

in the 2nd millennium B.C. In 500 B.C. the Nabataeans, nomads who had come from the south, drove this population out and made Petra their capital. Strategically situated at the junction of ancient trade routes, Petra was filled with merchants who transported their wares from Damascus, Arabia, the Mediterranean and Egypt. Using this virtually impenetrable city as their base, the Nabataeans controlled the caravan route and amassed riches, thus giving rise to a flourishing civilization. The rocky terrain was no problem for this population. In fact, their chief divinity, Dushara, was symbolized by masses of stone and obelisks scattered in the Siq, the narrow gorge of Petra, and throughout the city itself.

In 63 B.C. the Romans tried to conquer the city through a surprise attack, but they finally managed to do so only in A.D. 106, when Petra became part of the Roman province of Arabia, seemingly without putting up any resistance. Despite the fact that the Nabataean dynasty had ended, the local population co-existed with the Romans for over a century, after which time the destiny of Petra was wrapped in mystery until 1812.

The capital of the ancient Nabataean kingdom, declared a World Heritage Site by UNESCO, has retained all its former splendor and spirit. Access to the city is the same as it was during Burckhardt's day, either on foot or horseback through the spectacular Siq gorge.

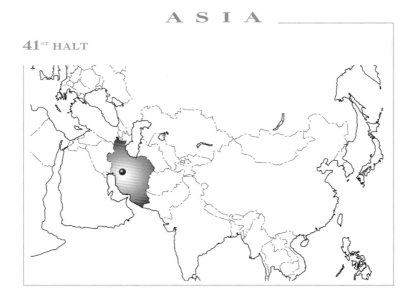

ISFAHAN
IRAN

According to the legend, the enchanting city of Isfahan rose up right in the middle of an oasis created by the gods. The entire area was nothing but desert, but one day, while the vizir Aznayv was taking none other than King Solomon himself on a stroll amid the skies of Persia to show him the beauty of his native country, both he and his guest were stunned to see, through the clouds, a large and luxuriant spring surrounded by palms. It was a magic site chosen on that occasion to found the city of wonders. This was Isfahan, traversed by the Zayandeh River with its bridges of a thousand arches and dominated by the ancient Zoroastrian Temple of Fire, which had already become known as Aspadana during the Greek geographer Strabo's time (1st century B.C.) and a flourishing trade center as early as the 5th century B.C.

But what most strikes one about this elegant city is the immense square. At 1650 ft (500 m) long and 495 ft (150 m) wide, the splendid Maidan-i Imam, also known as Maidan-i Naghsh-i Jahan, is one of the largest squares in the world and a grandiose example of town planning. Laid out in 1612, it is lined with some of the most stunning monuments in Isfahan. Towering over the south side of the square is the so-called Friday Mosque, whose exterior and interior are completely dressed with light blue majolica tiles with inlay with cream and yellow colors that are the city's symbol and that change color according to the light, offering ever-new emotions.

The entrance portal, flanked by two identical minarets, looks directly onto the square, while the main body of the mosque is oriented in the direction of Mecca. Shah Abbas the Great, the most famous leader of the Safavid dynasty of Sufi teachers, who succeeded in reconquering most of Persia from the Uzbeks and Ottoman Turks, commissioned the construction of the Friday Mosque, which took 26 years to build and was finished in 1638. Once past the imposing portal and the following corridor, one enters the hall the leads into the inner courtyards, which is surrounded by four *iwans* or colonnaded atriums. Each of these leads to a prayer hall with its vaulted ceiling, against the backdrop of the large decorated dome that towers over the mosque.

The sides of the square shine with the brilliant majolica tiles that decorate the bazaars and the 18th-century Ali Qapu Palace, a sort of noble residence for the Shahs' important guests.

150 left Detail of the main façade of the Friday Mosque, which is covered with polychrome mosaics and was built for Shah Abbas the Great on the main square of Isfahan.

150 center The fountain inside the mosque is richly decorated with sunken scale-work of amazing elegance that symbolizes the purification ritual.

150 right The inner arcades are distinguished for their decoration of tiny inlaid tesserae that are azure, blue and cream, the dominant colors of the mosque itself.

150-151 and 151 bottom The mosque, with twin minarets and a courtyard with an enormous fountain, faces the Maidan-i Imam, one of the largest squares in the world.

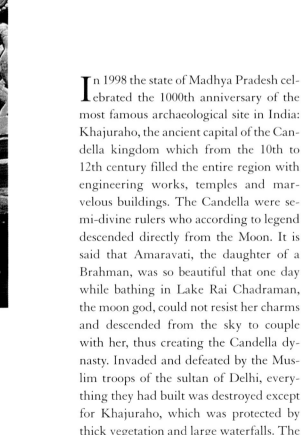

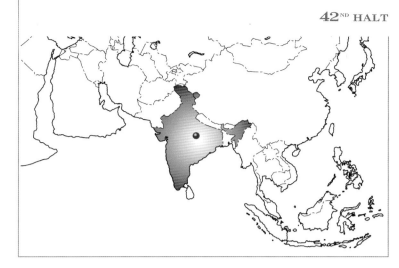
KHAJURAHO
INDIA

In 1998 the state of Madhya Pradesh celebrated the 1000th anniversary of the most famous archaeological site in India: Khajuraho, the ancient capital of the Candella kingdom which from the 10th to 12th century filled the entire region with engineering works, temples and marvelous buildings. The Candella were semi-divine rulers who according to legend descended directly from the Moon. It is said that Amaravati, the daughter of a Brahman, was so beautiful that one day while bathing in Lake Rai Chadraman, the moon god, could not resist her charms and descended from the sky to couple with her, thus creating the Candella dynasty. Invaded and defeated by the Muslim troops of the sultan of Delhi, everything they had built was destroyed except for Khajuraho, which was protected by thick vegetation and large waterfalls. The site was then overlooked, as it were, by the fierce Moghul conquerors and it was only during British domination that Khajuraho began to be rediscovered.

Although only 22 of the legendary 85 Candella have survived in the lavish sculpture decoration, these are enough to evoke the spirit of what was one of the most prosperous and fruitful periods in the area. This was especially true after the latest restoration, which cleaned the bas-reliefs damaged by violent monsoons that narrate the history of the people, their fears and aspirations. The sculptures depict musicians, dancers, hunters, religious feats, dramas of jealousy and a host of erotic scenes that all illustrate with one glance the everyday life of the time and the basic principles of Tantrism, that is, that branch of Hindu philosophy that celebrates the body as a path to the higher spheres of spirituality. The highest expression is the *mithuna*, union with the gods, which generates vital energy. In the Tantric system the sexual act becomes a rite in which the man and woman incarnate Shiva and Shakti, the male and female principles, even by means of apparently acrobatic positions of coitus that draw inspiration from yoga.

Those who spend a little time strolling through the temples surrounded by bougainvillea and scattered over an area of 8 sq. miles (13 sq. km), will find themselves encircled by divinities – beginning with the Trinity of Brahma the creator, Vishnu the preserver, and Shiva the destroyer – musicians, warriors and worshippers, scenes from the Kamasutra, and hundreds of fantastic animals. Then there is a multitude of Apsares, the mythological dancers descended from the sky who are sensual and alluring but always distinguished by that grace and charm that makes even the most provocative Indian sexual scene a minor masterpiece. One can easily imagine hearing the music of the sitar that leads the dances of these sinuous statues,

154 top The portal and altar of the Parsvanatha Temple, with the statue of the divinity in the middle; the walls are covered with friezes depicting scenes from sacred Hindu texts.

154 center This photo shows the interior of one of the largest temples in Khajuraho, the capital of the Candella dynasty: the Kandariya Mahadeva, which is distinguished for its tall inlaid colonnades.

154 bottom A part of the façade of the Lakshamana Temple has delicate scenes of lovemaking among the divinities that generate vital Tantric energy.

155 All the female figures at Khajuraho are wearing jewels and the details of their clothing are exquisitely sculpted.

A S I A

which have the same poses and facial expressions used today in the classical national dance, including the makeup that lengthens the eyes.

The red granite or sandstone temples that turn yellow and pastel pink with the changing light all have their entrances facing east and are built on tall platforms, thus giving the impression of soaring into the air. The most famous is the Kandarya Mahadeva, which is 102 ft (31 m) high. And then there are the most ancient temples in the complex, the Caunsat Yogini (the name of a sort of 'nymph' who was a follower of Kali); the Temple of Devi Jagadambi, the mother goddess; the temple of the sun god Chitragupt and of Vishvanatha, on the walls of which are depicted Brahma and his wife Saraswati; the Caturbhuja temple, which boasts a colossal sculpture of Vishnu; and the Duladeo temple. To complete your visit, you should go to the local archaeological museum, which houses restored Jain and Buddhist sculptures and bas-reliefs.

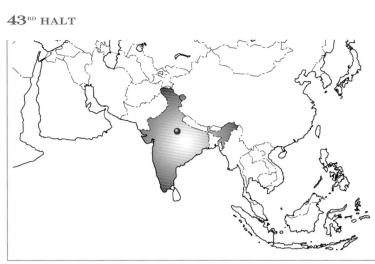

TAJ MAHAL
AGRA, INDIA

156 The entrance to the most famous monument in India, built in the early 1600s with highly prized marble and precious stones at the behest of the emperor Shan Jahan to honor his beloved wife.

157 The avenue leading to the Taj Mahal has a pool with a reflection of the grand mausoleum. The pink hues, which at sunset tend toward red, are due to the composition of the sandstone of the edifice.

On the banks of the Jumna River, 125 miles (200 km) south of New Delhi, the Muslims founded the capital of the Moghul Empire. From the 16th to the 18th century Agra was a flourishing cultural center protected by the massive walls of the Red Fort, so named after the ruby hues of the local sandstone at sunset, and later became a holy site with the construction of the most lavish mausoleum the world has ever known. This is the Taj Mahal, or Palace of the Crown, which is dressed with fine marble dotted with precious stones.

The monument seems to come from a fable in *Thousand and One Nights* and since 1631 has stood on the bank of the river to commemorate the emperor Shah Jahan and his lovely wife Mumtaz Mahal. According to the legend, the Moghul sovereign was persuaded by his young consort to promise to do four things should she die before he did: remarry so that their fourteen children should have a mother, treat the children well, visit her tomb every year, and build a palace in her memory. And in fact she died seventeen years after their marriage. The grief-stricken emperor was well versed in art and architecture — among other things, he had the Jama Mashid mosque built in Dehli and the Shalimar park laid out at Lahore. He summoned the best Persian, Afghan and even Venetian architects to his court to design the mausoleum and had skillful engravers cover the walls with verses from the Koran. Furthermore, he hired 20,000 laborers and artisans, who worked day and night for 22 years to build the complex, which had mosques and minarets designed by an architect from Samarkand. A ramp almost 2 miles (3 km) long was built to transport the marble, and in order to avoid any risk of the building collapsing on the tomb of the beautiful Mumtaz Mahal and on his own tomb, since he wanted to be buried beside her, the emperor asked that the minarets on the corners lean a bit out-

ASIA

ward, just enough so that in case of an earthquake the stones would fall outside the walled enclosure.

This is a monument to eternal love more than a luxurious family chapel "designed by the gods and built by jewelers," as the Indians say. And indeed the external decoration – made of white marble from the quarries of Makrana, over 185 miles (300 km) from Agra and transported on carts drawn by elephants, and also used to case the domes – seems to be the work of a goldsmith. The chemical composition of this mineral imparts a unique fascination, because as if by magic it changes color according to the hour of day and meteorological conditions. Moreover, the marble is inlaid with tiny stones of agate, jade and garnets that form lovely, delicate floral motifs. Multicolored twigs, garlands and flower buds line the walls of the building, which in the morning has a cream color that then becomes pink and gradually goes from gold to light blue, until the moonlight creates silver hues on the veins of the marble.

The Taj Mahal is reflected in the waters of the Jumna River and, in an endless play of reflections that dominates the style of the mausoleum complex, the central dome is reflected in the large fountain pool in the middle of the garden. From here one arrives at the twin mosques surrounded by soaring minarets and built on a terrace whose pavement is also lined with marble with the above-mentioned multicolor effect. This is the prayer hall for the hundreds of faithful who arrive at Agra from nearby places for the traditional pilgrimage. Tourists, on the other hand, prefer the large area in front of the mausoleum, which lies toward the back of the garden and is also embellished with a series of huge niches and small towers surmounted by tiny domes. Of the original complex, only the legendary silver-clad stairways have not been preserved. Otherwise, the building has remained just as it was when the love-stricken emperor saw it for the last time: when he died at the age of 74 he was found with his eyes open, looking at the Taj Mahal and the soul of his beloved.

160-161 and 161 The summit of K2, 28,250 ft (8611 m), dominates the Karakorum mountain range. In 2004 there were celebrations of the 50th anniversary of the conquest of the peak on the part of the expedition led by the Italian Ardito Desio.

160 bottom A line of porters heads toward one of the upper camps, where the climbers will rest for a few days in order to allow their bodies to adapt to the rarified air before attempting the final climb.

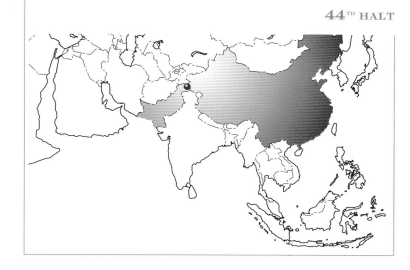

K2
CHINA, PAKISTAN

Towering over the Chinese-Kashmir border, K2 stands out among the other peaks of the Karakorum mountain range, almost touching the sky and penetrating the clouds with its height of 28,416 ft (8611 m). It is also called Mt. Godwin-Austen, in honor of the geographer who made the first geological survey there in 1856, and Dapsang or Chogori in the local dialects. For over a century it has been a favorite with climbers, who are irresistibly attracted by the unforgettable Himalayan scenery. This is especially true of the Italians. They were the first to attempt to conquer the summit in 1902, when the team of rope climbers led by Luigi Amedeo of Savoy, Duke of the Abruzzi, conquered the east spur of the mountain and named it the Abruzzi Spur, while Lino Lacedelli and Cesare Compagnoni were members of the historic Ardito Desio expedition that finally reached the summit in 1954.

The best-known slopes for the heroic climb are the Pakistani one and the much less explored one on the Chinese side. On the latter climbers cannot be accompanied by the local porters, and for the less expert it is the least recommended route – not so much to reach the peak (considered almost impossible and to date conquered by fewer than 200 heroic mountaineers, including five women) but just to enjoy one of the world's most exhilarating panoramas at accessible altitudes and without the aid of oxygen tanks.

K2 does not attract only climbers, but also geology buffs and experts following the tracks of the Italian geologist Bruno Zanettin, the first person to theorize the tectonic origin of this peak. According to this scientist, who was a member of the Desio expedition of 1954, it was precisely in this point of Asia that the impact between the Indian and Asian plates took place, with the monumental creation of very high mountains (there are only fourteen peaks in the world over 26,400 ft (8000 m). And in fact on the ridges of K2 one can still find the remains of sea beds, fossils of algae and primeval organisms that were pushed upward 10 million years ago by an enormous mass of the earth's crust. Scientists say that this natural phenomenon lasted over 2 million years, continuing at an ever slower pace up to the present, as is demonstrated by the ore samples and rocks on the glaciers. Furthermore, it was a mere accident that prevented K2 from becoming a volcano instead of a simple mountain. The intense heat the developed during the collision of the two plates, over 700°C, liquidized the minerals in the rocks, creating a column of incandescent liquid that might easily have been transformed into lava. However, having been pushed up to high altitudes and therefore at low temperatures, the magma solidified, giving rise to those marvelous strata of glossy dark gneiss that greet hundreds of climbers every year.

45ᵀᴴ HALT

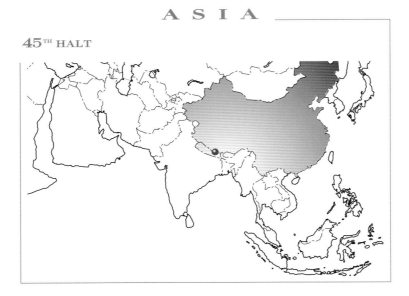

MOUNT EVEREST
NEPAL, CHINA

The highest mountain in the world was named after Sir George Everest, an English surveyor who worked for some time in India for the British Crown. The Nepalese call it Sagarmatha, or God of the Sky, and the Tibetan name is Chomo Langma, or Mother Goddess of the Universe. Mt. Everest (29,028 ft/8848 m) high, dominates the Himalayas; but has rather negotiable paths that even non-expert climbers can handle. In 1978 Reinhold Messner and Peter Habeler succeeded in reaching the summit without the use of oxygen cylinders, but the first successful climb to the top took place in 1953, when the New Zealander Edmund Hillary and the Sherpa Tenzing Norgay managed to go up the south face of the mountain. This is the favorite ascent for climbers, lying on the Nepalese slope of the mountain, while the other, north side is in Tibet and is more difficult to climb.

In order to enjoy the climb even if not going to very high altitudes, it is best to organize the trek in the spring so as to avoid the summer monsoons, which, by the way, cause an interesting geo-physical phenomenon. The wind travels as a current at about 4.5 to 6.2 mph (ca. 7 to 10 km/h) only a few feet above the ground and is so persistent that is has been called 'jet stream.' Besides being very annoying, it also considerably reduces the climbers' speed.

The classic route entails going to Lukla by airplane and then proceeding to the base camp in Nepal in one week in order to adapt to the difference in altitude from 9450 to 17,750 feet (2860 to 5380 m). From here, porters and yaks accompany the climbers are accompanied to the next camp, situated on the Khumbu glacier, which should be climbed at dawn, when the blocks of ice are more stable and less slippery. Once past this barrier, ropes and rope ladders fixed to the rock faces help the climbers to reach the most fascinating part of Mt. Everest, the Western Cwm, also known as the Valley of Silence because it is so enclosed that the wind cannot enter and sounds are so muffled that the landscape seems surreal. Once at an altitude of 26,400 ft (8000 m) you are in the so-called dead zone, the area where there is great risk of hypoxia and fierce of wind currents often make it impossible to reach the summit.

For those who prefer the climb from Tibet, the northern slope also offers an amazing spectacle. Here the series of grav-elly plateaus and light blue glaciers is almost unbelievable, and immediately afterwards there is a wholly different type of scenery, which is really frightening, just past Camp 5. At an altitude of 25,657 ft (7775 m) there suddenly appears before you a series of chasms and crevices that are an invitation to surrender. But those who get past this seemingly impassable area, which is like a rite of passage, are rewarded by a true paradise – a series of smooth rock steps that seems to have been carved to make the last stretch easier.

It is estimated that to date at least 1500 persons have managed to reach the summit of Everest, but there is a much greater number of men and women from all over the world who go to the bases to tackle only the first stage of the climb to enjoy the enchanting panorama. Unfortunately, this natural treasure is now jeopardized by the greenhouse effect, which has increased the speed of the melting of the glaciers, causing floods in the Himalayan lakes. Those who suffer most from this change are the Sherpas, the Tibetan shepherds who make their living mostly from tourism and serving as porters for the climbs and for their expert knowledge of the climbs. Furthermore, they are blessed with a natural gift: their cardio-circulatory system is very flexible, which allows them to adapt readily to the continuous changes in altitude.

162 *In this romantic picture, the top of Mt. Everest is enveloped in pink clouds. This 29,028 ft (8848 m) peak has long been revered by the local populations and is a favorite with mountaineers, even though the climb is treacherous.*

162-163 *Above the dead zone (26,400 ft/8000 m), the rarified air makes Mt. Everest's north face dangerous. Climbers may hallucinate; they need oxygen for safety.*

163 bottom *This aerial view of Mt. Everest and the surrounding peaks reminds one of a cut diamond.*

164-165 *An evocative photograph of the summit of Mt. Everest, which is constantly battered by icy winds that make the climb virtually impossible.*

166-167 and 167 The Potala Palace lies on the Martori, also known as the Red Hill, almost 100 meters top Lhasa. The name derives from the Sanskrit word for 'mountain of Buddha.'

166 bottom left The Potala Palace rises 13 stories, is 3.85 million sq. ft (360,000 sq. m) in area, and is 386 ft (117 m) high. It also used to house the Tibetan government offices.

166 bottom right This building was used by the civil servants. The palace was not only the seat of the government, but also included many public services such as schools and libraries.

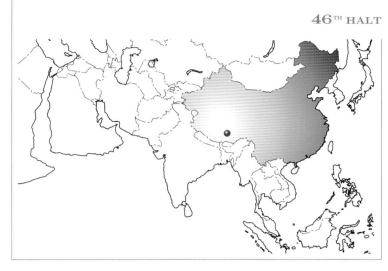

THE POTALA
LASHA, AUTONOMOUS REPUBLIC OF TIBET

In the heart of Tibet, at an altitude of 12,210 ft (3700 m), is the Red Hill of Lhasa, which has one of the most important monuments in Asia, the Potala, the sacred edifice of the Buddhists built in 631 by Songtsen Gampo that houses the remains of the thirteen Dalai Lamas that have succeeded one another in Tibet from 1300 to the present. The name derives from the Sanskrit *Potalaka*, the mythological Indian mountain consecrated to Chenrezig, the Bodhisattva of Compassion. Whoever has the good luck to see this grandiose edifice, which seems to be suspended in nothingness and stands out against an ever clear sky to announce the approach to the capital of Tibet from many miles away, cannot help being both stunned and awe-struck. This site has a surface area of 3.85 million sq-ft (360,000 sq. m), one-third of which is roofed, and is made up of various buildings superposed along the slopes of the hill. These are granite structures with gilded decoration, such as the pagoda roofs and the vases that dot the walls in a blaze of very bright red, yellow and cream that emit energy and also pacify those predisposed to meditation and to the veneration of Buddha. The palace has thirteen stories and is 386 ft (117 m) high, but it was once even busier because it housed a monastery, many Tantric Buddhist chapels, and government departments. The circumambulation takes place around the palace, with the faithful holding hands and walking in silent prayer for over a kilometer (just under three-quarters of a mile), some even prostrating themselves repeatedly during the ritual.

Steep steps link the different levels of the Potala Palace. But the fatigue is worth your while, because you can admire the splendid chapels of Maitreia, of the three-dimensional Manadala, of Kalachakra, and of the sacred tombs of the Dalai Lamas (including the 13th, who in 1912 proclaimed the independence of Tibet and left his body, as the Buddhists say, on 17 December 1933). And then the palace has a rich treasure gathered over the centuries, the cream of Buddhist art: objects and statuettes made of jade; fine glazed porcelain; gold seals the Chinese emperors donated to the Dalai Lamas to demonstrate their respect for and admiration of the Tibetan sovereigns; hundreds of bell-shaped stupas and votive paintings. But the treasure of Potala also comprises hundreds of Buddhist writings, including the precious Sutras concerning the Hinayana Buddhist canon, which illustrate the teaching of Buddha, the rule of monastic life, and the philosophic elaboration of the doctrine. Lhasa is also world famous as 'the home of the gods' because of its solemn atmosphere, which strikes even the most inveterate atheists.

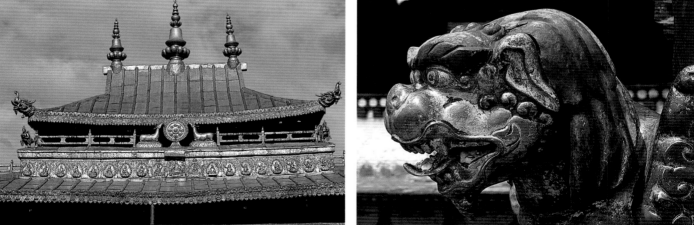

168 top This door belongs to the rich collection of Buddhist art kept in the Potala Palace, which has been converted into a museum. Among the most precious objects are the writings with the rule of the Tibetan monks.

168-169 Yellow and brown dominate the top floor of the palace. To get to the top of the hill there are paths and stairs dating from the 1600s, when the Fifth Dalai Lama rebuilt on this site the palace of the Tibetan king Songtsen Gampo, which had been destroyed in the 8th century.

168 bottom left The typical gilded and inlaid pagoda roofs stand out among the more ancient edifices.

168 bottom right A decorative sculpture 'keeps guard' over the palace.

169 top This meditation corridor faces the inner courtyard; it serves as a cloister.

169 bottom A precious statue of Buddha that is one of the more than 200,000 sacred sculpture pieces in the Potala Palace.

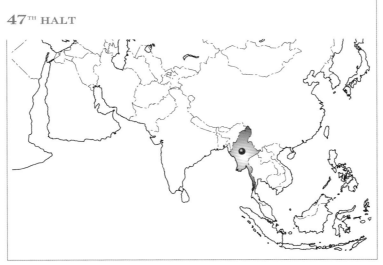

PAGAN

BURMA

Pagan (modern Bagan), the capital of the ancient Burmese kingdom, rose up along the left bank of the Irrawaddy River, in the middle of Burma, when in the mid-11th century King Anawratha attacked the populations of the south and transferred the Mon dynasty royal family, monks, workmen and artisans from Thaton to Pagan, thus marking the beginning of the unification of the various local cultures. For Pagan this was a golden age, and the flourishing economy was accompanied by innumerable feasts and, above all, religious ceremonies. This period witnessed the construction of an amazing number of temples and stupas scattered over an area of 8 sq. miles (20 sq. km). In fact, about 2000 structures were built during the reign of Aniruddha and up to the Mongol conquest led by Khubilai Khan in 1287. Pagan was transformed into an open-air construction yard, and since the religious monuments were made of masonry instead of the teak wood used for the civil architecture, they have been preserved intact. The white stucco friezes in the shape of lotuses, flowers and garlands as well as the flamboyant gilded inlay, all characteristic features of Burmese monuments, have also been come down to us in good condition. Examples of this are the Shwezigon, the bell-shaped stupa adorned with gold leaf and precious stones, and the square Ananda temple of "great wisdom," with gigantic sculptures of Buddha and 1400 detailed bas-reliefs with episodes from his life taken from the *Jataka*, the book consisting of a collection of 550 tales and teachings of the Buddha. The Ananda temple is the most striking example of syncretism of the Indian, Buddhist, Khmer and Mon cultures, just as the Mahabodi temple was greatly influenced by Hinduism. Then there are the luxurious four-story votive constructions such as the Thatbyinnyu, with gilded roofs, and monasteries such as Upali-Thein, which are completely decorated with Tantric frescoes.

Experts consider nothing less than amazing the construction, in such a short time, of so many edifices that were so different from one another. The most widespread style is that of the Mon King Anawrata, who favored what could be called an austere form (small windows with grilles, rather dark corridors, sloping roofs) that was quite distinct from the subsequent architectural styles, in which the abundance of paintings, sculptures and well-illuminat-ed corridors on different levels imparted a much more magnificent aura to the religious buildings. In any case, the galleries were always carefully conceived to allow for the most comfortable circumambulation, the clockwise walk the faithful made around the temple to admire the holy images and draw inspiration for prayer. Even those with no knowledge of Burmese art are immediately struck by the beauty of the shrines, which are presented in more variety here than in any other country in Southeast Asia. They are onion-shaped much like the Tibetan chorten, campaniform, octagonal, and round, representing Mt. Meru, the Hindu Olympus populated by fantastic spirits and animals. The foundations of the stupas here are therefore a sort of protection for the structure itself and for the worshippers who pray around them: In like manner, the stairways symbolize the ideal union between earth and sky, the small stupas that are often located around the larger ones represent the low mountains that surround Mt. Meru, and the sloped roofs symbolize the sky of Brahma.

The typical references made by sacred art do not end here. We need only think of the interior of the temples, consisting of rooms that reproduce the grottoes where the Buddhist monks pray, while the dragons symbolize the purification of the flowing water.

170 and 170-171 Pagan is the ancient capital of the kingdom that around the year 1000 entered a period of splendor and was beautified with a gigantic complex of sacred monuments.

171 bottom left This temple was built on a sort of stepped platform to underscore the divine status of the site. The walls mark the circuit the faithful make.

171 bottom right A detail of the characteristic elongated roofs that are more or less rounded at the base. They symbolize the connection with the sky and the divinities.

172-173 Aerial view of the archaeological park of Pagan, which boasts over 2000 constructions of various sizes built in different architectural styles in the course of two centuries.

174-175 The Royal Palace complex in Bangkok has many marvelous structures.It is completely surrounded by decorated walls. In this middle of this photograph is the Wat Phra Kaew Buddhist temple.

174 bottom Worshippers praying in front of one of the solid gold votive statues of Buddha. Next to the temple entrance, a woman is holding a bunch of incense sticks that are to be burned as a sign of devotion.

175 left The towers of other religious edifices surround the temple. These structures include the Phra Si Ratana Chedi, the gilded reliquary of Buddha, the library of sacred texts, and the royal mausoleum.

175 right The Emerald Buddha is one of the most venerated statues in Buddhism. It is only 14 inches (60 cm) high, was carved out of a single block of jade, and is kept on a very tall gilded altar.

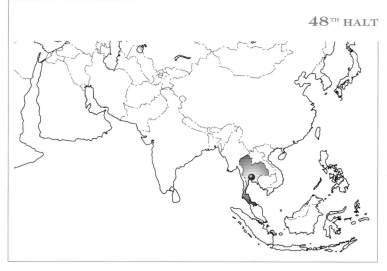

WAT PHRA KAEW
BANGKOK, THAILAND

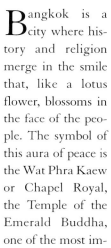

Bangkok is a city where history and religion merge in the smile that, like a lotus flower, blossoms in the face of the people. The symbol of this aura of peace is the Wat Phra Kaew or Chapel Royal, the Temple of the Emerald Buddha, one of the most important and most beautiful sanctuaries in the world. It lies in the Royal Palace, a complex with a surface area of 261,600 sq. yards (218,000 sq. m) and a castellated wall perimeter almost 1.25 miles (2 km) long that was built in the second half of the 18th century. The temple is one of city's main sights.

In the palace complex is a series of buildings erected in different periods and in different styles, from classical Thai to Victorian. Some of the edifices are open to the public. One is the large Audience Hall with the tombs of the kings, and the Hall of the Court, where the sumptuous coronation ceremonies are held.

A short distance away, at the left-hand end of the complex, in the shadow of the campaniles, *prangs* (conical towers) and Khmer towers, is the Wat Phra Kaew, surrounded by a wall in the shape of a Greek cross. This monument differs from the other edifices in the complex for its polychrome green and orange roofs and brilliant gilded cusps. At the entrance are two distinguished large statues decorated with green, white and red motifs in relief that represent the Yaska, the demons that Buddha converted and that became temple guardians. The entrance leads to the colonnade completely decorated with battle scenes (to be read counterclockwise, starting from the north wall), portraits of divinities, and scenes of daily life (including opium smokers and gamblers) whose allegorical content is explained in the marble tablets under the paintings.

The sanctuary is a rectangle about 231 ft by 99 ft (70 m by 30 m), a lavish reliquary built inside the Royal Palace complex at the behest of Rama I (who reigned from 1782 to 1809) to house the statue of the Emerald Buddha. The chapel is richly decorated with mosaics, gilded incense altars, and an elegant pavement with ocher, cream- and tobacco-colored marble tesserae, over which are red carpets with silk borders used for meditation. The walls, marked by mother-of-pearl decoration, have paintings of mythological scenes from the *Ramakirti*, the Thai version of the *Ramayana*. Among the other decorative furnishings are votive sculptures of the Garuda - mythical birds, considered the mounts of Vishnu - the Kinnara celestial musicians with human face and bodies of horses and birds, and innumerable nymphs. Nearby is the venerable statue of the Emerald Buddha, which is 24 inches (60 cm) high, and carved from green jade.

The history of this famous cult image is wrapped in mystery and the first documented traces of its existence date only to

176 top This row of guardian statues is situated in the sacred precinct of the Royal Palace, a small, hidden enclosure at the western end of the complex, which is important from an artistic, religious and political standpoint.

176 bottom left These gilded bronze statues and friezes are on the roof of the Wat Phra Kaew, which is completely cased with green and orange majolica tiles and decorated with small bells that ring every time the wind blows.

176 bottom right One of the many anthropomorphic statues placed around the temple. These are the royal sentinels who keep watch over the reliquary, the mausoleum and the sacred library.

177 The architecture of the temple entrance is impressive and lavish. In the interior, besides common citizens, one may come upon members of the royal family during solemn official ceremonies.

1436. It was moved here and there, following the Thai royal court in the various stages of its expansion, until it found its present home in the Wat Phra Kaew, on the large, 36-ft (11-m) high gilded altar, surmounted by a nine-layer ceremonial umbrella. The Emerald Buddha thus became the symbol of the link between the present dynasty and Buddhism. In fact, with every change of season the king himself leads the changing of the decorative hangings: a gold tunic studded with diamonds when the hot season begins, a gilded robe for the rainy season, and another robe made of enamel and solid gold for the spring. Around the temple there are other, smaller sacred structures that are not open to the public: the Phra Si Ratana Chedi, which is also gilded, built for Rama IV to house a holy relic of Buddha – a piece of his breastbone; the Phra Mondop, completely surrounded by statues of white elephants, the home of the library of Buddhist writings; and the Prasad Phra Thep Bidom. Outside the temple precinct one can still find the local clairvoyants who predict the future with their wooden canes, long rows of bowls to collect offerings of coins or handfuls of rice that the monks keep in their orange tunics, and cages with multicolored birds that are let free at sunset as a sign of peace.

178-179 A general view of what is commonly considered the most important example of Hindu architecture: the temple of Angkor, situated inside the complex of the same name, which contains religious and civil edifices of the Khmer empire.

178 bottom left The Cambodian complex of Angkor, located along the Mekong River, was left is a state of total abandon for centuries and buried under the vegetation. The first series of restoration work began in the 1800s.

178 bottom right This entrance leads to the principal temple in the area, Angkor Wat. Built in the 12th century in honor of Vishnu, the divinity of whom the Khmer rulers claimed to be the reincarnation, it is probably the mausoleum of Suryavarman II.

179 High relief sculpture in stone that narrates the life of the Hindu divinities and the exploits of the Khmer soldiers. They cover most of the building façades, and it has been estimated that thousands of stonecutters were needed to carve them.

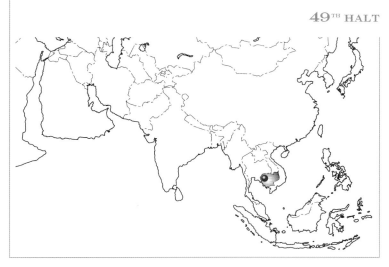

ANGKOR WAT
CAMBODIA

Archaeologists needed NASA's highly sophisticated tracking stations to find the remains of ancient Angkor Wat buried in the thick tropical vegetation that for centuries had safeguarded most of the temples from plunderers in search of archaeological finds. But today, after years of study, the site of the imperial Khmer city has been almost completely explored and uncovered. This is an area of 60 sq. miles (150 sq. km) in which the kings of Angkor had mastodonic temples built from the 9th to the 14th century to underscore the divine origin of their investiture. And this has given humanity one of the most fascinating and extraordinary archaeological sites on Earth.

Here, the religious and civil edifices had been abandoned since the year 1430, after the fall of the Khmer dynasty and the conquest of the city on the part of the Thai, who then transferred the 'capital' (this is in fact the meaning of the word

Angkor) to Phnom Penh. It was discovered only 400 years later, thanks to the efforts of the French naturalist Henri Mouhot, who in the late 19th century published his *Voyage au Siam et dans la Cambodge*, which aroused the interest of scholars. Since that time archaeologists from all over the world, in cooperation with the local authorities, have literally wrested the monuments stone by stone from their mantle of lianas and vines.

First of all there is Angkor Wat, the largest and best-preserved temple, with five 215-ft (65-m) towers. It is the only one facing West, which has led archaeologists to presume that this is really a funerary monument. It was built in the 12th century for Suryavarman II, during whose reign the Angkor civilization attained its golden age, and was originally dedicated to the god Vishnu; it was later converted into a Buddhist temple. All the other structures, including a

grandiose system of cisterns and plumbing worthy of the most modern hydraulic networks, face the East.

But let us get back to Angkor Wat. Its 2640 ft (800 m) of enclosure walls are dotted with bas-reliefs that narrate the exploits of Krishna, Rama and the Khmer armies. But they also celebrate the divinity of the king, who personifies Vishnu, who uses a serpent to stir the fluid of immortality from which 1700 dancers rise up to symbolize the myth of creation. The five majestic central towers represent the peaks of the holy Hindu mountain, Meru, and the outer moats complete the metaphor of the temple as the center of the world by evoking the depth of the oceans.

The Bridge of the Naga, powerful hundred-headed serpents, leads to the walled city of Angkor Thom, a sort of religious enclave of Mahayana Buddhism conceived by the Khmer king

180-181 A detail of the towers on the top of the Bayon temple, a pyramid-shaped structure with 54 stone columns on its roof that are crowned with cyclopean heads of divinities.

180 bottom The Bayon temple was built on a large stone base and has an arcade supported by slender columns and decorated with detailed battle scenes.

ASIA

181 top This portrait was sculpted on a side tower of the Bayon edifice. The construction of the temple was ordered by King Jayavarman VII (1181-1219), who had just converted to Buddhism.

181 bottom Detail of the bas-reliefs in the Bayon temple, with scenes of daily life rendered poetically and with a wealth of details that have allowed scholars to reconstruct the customs of the time.

Jayavarman VII, who summoned 5000 men to fortify a sacred precinct of 5 sq. miles (12 sq. km).

This is the heart of the splendid complex of 70 temples that is the leading tourist attraction in Cambodia and that includes the Bayon monument with its 54 tall towers and thousand heads of Bodhisattvas that seem to envelop visitors with their thousand smiles. This monument was also built by Jayavarman, who converted to Buddhism because he felt that the Hindu divinities had not been able to protect Angkor.

The only remains of the Ta Prohm monastery, which is almost covered with vegetation, are some ruins popping up from the foliage, strangled by the gigantic centuries-old *Bombacaceae* roots.

And then there are the Ta Keo, which reminds one of the Maya pyramids and is totally without decoration, a kind of presage of modern Minimalist design; the labyrinthine Preah Kahn temple; the Phnom Bareng dedicated to the Hindu god Shiva; and the Terrace of Elephants and the Terrace of the Leper King, which are covered with perfectly preserved bas-reliefs. And all this is only a sample of what is store for visitors to Angkor.

182-183 This monumental statue of Buddha is in the archaeological site of Borobudur. In the background are some of the stupas that decorate the temples of Java and house votive sculptures.

182 bottom The Borobudur complex comprises five quadrangular terraces surmounted by three round elements to form a pyramidal structure that represents the Pantheon of Indian divinities: Mount Meru.

183 left The grand stairway goes up the sacred monument and leads to the numerous temples. Borobudur means 'Buddhist monastery on a hill,' referring to the great quantity of portraits of Buddha here.

183 right The terraces at Borobudur symbolically represent, from the bottom to the top, the various stages in the quest for purity and perfection, the intermediate phases of purification, leading from our worldly life to Nirvana.

BOROBODUR
JAVA, INDONESIA

The name of this monument derives from the Sanskrit appellation, Vihara Buddha Uhr, which means 'Buddhist monastery on a hill.' And the largest sacred construction in the world dedicated to the Enlighted One and visited by thousands of worshippers from all Southeast Asia lies precisely on top of a small mountain on the luxuriant Indonesia island of Java. The monument was built in the late 8th century by the Sailendra rulers, but for a thousand years, from the year 856 when it was abandoned after the dynasty fell, to 1814, when the British governor Sir Thomas Raffles supervised the campaign to rediscover it, all Borobodur lay buried under the thick vegetation of palms and the volcanic detritus of Mt. Gunnung Derapi, which had covered the area with a thick layer of ash. The terrible monsoons and frequent earthquakes that strike this section of Indonesia made archaeological digs difficult, and this was even more the case

with the restoration begun by the Dutch archaeologist Van Erp in the early 20th century and finished only in 1983 thanks to the generous economic aid given by many international institutions such as UNESCO.

Today Borobodur has regained its former splendor and in the early morning, when the heat is still bearable and the steep climb up the step pyramid is easier to make, a multitude of tourists and worshippers pay homage to the monument in respectful silence. Built in the vicinity of two rivers in keeping with Hindu tradition but bearing Mesopotamian and even Hellenistic influences, the Borobodur shrine has greatly intrigued the experts. Its heterogeneous features and huge size are not at all common, but scholars do agree on one point. The choice of the exact site of the monastery was based on the perfect consonance of the natural elements with the holy sites of Hindu and Buddhist tradition: the confluence of the two rivers reminds us of

the sacred union of the Ganges and the Jumna, while the mountains on the horizon evoke the Himalayan peaks.

But leaving aside its symbolism, the spectacle of this monument is simply grandiose. From the top, surmounted by a gigantic stupa or burial mound with a round base of a diameter of 50 ft (15 m), it dominates the valley filled with rice paddies. In order to get there you have to go up the stairs on each side of the pyramid, which has a quadrangular base whose sides are over 396 ft (120 m) wide and 126 ft (42 m) high and which is traversed by ten terraces used for meditation and lined with bas-reliefs illustrating the life of Buddha. However, many of these sculptures are covered with large stones as if to hide them, and none of the many scholars of Asiatic art has ever discovered the reason for this. Only the ones on the south side are perfectly visible; these depict in a highly ironic vein the temptations of the spirit offered to Man

184 top Unlike the Japanese or Tibetan portraits of Buddha, in this statue he seems younger and thin. Furthermore, at Borobudur he is always depicted with curly hair and wrapped in a cloth that covers only one shoulder.

184 center and bottom The bas-reliefs that decorate the over 9 miles (15 km) of galleries and corridors represent scenes of the terrestrial life of Buddha and the stages of his spiritual ascent and attainment of enlightenment.

184-185 Here the face of Buddha is surrounded by flowers. Among the different versions of the sculpted portraits of the god at Borobudur, there is also the very popular one of him holding the wheel of dharma.

185 bottom The three faces depict different levels of Nirvana, the mental and spiritual state represented at the ninth and final level of the Borobudur shrine by an isolated and empty temple that celebrates the Absolute Void.

ASIA

during his terrestrial life, all-consuming passions that draw him away from the noble aim of emancipation from greed (*rupadhatu*) and even more from the purification of the eternal void (*arupadhatu*).

The last terraces, those closest to Buddhist Paradise, are round and decorated with small bell-shaped stupas intricately carved like embroidery to underscore the beatitude and harmony one attains the more one ascends toward the heavens. As the local guides explain so patiently and meticulously (they deal mainly with European and American tourists who have little knowledge of Buddhist philosophy), the number of terraces corresponds to the stages in the ascent toward perfection. These range from the recognition of worldly desires to the gradual separation from them in order ascend to the sky; and the more one is aware of the ephemeral nature of all things and all states of mind, the more one can hope to be reborn in a more elevated form of life. This awareness frees one from craving and attachment and wraps the spirit in the Buddha's state of transcendence – nirvana or enlightenment.

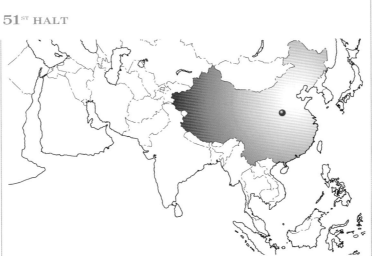

186-187 This row of terracotta warriors lies in underground corridors protected by wooden roofs that have both preserved and hidden them for centuries. The sculptures were discovered only thirty years ago, over 2000 years after their creation.

187 top The clothing, armor, faces and hats of footmen, officers and generals were executed with great precision, so much so that experts were able to ascertain the different ethnic groups and ages of the soldiers.

THE TERRACOTTA ARMY
XI'AN, CHINA

As early as the 2nd century B.C. there was documentation of the existence in China of a marvelous building, the royal tomb of the Qin emperor Shi Huangdi (d. 210 B.C.), constructed and decorated by over 700,000 laborers and artisans from all over the country. And yet for years archaeologists carried out digs in the Xi'an area to no avail, despite the fact that they had slavishly followed the indications given by the most authoritative historian of the time, the eminent Shima Qian. This activity continued in vain until 1974, when by pure chance (as usually occurs with the most important archaeological discoveries), some farmers who were digging a well unearthed a strange and surprising series of human heads. They were all made of terracotta and were the 'tip of the iceberg' of an amazing treasure – the terracotta army placed near the tomb of Shi Huangdi, which archaeologists later found. This consists of 8000 life-size soldiers (footmen, archers, knights, etc.) with their horses, chariots and weapons that presumably were there to guard the nearby tomb of the emperor, protection that was of course more symbolic than effective.

It is not clear just how this multitude of powerful warriors – each of which is in perfect fighting trim, with a bellicose expression, a rather proud look, and different facial features that underscore the uniqueness of each one – could have really been meant to frighten anyone, since they were hidden under the ground. In fact, the en-

ASIA

tire army, arranged carefully in rows, was found buried with a protective roof covered with earth that preserved it intact for over 2000 years. Therefore, most scholars feel that the army was most probably an art collection placed at that site for votive and thaumaturgic purposes. Perhaps the truth will never be known, and in any case we will have to wait at least until the restoration of the statues is completed. What matters is that Xi'an is truly splendid and has even been called the Eighth Wonder of the World. At first glance it evokes the atmosphere of ancient times, when this city flourished (it had one of the largest populations in the world, with a little less than 1 million inhabitants) and was still the political center of China. In fact, Xi'an was the capital of eleven imperial dynasties from the 11th century B.C. to the late 10th century A.D., including of course the Qin Dynasty of Shi Huangdi.

According to archaeologists, the tomb of this emperor – who is best known in history for the cultural-political revolution he effected by ordering the destruction of all existing historic-political literature and codifying both the court ceremonies and the standards of weights and measures – was the only tomb in the Xi'an area never to be violated. And since this region is filled with tumuli and the tomb is nearly a mile away from the terracotta army, it is thought that the warriors carried out their task of vigilance to the full. However, it now remains to be seen whether the guards and archers, charioteers, footmen in heavy uniforms and knights with sharp lances will be able to protect themselves. Since they have been brought to light some statues have begun to discolor and there is the risk they may slowly crumble. In order to avoid this, a team of German chemists has already begun experimenting with a protective liquid, an organic solution of hydroxyethyl methacrylate, whose tiny molecules can easily penetrate the vitreous film that covers the sculptures. At this point the statues will be delicately placed in a particle accelerator and bombarded with electrons so that the methacrylate can be spread uniformly and then solidify, creating a sort of plastic film that will serve as an invisible protective glue for the prodigious warriors.

190 top Two warriors depicted in a very plastic and natural pose. Note in particular the side torsion of the bust in the sculpture at right, which shows the skill of the artists who executed these fine sculpture pieces, some of whom even carved their names on the statues.

190-191 This horse-drawn chariot was found during the archaeological digs at Xi'an. Seen from a distance, the chariots and horses with their rich harnesses must have given the impression of the wealth and power of the imperial army.

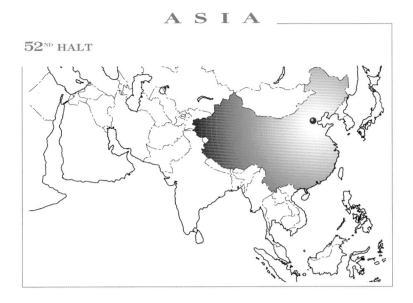

THE FORBIDDEN CITY
BEIJING, CHINA

Beijing is the capital of the People's Republic of China and the political heart of the country. The first settlements there date back to the 11th century B.C. Over the centuries the city was rebuilt three times, and only in 1421 did it take on the name of Peking (Beijing), meaning Northern Capital. This period, during the Ming Dynasty, witnessed the construction of almost all the monuments we see today, including the Imperial City, better known as the Forbidden City because the common people were not allowed to enter.

The Forbidden City is a city within a city that in the configuration of its buildings reflects the absolute power and cosmic role of the emperor, the Son of Heaven. In the span of five centuries, the Purple City – where the Manchu Qing (Ch'ing) dynasty settled in 1644 – became the pulsating sacred seat of the Middle Empire. In five centuries, de-

spite political changes, the evolution of society and historical vicissitudes, the ritualized life in the Forbidden City stubbornly continued to follow a model that defied time. It seemed to be a mold of the very destiny of China and its age-old traditions. It took one million workmen over fourteen years to build it. Only eunuchs were allowed to remain in the Palace after a certain hour, together with the members of the imperial family, of course. This pattern of life went on until 1911, when the last emperor, Pu Yi, was overthrown by a revolution led by Sun Yat-Sen.

The Forbidden City has a surface area of 864,000 sq. yards (720,000 sq. m), and its 9999 rooms make it the largest museum in China. The main gate (Wu-men) is about 132 ft (40 m) high and is crowned by a huge photograph of Mao Zedong. Once past the gate you are in an enormous courtyard paved with light

grey stone and crossed by the River of the Golden Waters, which symbolizes life in the imperial court. Passing over one of the five bridges that cross over the stream, you reach the Gate of Supreme Harmony, where huge columns and splendid decoration in the classic blue and gold lead to the Court of the Imperial Palace. Majestic bronze jars contained water and the court was permeated with the strong scent of 18 incense burners (the number of Chinese provinces).

But the largest and most important hall was the Hall of Supreme Harmony (Taihedian), 115.5 ft (35 m) tall, which was reserved for the emperor alone. Seventy-two columns, six of which are 3.3 ft (1 m) in diameter, support the roof, which is decorated and lacquered with traditional Chinese images, a true compendium of the centuries-old architectural experience of this nation. Part of

192 left One of the many pavilions in the Forbidden City, which is reached by means of one of the five marble bridges that cross over the moat and that represent the Five Virtues.

192 right This frieze is quite characteristic of the decoration in the interiors of the buildings, which drew inspiration from ancient Chinese iconography. For the most part the motifs are mythological animals such as dragons and gigantic serpents.

192-193 The Forbidden City viewed from above displays all its majesty and grandeur.

193 bottom The edifice at left serves as a vestibule to the central body of

the imperial citadel, which is now a museum. The Forbidden City is an enclave protected by a quadrangular enclosure wall (right). Entry was reserved for the imperial family and members of the government.

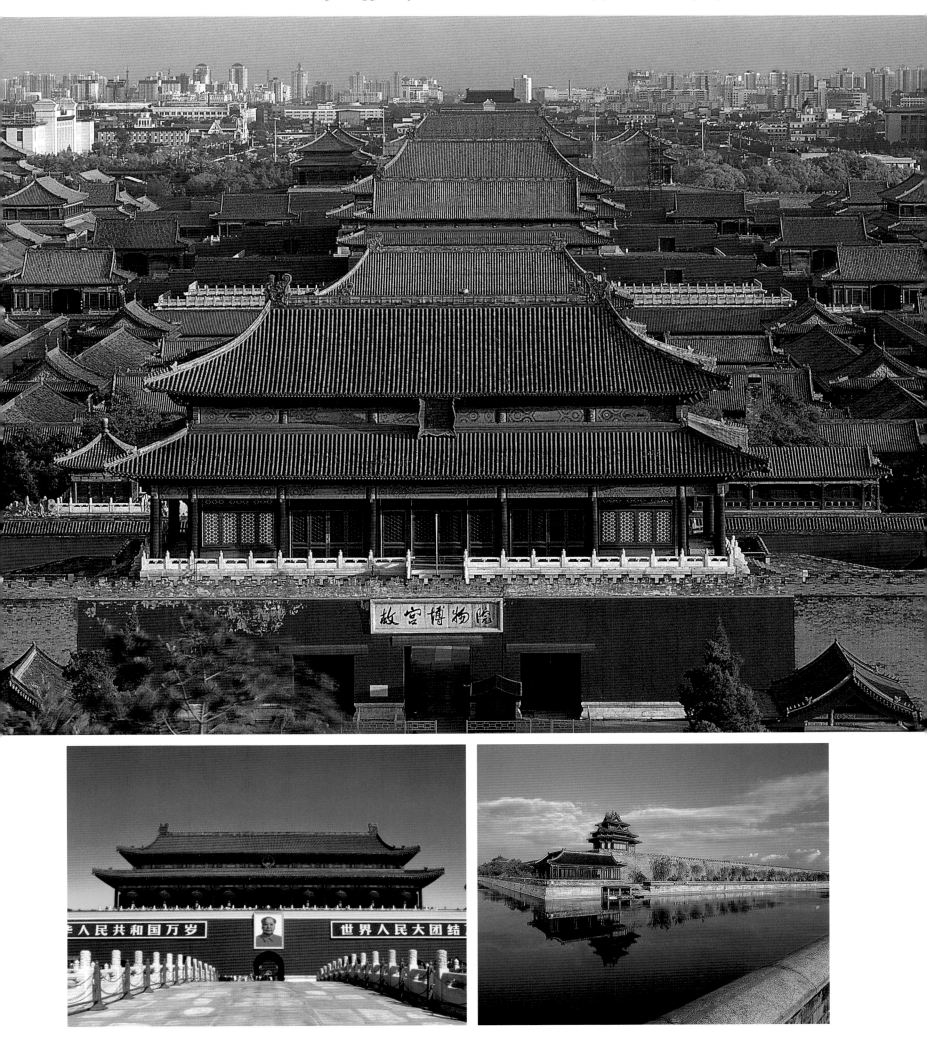

194 top *Fine sculptural
decoration crowns the roofs of the
Forbidden City: it represents the
sentinels at the emperor's
residence accompanied by
guardian animals.*

194 bottom *The entrances to the
numerous pavilions in the Forbidden
City always face south, so that they are
sheltered from the strong winds from
Siberia and, on a symbolic level, from
negative energy.*

ASIA

the decoration consists of dragons, which are nothing less than marvelous and are the largest in the
entire palace, dominated by the Throne of the
Dragon. The hall was used for marriages, births
and coronations, as well as banquets and meetings
with important guests such as ambassadors. Since
the Palace extends on a north-south axis with the
main buildings in the middle and the secondary
ones on either side, the best way to visit it is always
to head north; once past various amazingly beautiful halls and doors, you are at the exit, the Shenwu-
man Gate.

The northwest district of Beijing consists of a
series of courts and buildings, not all of which are
open to the public, where the concubines, favorites
and eunuchs lived. Today most of these buildings
are used as a museum featuring collections of precious objects made of ivory, silk, porcelain, gold
and stones that were once part of the imperial
treasure.

194-195 *A large sculpture of a lion, the symbol of power and riches.*

195 *bottom left* *The finish was the work of the best Chinese artisans of the*

time, who were summoned to the imperial court even from distant places to embellish the edifices with precious woodwork, stuccowork and brilliant lacquer.

195 *bottom right* *At the entrances of all the houses, as well as those of the temples, reception halls and state buildings, there are sculptures like these that symbolically welcome guests.*

196 top *The Imperial Palace is still decorated with fine statues and objects from different periods made of gold, silver and precious stones. Collected by various emperors, these treasures were saved from Japanese looting during the occupation of China before and during the Second World War.*

196 bottom *The throne room has imitation walls and slender decorative columns with gilded chiseling. The cobalt-colored vases are among the most precious pieces in the collection, which boasts a repertory of priceless ancient ceramics.*

ASIA

196-197 *A detail of the ceilings that decorate the concubines' chambers. They are made of inlaid wood painted with complex motifs, an alternation of geometric patterns and graceful, fantastic figures.*

197 bottom *This throne dominates one of the halls used for imperial audiences.*

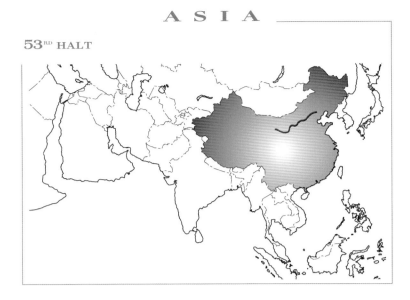

THE GREAT WALL
CHINA

The Chinese name for the Great Wall of China is Wanli Chang-chang, which means 'the long wall of 10,000 li,' the word *li* indicating the ancient Chinese unit of measurement equal to 1650 ft (500 m). Simple calculation therefore shows that this wall was 3100 miles (5000 km) However, modern measurements of the various sections of the wall demonstrated that there are 3720 miles (6000 km) of earth and stone that cross entire valleys and plains, and a more recent, definitive estimate increased the length to 4460 miles (7193 km), because a large section of the wall was discovered between Kansu and Xinjiang Uygur. Moreover, to this figure there must be added the 1550 miles (2500 km) of ramifications that extend into the interior. In short, the wall is unbelievably vast. Its height ranges from 26 to 36 ft (8 to 11 m), while the average width is about 23 ft (7 m).

According to some Chinese historians, the wall was built in 10-15 years, and many men lost their lives in the task. It is impressive to see the Great Wall on a map, extending from the Gulf of Chihli (Bo Hai), near the city of Qinhuangdao (east of Tianjin), and running without interruption up to the western borders of Gansu province (at Dunhuang, over 1550 miles/2500 km away). And it is very ancient, built in the late 3rd century B.C. by Qin Shi Huangdi, the first emperor of unified China, who connected all the stretches of walls that had already been built in previous centuries by the various Chinese states to protect their provinces. As a complement to the linking of the walls and in order to reinforce the Great Wall, another wall was built inside it and the space between the two was filled with beaten earth. The wall as it appears today represents large amounts of later work completed under the Ming Dynasty (1368-1644).

From a military standpoint, the Great Wall never checked such major invasions as those of the Liao, Mongols and Manchu, but it was at least an efficient barrier and deterrent to minor raids along the frontier. In order for the Great Wall to perform its main function of defending the nation against invaders, it has a paved road on its top, on the area between the two walls, that allowed the messengers on the watchtowers (which were 3 miles (5 km) apart) to sound the alarm and reach the troops quickly.

The Great Wall is special in that it was built on the outer edges of the area whose climate and configuration allowed for the development of the Chinese agricultural system, which is still operating. This division indicates the physical border between two major methods of exploiting natural resources as expressed in the Far East: the sedentary procedure of the Chinese, consisting of intensive farming, and the nomadic and semi-nomadic method used by the Turco-Mongol populations. As for the political border, the Great Wall never served this purpose, since all the great Chinese dynasties extended their dominion way beyond the wall itself. More than anything else, it represented the will of a people, or better, of its rulers, to maintain at all costs the integrity and age-old traditions of the vast Chinese territory.

198 One of the watchtowers built on the 3720-mile (6000-km) Great Wall of China, which was once almost twice as long.

198-199 The Great Wall bifurcates near Nan-K'ou and then becomes a single wall again in Shanxi. The cyclopean construction built to defend the Chinese Empire follows the natural configuration of the hills, rivers and valleys, creating a sinuous and harmonious effect.

199 bottom left According to experts, the construction of the Great Wall required the labor of at least 300,000 men.

199 bottom right The castellated wall is perfectly paved for its entire length to allow for fast and easy communication. The wall is from 16.5 to 33 ft (5 to 10 m) high and dotted with towers from which the guards used fire signals to warn of impending danger. The best preserved section is around Badaling, about 50 miles (80 km) from Beijing).

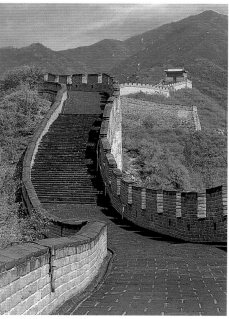

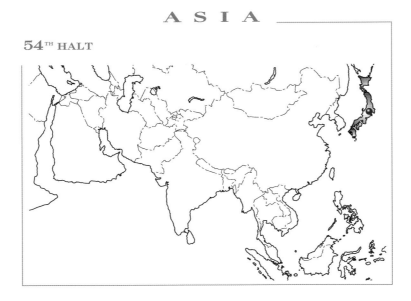

THE GINZA DISTRICT
TOKYO, JAPAN

Vital, energetic and constantly changing, Tokyo is one of the most exciting cities in the world. The Ginza district, which literally means "place of silver," is now famous as the center of luxury shopping. Here the large, converging streets are filled with sounds, lights and colors and are lined with buildings housing the shops of internationally famous designers and the most popular and expensive department stores in Japan. The symbol of Ginza is the Hattori Clock Tower, installed in 1894 on the top of the Wako department store at the corner of Harumi Dori Street and Ginza Dori Street.

Not everybody knows that centuries ago the Ginza quarter was the home of the state Mint (in fact, the name Ginza refers to the place where silver coins were struck), built in 1612. This district was remodeled and renewed in the second half of the 19th century in 'Western style' and was the first to have shops with brightly lit window displays. During the post-war reconstruction stress was laid on pragmatism, with a cityscape that left little room for aesthetic considerations.

The best way to take in the most interesting facets of the Ginza district is to plunge into its bustling chaos and then enjoy its oases of peace and quiet. Ginza is full of life, as can be seen by the many small private art galleries that alternate with the shops. The Ueno-koen Park has some of the most interesting museums in Japan. The Tokyo National Museum houses the world's largest collection of Japanese art, the National Sci-ence Museum is a vast complex with an exhaustive display, and the Shitamachi History Museum boasts reproductions of the lower-class neighborhoods of old Tokyo. Besides its shops, the Ginza area also has the Kabukiza Theater, the most famous Kabuki theater in Tokyo, built in 1889. The special feature of this theater is that you can purchase a ticket valid for only parts of the performance, which naturally costs less than one for the entire show.

Equally spectacular is the night scene of the Ginza, with its illuminated skyscrapers that offer other facets of this district: tiny cafés with long counters, characteristic restaurants featuring first-rate tofu, night clubs, and limousines that have to weave their way through the heavy traffic.

200 left A row of skyscrapers in the Ginza district of Tokyo, which has become a sort of permanent laboratory for architects and designers, who continuously design and construct bright and tall buildings there.

200 right and 200-201 Two views of the most famous district in Tokyo, the headquarters of the Japanese business world, where every firm wants to be represented by a shop or agency.

201 bottom left At any hour of the day the Ginza is teeming with passersby and working people.

201 bottom right The light railway crosses the district, transporting thousands of persons every day.

202-203 The quarter that was once the home of the Tokyo Mint was transformed in the last century into a luxury area, a sort of permanent exhibition of high-class shopping.

202 bottom Pastry shops, delicatessens, restaurants and boutiques delight passersby all day long with their tempting shop windows.

ASIA _____

203 top This modern three-story cafeteria was built with panoramic glass walls so that the clients could admire the surroundings while having a cup of tea.

203 bottom In the center of Ginza what strikes one is the sheer variety of materials used in the construction of the skyscrapers: the various offices, cinemas, theaters, art galleries and museums are made of glass, cement, aluminum, granite and steel of every type.

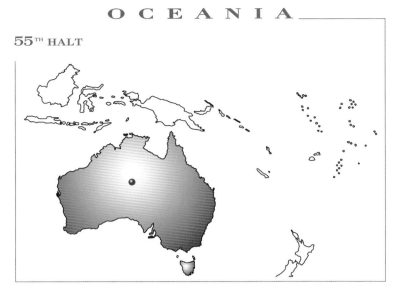

AYER'S ROCK AND THE OLGAS
AUSTRALIA

Ayer's Rock, called Uluru by the aborigines, is the most famous rock in the world. Its mass extends for 2.25 miles (3.6 km) and it is perhaps Australia's leading tourist attraction. This enormous red sandstone monolith, which has a circumference of over 5.5 miles (9 km) and rises 1150 ft (348 m) above the surrounding desert plain, is surrounded by half-hidden springs that since the dawn of time have been a precious source of water for the local population. The rock has become a holy site. Every crevice, cavern, niche, protuberance and band and furrow of its surface has a specific sacred meaning. At the base of the rock there are separate prayer areas for men and women decorated with delicate rock frescoes that are amazing in such a wild place surrounded by an expanse of desert and scrub.

But everything is transformed at dawn and sunset, when Ayer's Rock offers one of the most thrilling spectacles on Earth. Under the grazing beams of sunlight this imposing mass becomes a dazzling display of resplendent color that literally seems to be on fire for a few minutes: a sort of ancient meteorite that twice a day takes on its former appearance and then returns to its 'normal life' as a peaceful, splendid and tame rock.

In the vicinity there is another natural wonder, the Olgas hill system, which consists of 36 rounded monoliths that, curiously enough, lie exactly 22 miles (36 km) from Ayer's Rock. This complex is a labyrinth of incredibly beautiful rocky domes engraved with crevices and paths. The aborigines call them *Katatjuta*, which means 'the place of the many domes,' and according to legend they represent the Pungalunga, fearful giants who once fed upon the natives.

The complex has great cultural importance for the local peoples, such as the Anangu, and is one of the most famous icons in the Australian interior. Given the cultural importance of the domes, which the aborigines consider to be a sort of local Olympus, the visitor should never attempt to climb them.

Some hills are in fact identified with the rain gods, while Ayer's Rock is the symbol *par excellence* of fertility, represented by the huge serpent of the kingdoms of the spirit that reputedly arrived on Earth on a rainbow. The aborigines believe that under the huge rock there is a sacred cavern containing the Tjukurpa spring of energy. This is what governs the Dream Time, in which the primordial heroes created the world.

These ancestral beings, semi-human giants who also take on the guise of plants or animals, were born specifically in natural springs, and then breathed the divine spirit into everything and generated life. This is why Ayer's Rock, besides being a precious natural treasure, is considered a sacred healing site around which persons of every faith and provenance gather in meditation.

204 and 206-207 The Olgas Hills lie near Ayer's Rock and for centuries geologists from all over the world have studied them for their unique configuration.

204-205 Despite its barren aspect Ayer's Rock is surrounded by many springs, which according to local legends are of divine origin. It has a perimeter of more than 5.5 miles (9 km) and is over 1150 ft (346 km) high.

205 bottom left The faces of Ayer's Rock are not very steep and can be climbed rather easily. Visitors from all over the world gather around the foot of the rock, because the site is considered to have miraculous healing potential.

205 bottom right The light of sunset strikes a rock face. At this time of day the color of the monolith becomes markedly reddish and the surface seems to be iridescent, much like velvet.

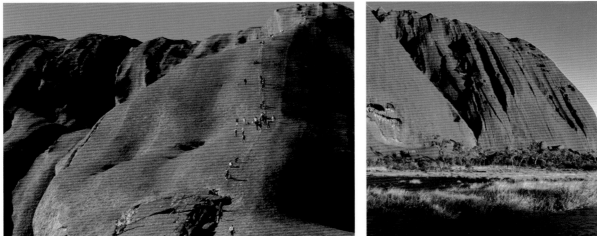

208-209 The Great Barrier Reef extends along the east coast of Australia from Cape York to Lady Elliot, creating enormous formations of over 1070 sq. ft (100 sq. m) with submerged walls up to 330 ft (100 m) high.

208 bottom These photographs were taken along the 1240 miles (2000 km) of the Great Barrier Reef, declared a biosphere reserve and marine park in 1975 and a UNESCO World Heritage Site in 1981.

209 left A belt of emerged sand stands over the coral reefs; it became an islet that in a short time was colonized by lush vegetation and inhabited by various species of birds.

209 right Here we have an example of the alternation of emergent and underwater reefs that create a sort of patchwork in the ocean that makes navigation quite difficult.

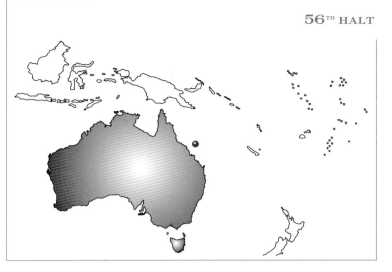

GREAT BARRIER REEF
AUSTRALIA

The origins of the Great Barrier Reef are very ancient, as scientists have dated the first formations at about 28 million years ago. This is the largest and most famous coral reel in the world, which extends for over 1240 miles (2000 km) along the northeast coast of Australia, from the Torres Strait to below the Tropic of Capricorn. The reef – which is separated from the mainland by a lagoon whose width varies greatly, from 198 ft (60 m) to 185 miles (300 km) – consists of about 400 species of corals and 600 islets, most of them uninhabited, along its perimeter. Most of the barrier lies under water, but in the highest points rather large coral agglomerations emerge that with time have been transformed into small, luxuriant islets that peep out of the sea and are covered with thick tropical vegetation. This scenery can be enjoyed from the coast, which at this point is only 198 ft (60 m) from the reef: the multicolored shallow water populated by multicolored fish and sinuous algae offer a unique sight indeed.

Now a national park, the Great Barrier Reef is the largest rock formation of organic origin in the Earth, with a surface area of 136,000 sq. miles (340,000 sq. km). It consists of several reefs of different shapes that create a series of canals and bends that are not always navigable. Its coralline structure is characterized by a multitude of shells of small organisms, madrepores, which settle in the first substratum of the sea. In order to effect photosynthesis, which is indispensable for their survival, the madrepores need light, and this is the reason why they cannot live at a depth of more than 132 ft (40 m).

The Great Barrier Reef is really divided into three main sections: the north zone, where the clear water is only 120 ft (36 m) deep; the central zone, which is deeper and has flat reefs that lie a certain distance from another; and the south zone, which has a depth of as much as 462 ft (145 m). This thick labyrinth of reefs separated only by narrow gorges favors the creation of strong, swift currents. Thus the water is always clear and perfectly oxygenated, forming an ideal habitat for hundreds of marine species that go to make up this extraordinary, invaluable haven for fish. Not only marvelous soft corals such as the brilliant alcyonarians, but also a host of tiny concretions, ramified formations that look like large trees, where the fish take refuge during their fecundation period or when they want to escape from such dangerous predators as the Australian sharks.

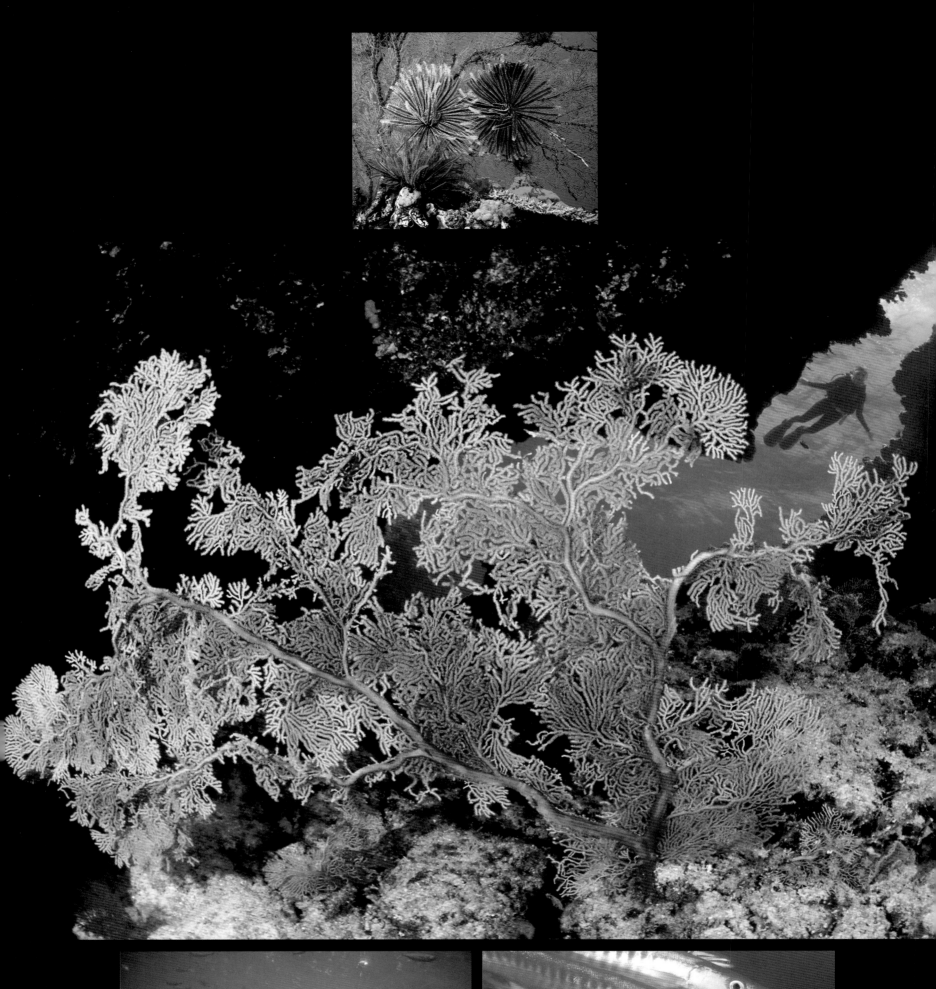

210 top The waters of the Great Barrier Reef are populated by mollusks of various shapes and colors. Here we can recognize some sea lilies.

210-211 and 211 top Over 400 types of coral have been identified in the

waters of the Great Barrier Reef. This photograph shows the fanlike shape of huge gorgonians.

210 bottom White sharks are the undisputed rulers of the Australian coasts, but the barracuda are also fierce predators.

211 bottom This photo documents the harmony of life in the shade of the Great Barrier Reef: a small clown fish lives in safety under the tentacles of an anemone, which sting everything except the fish itself.

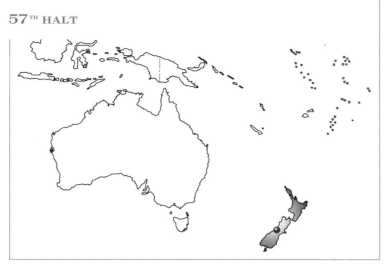

MOUNT COOK
NEW ZEALAND

In the Maori language this mountain is called Aorangi, which means 'cloud piercer.' At 12,421 ft (3764 m) Mt. Cook, a peak in New Zealand's southern Alps, is the highest in Oceania. It is a fascinating site thanks to its luxuriant and extremely varied vegetation. Scientists have classified about 1500 species of indigenous plants, accompanied by hundreds of rare species of animals. In fact, the environment of New Zealand differs from any other region on Earth precisely because, being an island, there has been no intrusions and crossbreeding among animal and plant species, and the genetic constitution of every species has been kept intact for centuries.

Fauna include red deer, rabbits, goats, boars, weasels, ferrets and opossums. The mountain is also the home of many other special animals such as the Tuatara serpent, which looks like a large lizard but according to experts is a direct descendant of dinosaurs. The area is also the nesting ground for splendid birds with little power of flight, such as the nocturnal kakapo parrot (*Strigops habroptilus*), which is green, tawny and yellow and which in the 1960s was declared an endangered species. The favorite prey of wildcats and kiores (large New Zealand rats), the kakapo mates only when the rimu tree bears fruit, every three or four years. This is the reason all attempts at repopulating this rare bird have been fraught with difficulty. However, over 200 specimens were counted recently along the steep flanks of the mountain that plunges onto the white ocean beaches.

Mount Cook offers breathtaking scenery. The terrain is sculpted by deep crevices and faults that cross all the surrounding area, highlighting the geomorphologic blocks that around 26 million years ago rose up, creating the present-day mountain ranges. There is still very intense volcanic activity here and the ancient craters have become large, enchanting lakes on the slopes of the mountain. Rivers flow down from the peaks of the mountain; one of them is the swift Clutha, which is 208 miles (336 km) long. The endemic forests dotting the west slope of Mount Cook are also fascinating, and their particularly humid microclimate favors the growth of lush and beautiful species of trees with highly prized wood: kauri, kahikatea and totara.

Considered by mountaineers one of the most exciting and treacherous mountains to climb because of the variable rainfall and abundance of snow on the summit, Mount Cook recently became even more famous when film director Peter Jackson chose its highlands as the setting for many scenes of his trilogy *The Lord of the Rings*.

212 Snow-capped Mount Cook photographed at dawn. The peak is 12,421 ft (3764 m) above sea level and is the highest in Oceania. The mountain is a major plant reserve in which hundreds of very rare species have been classified.

212-213 The summit of Mount Cook is popular with climbers and mountaineers as a great challenge and adventure because of the variable and treacherous weather conditions. The peak was first conquered in 1894 by three New Zealanders.

213 bottom Two hikers on the slopes of Mount Cook at sunset. The panoramic view from this point is nothing less than astounding, ranging from the woods to the torrents formed by the melted snow, the peak and the Pacific coastline.

BORA-BORA
FRENCH POLYNESIA

Bora-Bora means 'first-born.' And in fact it is thought that this was the first island in Polynesia to rise up from the geological upheavals that occurred many millions of years ago. Like all islands here, it was the theater of violent and endless struggles among the indigenous tribes until the arrival of the colonists. Situated 167 miles (270 km) northwest of Tahiti, it is a mountainous massif surrounded by a lagoon and a coral reef that earn it the name of 'Pearl of the Pacific.' According to legend, the island was once called Vavau, then Pora-Pora, and it is though that it began to be populated in the 9th century A.D. It played a fundamental role in Polynesian political and religious life, even though it was subject to vicious rivalry among the various pretenders to the throne. In the 18th century, after many a violent

battle the great King Puni of Faanui managed to unify the different tribes that lived on Bora-Bora. He went on to conquer all the Society Islands except for Huahine. The last ruler was a woman, Maevarva, who reigned until 1888, when the island became part of French Polynesia.

Bora-Bora, with its enchanting lagoon that has no equal in the whole world, offers extraordinarily moving scenery thanks to its crystal-clear sea, beaches with fine white sand, and the coral reef that surrounds it. In recent years the island has witnessed the rapid development of tourism, which has sparked the construction of fantastic hotels and resorts. The climate has a strong influence on the flora in this gem of French Polynesia, which offers visitors spectacular luxuriant vegetation that in-

cludes coconut trees, Australian pines, bread trees and giant bamboo. The fauna is no less impressive, especially in the sea. Hosts of fish of every species and shape, coral, turtles, manta rays, moray eels, groupers and gigantic algae color the bed of the sea with veritable rainbows that are also lit at night by the moonlight.

Blessed with a basically mild climate and greatly influenced by the trade winds from the Pacific Ocean, Bora-Bora has an average temperature of about 27°C and, since the temperature of the sea is 25-26°C, the island is seventh heaven for swimmers and ideal for divers, who can admire the sea floor and its life for hours on end. Another advantage here is that the rainfall occurs only from December to March.

In other words, this is a paradise, not a mere atoll.

214 This aerial view shows some of the coral islets around the 'Pearl of the Pacific,' Bora Bora, which is situated in the Leeward Islands, an hour by airplane from Papeete.

214-215 The configuration of Bora Bora is the result of the folding of the Earth's crust due to plate tectonics, which created a large coral reef around the island.

215 bottom Bora Bora is surrounded by a lagoon and coral islets - called motu *by the locals - that are large enough to accommodate an airport and some tourist villages. There is only one crossing through the reef, in front of the village of Vaitape.*

216-217 The temperature of the ocean around Bora Bora is pleasantly tepid all year long, so that divers can spend hours in company of amazing multicolored fish, rays and turtles.

218 Two views of the peak of Mt. Kilauea a few weeks after a rather strong eruption that created rivers and pools of hot lava. The volcano is 3960 ft (1200 m) high and is situated in the southwestern region of Big Island.

219 A helicopter monitoring and measuring the volcanic activity of Mt. Kilauea. Each of the two main craters has a fissure, in which the lava flows directly down to the ocean.

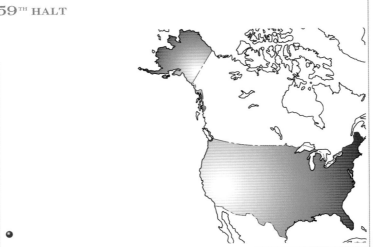

MT. KILAUEA
HAWAII, USA

Mt. Kilauea is part of the Hawaii Volcanoes National Park, which UNESCO made a World Heritage Site in 1987, and is one of the most active volcanoes in the world. Hawaiian legend narrates that the archipelago was created by the goddess Pele who, after distributing craters along the entire Pacific Ocean with her magic hoe, decided to live forever in the Halemaumau fire pit of the Kilauea crater. The geological explanation is that the intense magmatic activity of the area formed volcanic cones in the ocean millions of years ago that later became emerged dry land, where the terrifying and venerated Mt. Kilauea rises up. It lies in the southeast part of the coast of Hawaii Island over which the national park extends, and according to experts its rocky cone is among the most active in the world. In fact, in recent years it has erupted more than 50 times, and the famous 1949 eruption was one of the longest in living memory, lasting five months. Another famous eruption took place in 1959, forming a fountain of fire about 1980 ft (600 m) high.

The shape of Kilauea reminds one of an upside down bowl on the top of which are two large fissures that extend along the slopes and that take in the rivers of hot lava during eruptions. One of these two rocky clefts is called 'leaf of fire' because of its elongated shape that widens in the middle and then becomes narrow, just like a huge boiling leaf that can be seen from a long distance. Then, the entire mountain is dotted with fiery lakes that are created after eruptions and for weeks produce extraordinarily beautiful plays of light and color effects, especially at night. The lake created after the 1959 explosion on the secondary slope of Kilauea was 396 ft (120 m) deep and took almost 25 years to solidify, an impressive phenomenon indeed.

The cooling of the basalt magma produces the classic ropy lava, which lends the rocks the harmonious appearance of drapery. This has no relation at all with the rapidity with which the lava swallows up and destroys everything in its way before solidifying. The forest is the area most exposed to this devastation: it is literally swept away, except for some small pockets of vegetation that are saved by the bends in the lava rivers. As if by magic, these curves, as well as topographic irregularities, spare the small islets of greenery, the famous *kipukas* of Kilauea, characteristic land formations surrounded by lava in the most recent eruptions along the slopes of this giant of fire.

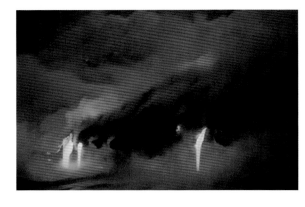

220 and 221 bottom These photos were taken at night along the slopes of the volcano, whose activity is so violent that it continuously creates new clefts. Climbing Mt. Kilauea is extremely dangerous because a violent eruption may occur unexpectedly.

220-221 Some rangers in the national park observing the scintillating lava of Kilauea, which can utterly destroy entire woods in a few hours. Visitors on guided tours of the volcano are provided with gas masks and informed about emergency measures.

222-223 On 27 May 1937 an impossible dream came true: the colossal 83,000-ton bridge spanned the Golden Gate, the broad channel between the Pacific and San Francisco Bay.

222 bottom Construction of the Golden Gate Bridge began in 1933 and was fraught with enormous difficulties caused by the great distance between the two banks, the strong wind, and the powerful and complex currents.

223 Every day over 100,000 automobiles cross over this huge structure. Until 1964 the Golden Gate Bridge was the longest suspension bridge in the world, with a total length of 98,032 ft (2737 m); the center span is 3840 ft (1280 m).

224-225 Emerging from the fog that envelops the bay is the top of one of the piers of Golden Gate Bridge. The bridge is 227 meters high and was painted in 'international orange' in order to be seen easily from the passing ships.

GOLDEN GATE BRIDGE
SAN FRANCISCO, CALIFORNIA, USA

Admiration and skepticism were the reactions to the project conceived in 1918 by the young engineer Joseph B. Strauss: an amazing suspension bridge to replace the ferries that connected San Francisco and the towns in Marin County across the entry to the bay. The strait between San Francisco Bay and the Pacific Ocean had been dubbed the Golden Gate in 1846 by Captain John Frémont, probably by analogy with the Golden Horn in Istanbul. However, the strait in the Bosporus is much narrower, and its waters are shallower and less turbulent than those of the Golden Gate. It took five years to overcome the opposition of the powerful ferry boat owners' lobby – more than 170 boats were operating at the time – and to persuade public opinion of the value of the investment, which at the time was estimated at $27 million and later actually cost $35 million. But there are other figures that were, and still are, even more impressive: the bridge is 9032 ft (2737 m) long, with a center span of 3840 feet (1280 m), 89 ft (27 m) wide and 221 ft (67 m) above sea level. The two huge steel piers, which are the equivalent of 64-story skyscrapers, bear the steel cables, which are 37.2 inches (93 cm) thick. Construction began in 1933 and was marked by enormous difficulties, the most important one being the pier bases and fenders, which were built 100 ft (almost 30 m) below the surface of the sea, as they had to withstand the complicated and powerful tidal flows and currents, and the bridge had to resist winds that were sometimes about 65 miles (100 km) per hour. On 27 May 1937 the impossible dream came true. The 83,000-ton colossus towered over the foggy bay like a flame. Strauss had decided to have it painted in 'international orange,' the color of smelted steel. That day, 200,000 persons, about 50 airplanes and dozens of ships celebrated the inauguration of the longest single-span bridge in the world, a record that was broken in 1964. The Golden Gate Bridge has resisted windstorms and earthquakes. Its gifted planner Strauss had said that crossing over the bridge would be like "riding in the sky," and in fact this it has been for over a thousand persons who unfortunately ended their lives tragically by diving into the ice-cold waters of the strait. Every day over 100,000 cars use the six-lane road, most of them transporting commuters who work in San Francisco. For them, and for most of the townspeople and tourists, the Golden Gate Bridge is the symbol of the city.

226 top and 226-227 The tepid, crystal-clear waters of the Pacific Ocean, the home of dolphins (above), wash the desert coastline of the narrow Mexican peninsula, which is 1050 miles (1700 km) long.

226 bottom In Baja or Lower California, various species of whales mate and give birth every winter, especially the humpback (left) and California gray whale (right).

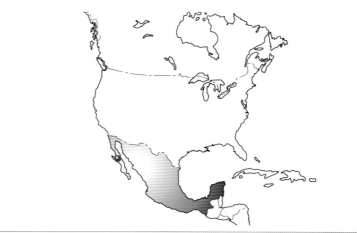

BAJA CALIFORNIA
MEXICO

*227 left Extending into the ocean with
its impressive granite stacks, Cabo San
Lucas, the southernmost tip of Baja
California, marks the passage between
the Gulf of California and the Pacific.*

*227 right The islands and more tranquil
bays are populated by the California sea
lion (Zalophus californianus), which lives
only along the warm coasts of the Pacific
and is the 'big brother' of the common seal.*

Cacti, desert, beaches and then more cacti, desert and beaches: this would seem to be rather monotonous scenery. Yet the narrow Mexican peninsula that separates the waves of the Pacific and the placid waters of the Gulf of California or Sea of Cortés offers an extraordinarily variegated landscape. Much of it has remained the same since it was explored and settled by the Milanese Jesuit Juan Maria Salvatierra, who landed at Bahia Concepción in 1697 and shortly afterward founded the mission of Loreto, the first of the many California missions. And a plaque on the small city hall reads: 'Historic capital of the Californias.' Suspended between the United States and Mexico, the long strip of land west of Central America was much admired by that indefatigable conquistador Cortés, who stubbornly insisted on searching for

pearls and gold in Baja California. The hot, arid land took its revenge on him, leaving him only the satisfaction of having the gulf to the east named after him.

In any case, this is a land of extremes that leaves a lasting impression on those who visit it. To begin with, there are the incredible contrasts and colors that accompany travelers along the Carretera no. 1, the road the runs the entire length of the peninsula for 1050 miles (1694 km), from Tijuana to Los Cabos. This road is marked by the missions founded by the Jesuits, who busied themselves with converting the locals, most of whom presumably died from the diseases contracted from the Europeans.

The Indian tribes left their rock paintings everywhere. On the Sierra de San Francisco, near San Ignacio, there are over 500 sites with stylized figures of

humans, animals and hunting scenes by Cochimì artists. The sea of 80,000 date palms that surrounds the oasis of the white San Ignacio Mission provides a means of sustenance to the community of the Castilian colonists' descendants.

The asphalt road penetrates a series of canyons filled with yellow and green cacti of every shape and size (the highest density on Earth lies precisely in the Desierto Central), on top of which are perched the *zopioltes* or buzzards. But the scenery changes quickly. One passes from the geometric sand dunes of the Desierto de los Chinos, past the mouth of the Colorado River, to towns with pastel colors and a vague French flavor, such as Santa Rosalía, on the Sea of Cortés: white wooden houses, built in the late 19th century for the miners who extracted copper from the bowels of the earth, and a small

228 *The sandy, rocky deserts are rich in endemic vegetation, including the gigantic, narrow cardon cactus (below), which rises up symbolically like a totem, attaining a height as great as 50 ft (15 m).*

229 *Most of the Lower California peninsula is virgin and provides interesting habitats for the fauna, which know how to take advantage of all the natural resources; for example, this Amphispiza bilineata sparrow is making use of the flowers of a cardon cactus.*

A M E R I C A

church made of iron designed by Gustave Eiffel. At San Telmo, toward the San Pedro Mártir Mts., where the National Astronomical Observatory stands at an altitude of 9250 ft (2800 m), pine, fir and cedar forests create an almost alpine landscape only a short distance from the Laguna Ojo de Liebre, a cove where from January to March hundreds of California gray whales (*Eschrichitius gibbosus*) come to winter. These cetaceans arrive from the Bering Sea to mate and breed. The Cedros and San Benito islands on the other hand are the headquarters of the California sea lion, the older brother of the common seal, which lives only along the warm Pacific coastline. The peaceful atmosphere of Baja California, which has a population of only 2 million persons makes it an ideal habitat for wildlife: from the raccoon to the coyote, red lynx, and mountain lion. The common loggerhead sea turtle lays its eggs on the tranquil beaches, while the steepest cliffs are the home of boobies, pelicans, frigates and gulls.

LAS VEGAS
NEVADA, USA

Something between a toyland and a mirage, Las Vegas is a city conceived for entertainment in the middle of the desert. It has become famous for its casinos, which are open 24 hours a day, its spectacular hotels, overnight marriages and equally fast divorces. The largest and most popular city in Nevada, surrounded by wild mountains inhabited by coyotes, Las Vegas is an enormous pinball machine. Since 1931, when the state government legalized gambling, the city began to attract visitors. The allure of success and easy winnings, the incarnation of the Far West, had found its capital. Every year almost 30 million people arrive here to try their luck and to be entertained.

Ironically, it was the Mormons who first settled here way back in 1855. Their mission, which they abandoned three years later, became a stage for the adventurers attracted by the gold and silver veins in this region. The city proper was founded on 15 May 1905 with the arrival of the railway, and saloons, stores and inns soon rose up there. Money has always circulated easily in Las Vegas, even during the Depression, thanks to such public works as the Union Pacific Railroad and the Hoover Dam on the Colorado River. And, obviously, thanks to gambling. The year 1941 witnessed the establishment of the first of the hotels that would make the fame of The Strip, the main city street, whose real name is Las Vegas Boulevard South. El Rancho Vegas was the first hotel and casino in one. Actually, in Las Vegas there are no hotels with casinos, but rather casinos with hotels.

The hotels are the true city monuments. Each period has had it own: from the Flamingo, built in 1946, with its unmistakable, huge neon sign in the shape of this bird, to the Riviera, the first skyscraper on the Strip, built in 1955, while that same year the Moulin Rouge was inaugurated as the first hotel open to clients of all races. The city became an enormous stage featuring shows and concerts with international stars at very low prices, since the rest of the cost was more than compensated by the profits made from gambling.

The latest development in Las Vegas was to transform it from a sin city into an entertainment venue for the family. It became an immense Disneyland, with the largest and most astonishing theme hotels in the world, from the Pyramid of Cheops to the Rome of the Ceasars, and the castle of Excalibur, with King Arthur who greets you at the entrance. As it was in the past, everything here is planned to attract and amaze the public.

230 and 230-231 The grandiose theme hotels are the new monuments in Las Vegas, which was founded in 1905 with the arrival of the railway line. The gambling capital of the world has thus become a huge fun park for the whole family, where you can find everything from the skyscrapers of New York (left) to the boulevards and Eiffel Tower of Paris (right). To make a journey in time, all you need to do is pass from one hotel to another.

231 bottom left Long John Silver and other fierce 18th-century pirates of the high seas are assaulting a British frigate. This free show is performed outside the Treasure Island Hotel.

231 bottom right Everything has always been easy at Las Vegas: it is easy to win and lose huge sums of money, easy to get married in one of the numerous chapels, and equally easy to get a divorce.

232-233 To spend the night in the castle all you need to do is knock at the door of the Excalibur, and King Arthur himself will open it for you.

232 bottom The Sphinx has arrived in America. Behind it are the Pyramid of Cheops made of glass and the Nile of Luxor, the immense hotel with 2526 rooms.

233 top The hotels in Las Vegas are symbols of different epochs: from the Flamingo (at left) to Caesar's Palace, the bizarre reconstruction of Imperial Rome (right).

233 bottom The Strip, the main street in town, is like a river overflowing with lights and neon signs.

234 and 235 *The overwhelming spectacle of Grand Canyon, in Arizona: 275 miles (445 km) of ravines and rock shaped by the rapid waters of the Colorado River. Five million years ago the river created an abyss that separates the Grand Canyon into two distinct zones: the silent, impervious North Rim, and the more luxuriant South Rim.*

236-237 *The thick clouds drift away while the glow of sunset blankets the steep rock faces. The Grand Canyon is like an open book on the geology of the American continent. In the more recent strata one can see corals, lichens and shells, which proves that the sea once covered the region.*

THE GRAND CANYON
ARIZONA, USA

"The Colorado River made it, but the instructions must have come from God," said the English author J.P. Priestley when he saw the Grand Canyon for the first time. And in fact the first impression one has is that of something supernatural. This gigantic gorge is a masterpiece of wild, majestic beauty, a labyrinth of rock that hides the secret of the birth of the world. For a stretch the Colorado River slowly eroded rock and earth, as if it wanted to reach the core of our planet. Indeed, the Grand Canyon is like an open book on the geology of the American continent. It begins at the bottom, with the black rock with red veins that date back to 1700 million years ago, and then on up to the Kaibab limestone filled with fossil shells that bear witness to the existence of the sea in Arizona. The canyon is 275 miles (445 km) long and from a few hundred feet to 15.5 miles (25 km) wide. Even its depth varies considerably, ranging from 9050 ft (2742 m) on the north side to 2415 ft (732 m) at Phantom Ranch. Viewed from above, the Grand Canyon looks like two facing mountains, at the feet of which flows the creator of majestic, deep chasms, into which it pours 857 cubic feet (659 cubic m) of water per second. The river once collected sediment in Utah that gave it a reddish color for its entire course (*colorado* is a Spanish word that means 'red'). The birth of the Grand Canyon, which became a national park in 1919, is no mystery. All the rocks that once occupied the zone were carried away by the Colorado River. But what astonishes geologists is that in its course the river did something unusual and apparently impossible: it cut through the Kaibab Plateau, a block 3016 ft (914 m) high. Waterways usually take the easiest path, skirting around such buttes, not crossing over or through them. Many theories have been propounded to explain this mystery. The most widely accepted one at present is that there were originally two rivers: the ancient Colorado, which headed toward Nevada, and another river that flowed toward California. This latter gradually began to erode the mountainous areas at the source, then extended northeast until it opened a path in the divide and absorbed the ancient Colorado. The newly formed river then flowed down rather steep terrain and was fed by the snow from the Rocky Mountains. Having become rapid, it began its drastic erosive activity. All this occurred five million years ago. The fascinating chasm separated the canyon into two distinct areas: the rainy, cold North Rim, usually covered with snow for months; and the mild, dry South Rim. The temperature rises as one descends into the canyon. On the North Rim there are poplar and fir forests populated by deer, coyotes, pumas, and the unusual white-tailed Kaibab squirrel. Upon entering the canyon, at an altitude of around 4950 ft (1500 m), you will see yucca, tea trees and cactus plants, around which rove kangaroo rats, desert bighorn sheep and jackrabbits. Farther down, only the typical desert flora is able to resist the heat, as the temperature there sometimes reaches 50°C. The North and South Rim also represent two different ways of viewing the Grand Canyon. The south side is the most popular and has paths that run parallel to the gorge. On the north side, which is much less frequented by tourists, there are superb pinnacles and ridges as thin as knife blades that hurl themselves into the chasm. The Navaho Indians gather on this solitary balcony for their spiritual retreats: their gods must not seem so far away from this vantage point.

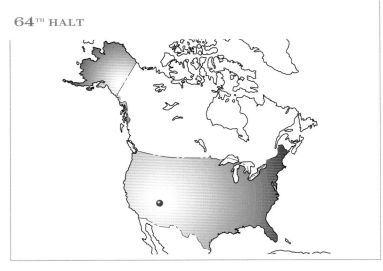

MONUMENT VALLEY
UTAH, ARIZONA, USA

"With beauty all around me may I walk" goes the refrain from an ancient Navajo Indian song that reveals the Native Americans' capacity to interpret the magic of Monument Valley in a few words. The valley consists of boundless arid plateaus and red deserts with massive, solitary stone monoliths that are splendid cathedrals, because those gigantic rock formations are natural monuments attesting to the miracle of creation. The wide valley extends for over 4800 sq. miles (12,000 sq. km) between the states of Arizona and Utah. Its extraordinary geological configuration is the result of 25 million years of erosion caused by rain and wind, awesome drought, and penetrating frost, as well as earthquakes and volcanic eruptions. Those rocky peaks that become fiery at sunset are the remains of the invasion of volcanic matter and crystalline rocks that broke free from

softer and less resistant marine sediment deposited when the entire zone was covered by an arm of the Gulf of Mexico in the Triassic era.

The whims of the rivers and the varying resistance of the layers of rock to the action of the atmosphere gave rise to bizarre rock formations and to the typical tableland with steep sides known as a mesa, which in Spanish means 'table.' The terrain rose up, creating other protuberances and crevices that became wider and deeper, generating canyons and narrow ravines. The result is an eternal, overwhelming monument whose landscape is very variegated in its profusion of colors and settings. Every hour of the day and every season of the year offer different panoramas. The summer here is torrid, while in winter the blood red pinnacles are tinged with white. And yet the Indians love their land.

The Monument Valley Navajo Tribal Park is part of the Navajo Indian Reservation, which lies in the northern quarter of Arizona and extends into Utah, Colorado and New Mexico. An area of about 41,540 sq. miles (67,000 sq. km) is the home of 250,000 descendants of those warriors who in the heart of Monument Valley, were defeated by the white soldiers of the US Army. Their ancestors gave names to the most curious rock formations. These include the Totem Pole, a spectacular stalagmite and the thinnest monolith in the United States, which is about 49.5 ft (150 m) high and casts a shadow 35 miles (56 km); others are the Three Sisters, the Elephant, the Thumb and the Camel. These sights can be seen quite easily by making a trip in a jeep or other off-road vehicle along the reserve's 99-mile (30-km) circuit.

238 and 239 *Situated in Arizona, near the Utah state line, Monument Valley is a vast expanse of arid land interrupted here and there by the strange dark orange rock formations. For 25,000,000 years, the* wind, rain and rivers have forged spectacular sculptures and mesas, the typical small isolated plateaus with level tops and vertical sides. A winding track about 19 miles (30 km) long runs through this majestic natural spectacle. Virtually unknown until the 1930s, the valley became the most famous movie set in the world after director John Ford used it to shoot Red River *and* Stagecoach, *starring John Wayne.*

240 *The valley is part of the vast reservation of the Navajo Indians, whose ancestors gave names to the most curious rock formations: the Three Sisters, the Elephant, and the Totem Pole, a stalagmite 495 ft (150 m) high.*

240-241 and 241 bottom *For centuries Monument Valley has been the cemetery of the Navajos, who would never abandon it, even though life there is virtually prohibitive. The summers are torrid and in winter the rocks are often blanketed with snow.*

A M E R I C A

For those who want see all the Monument Valley Navajo Tribal Park from an elevated lookout, the place to go is John Ford Point, where the famous American film director shot the most memorable scenes in masterpieces such as *Red River* and *Stagecoach*, starring John Wayne. The view is unrivaled: the vast spaces, an immense sky, the monumental plastic quality of the rocks and spires standing in the red dust—make for an impressive and archaic sight.

For centuries Monument Valley has been the mausoleum of the Navajo Indians. But this remote corner of the Earth became world famous thanks to Ford's films. Since 1938, innumerable features and commercials have been set in this symbol of the Wild West and of the American Dream. The last subtitle of one of the first films set in Monumental Valley reads as follows: "Men come, live their hour and then pass on, but the grandiose setting remains."

242 top Mammoth Hot Springs is a monument to the volcanic activity of Yellowstone Park. The limestone terraces have been sculpted for thousands of years by the water flowing from the hot springs.

242-243, 242 bottom and 243 The oldest national park in the world is an area with about 10,000 geothermic phenomena, the highest concentration in the world. It includes 200 geysers and a hot-water river frequented in winter by buffaloes.

THE YELLOWSTONE NATIONAL PARK GEYSERS
WYOMING, USA

"The dreams of a madman who has been away from civilized life for too long." This was the reaction of American scholars in 1811 to the description made by John Colter, one of the first persons to go to the Yellowstone area. The explorer swore he had discovered a valley filled with lakes of boiling mud holes, vents, fumaroles worthy to be part of Dante's *Inferno*, and jets of steam up to 165 ft (50 m) high that suddenly burst out of the ground. It took another 60 years and three official expeditions to convince people and the members of Congress that this place really existed and had to be protected. Thus, in 1872 the area of almost 6600 sq. miles (9000 sq. km) in northwest Wyoming was declared a national park.

Yellowstone is the world's first national park, the model for all the successive ones. In the past as in the present, its awesome hydrothermal activity continues to captivate visitors. For over 8000 years the spectacle produced by 10,000 geothermal phenomena has been repeated day after day — the highest and most varied visible concentration of its kind in the world. At Yellowstone it is as if the Earth was breathing. In general the Earth's crust is about 31 miles (50 km) thick, while in Yellowstone it is much thinner because of a series of volcanic explosions that took place in the last 17 million years (the most violent one occurred 600,000 years ago). Later on a caldera, measuring 28 by 47 miles (45 by 76 km) and several hundred feet deep, was formed. Subsequent eruptions partly filled-in the crater and made its walls less visible. The shape of the caldera was also altered by the ice flow that in the Pleistocene era covered the Rocky Mountains. In the course of 17 million years the area was the theater of a series of eruptions caused by the same hot point, an outcrop of fused material that had made its way into the Earth's crust. In the meantime the continent had moved, like a sheet of steel over an oxyhydrogen flame. At present this flame is burning under the geysers and hot springs. The Earth's crust here is from 2.5 to 3 miles (4 to 5 km) thick, which favors the penetration of water up to the mantle, where contact with the magma

244 and 245 *There are hundreds of thermal pools, hot-mud holes, fumaroles and hot spring falls, all with a host of colors. But nothing can equal the extraordinary range of hues in the Grand Prismatic Spring.*

246-247 *The Grand Prismatic Spring, which is 90 meters wide, is the largest hot spring in Yellowstone. Its color is due to the algae and microorganisms that live in its water and to the mineral deposits on the banks.*

AMERICA

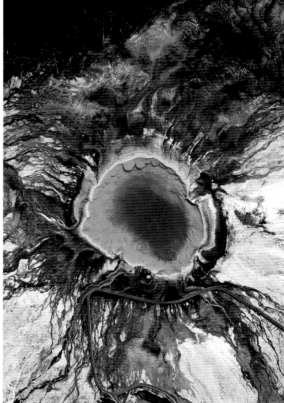

and the very high temperatures generate those impressive jets of hot water and steam. There are 200 geysers, which create an ever-changing landscape. In the Mammoth Hot Springs and Geyser Country the panorama may vary overnight, even from one hour to the next, and sometimes in the most unpredictable fashion. In fact, there are geysers that erupt almost regularly. This is the case with Old Faithful, which like a Swiss clock burbles like a pressure cooker every 94 minutes and then explodes into a jet of water and steam that spurts toward the sky for about 132 ft (40 m). Old Faithful is the most famous geyser, but the tallest one in the world is Steamboat, which sometimes reaches a height of 380 ft (115 m), accompanied by frightful rumbling. However, its bursts are only occasional; years may pass before it belches once again. On the other hand, the area where Steamboat is found, the Norris Geyser Basin, has extremely intense eruptive activity, with hundreds of thermal pools, hot-mud holes, smaller geysers that are always puffing, and even a river of hot water. The Firehole begins as a common mountain torrent, but

once it reaches the basin of geysers its waters become warm and never freeze over, not even during the long, bitterly cold winters. This is when it is easy to spot buffaloes and moose warming themselves along the banks. Indeed, Yellowstone National Park is the home of about 60 species of mammals, including the grizzly bear. The riverbed is warmed by a series of boiling springs. The same phenomenon creates the Mammoth Hot Springs, consisting of five spectacular limestone terraces carved by the boiling water for thousands of years. This gigantic, dazzling white natural architecture makes for a striking contrast with the pools and small falls, which take on different hues, depending on the water temperature and the type of bacteria and algae that flourish there. These microorganisms are able to transform a water hole into an abstract painting with incredible colors. Some of these are amazingly large, such as the Grand Prismatic Spring. Some 300 ft (90 m) wide, it is the largest spring in Yellowstone and, like the Old Faithful, is the symbol of the world's oldest national park.

248-249 Immense forests of Douglas fir trees (Pseudotsuga menziesii) cover the slopes of the mountains in Banff National Park, the second oldest park in the world after Yellowstone.

248 bottom Established in 1885, Banff National Park, together with the nearby Jasper National Park and other minor reserves, preserves almost 5 million acres (over 2 million hectares) in the Canadian Rockies. The altitude of the vast ramparts

formed between the Precambrian and Cretaceous eras varies from 3300 ft (1000 m) to Mt. Robson's 13,050 ft (3954 m). This is still a wild area that has remained as it was during the time of the pioneers.

249 The protected area comprises numerous lakes that are fed by large glaciers. The most impressive of these latter is the Columbia Ice Field, a carpet of ice covering an area of 170 sq. miles (325 sq. km).

BANFF AND JASPER NATIONAL PARKS
CANADA

Snow-capped peaks whose slopes are covered with Douglas fir forests that are mirrored in crystal-clear lakes: this is the image most used on boxes of chocolates. And it is the image that is repeated continuously in the Canadian Rocky Mountains. These grandiose ramparts divide the boundless plain of North America from the western side of the continent, separating the domain of wild nature from the civilized world.

The borderline was first marked out in 1885, when the Banff National Park was established, becoming the world's second oldest national park after Yellowstone. The Canadian government then extended its conservation efforts by founding the Jasper National Park and other protected areas, which now comprise about 7800 sq. miles (20,280 sq. km) of territory – a veritable country within a country, which the visitor can travel by car along the spectacular highway that runs northward from Banff for 175 miles (280 km) to Jasper. From the window you can see splendid mountain scenery that is reflected in the many large and small lakes, a fascinating panorama every season of the year. In spring and summer there is the pink of the willow herb and the light blue of the wild lupines, while the fall offers the blazing colors of the maple, sycamore and poplar trees, and winter blankets everything with snow. Even if you stay in your car you will spot bighorns, reindeer with gigantic antlers, caribou, gangling moose, fallow deer, marmots with their un-mistakable whistle, and Rocky Mountain goats with their white coats. These are only some of the 53 species of mammals that enjoy protected lives here, along with 280 species of birds, from the three-toed woodpecker to the golden eagle. If you want to see grizzly bears and grey wolves, on the other hand, you have to go on foot along the hundreds of miles of marked trails in the parks. To relax there is nothing better than a dive in one of the many hot springs in the Rocky Mountains. This natural phenomenon is well-known: the rain penetrates the rock and at a certain depth is heated, then emerging in the form of wholesome steam, what the Kootenay Indians so aptly described as 'the breath of the Great Spirit.' Proceeding northward, one skirts the large high-altitude glaciers up to the immense, flat Athabasca glacier, which can also be reached by coach. Other spectacular light-blue ice caps surround Lake Maligne, certainly a misnomer for such a splendid sheet of water with its changing colors.

250-251 Lake Peyto is one of the most spectacular bodies of water in the Rocky Mountains.

250 bottom The most impenetrable forests are the domain of the grizzly bear. In order to see this creature you have to follow the well-marked paths either on foot or horseback.

251 top The park is the home of a many animals - 53 species of mammals (including moose) and 260 species of birds.

251 bottom The Sunwapta River runs swiftly in a deep canyon, becoming a series of small waterfalls.

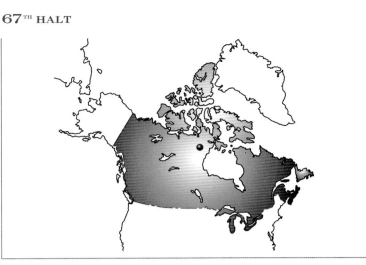

THE CANADIAN ARCTIC
CANADA

Remote, terribly cold, and covered with ice, the Arctic does not appear to be a place fit for humans. And yet 40,000 years ago the first inhabitants arrived even there. At that time, the Bering Strait did not exist and a land link between present-day Alaska and Siberia favored the migration of Asian populations to the northern regions of modern Canada. Their descendants are the most important indigenous people today. The Canadian Inuit (a name they prefer to Eskimos) number about 23,000, and they are the undisputed lords of this stretch of the Earth; since 1 April 1999 they have directly governed the province of Nunavut, which in the Inuit language means 'Our Land.' This is a region of ice and tundra measuring almost 800,000 square miles (2 million square kilometers) that, together with the Yukon and Northwest Territories, lies among a myriad of islands on the Arctic Circle – a wild land that extends beyond the tree line of Hudson Bay almost to the North Pole.

At this high latitude the certainties of everyday life, such as time, colors and orientation, do not exist. Above all, there is no such thing as a fixed division or clear status: day and night, sea and land, stable and mobile things are virtually indistinguishable. In the Arctic everything is relative. The location of places and the separation between water and terra firma are indefinite because the ice pack moves. The same is true of the flow of time, since in the summer the sun remains in the sky all day for months. During the long winter nights, on the other hand, the sky is suddenly illuminated with green, pink and violet hues, a display of patches of light that wander about like variable clouds and then disappear. This phenomenon, known as the *aurora borealis* or "Northern Lights," is caused by gases that are electrically charged in the upper layers of the atmosphere, at an altitude of 62 to 124 miles (100 to 200 km).

In this white universe – the Inuits have 41 words that indicate the various types of snow and ice – nature seems to be literally frozen in time. This is due to the climate, of course, but credit is also due to the Canadian authorities, who have turned vast areas into parks. One of these is the Auyuittuq National Park, the third largest in Canada, which includes Mount Thor, the highest cliff in the world (4950 ft; 1500 m).

Whales, seals and walruses swim among the icebergs, while dozens of species of sea birds whirl about them. There is a particularly large number of birds here, from the peregrine falcon to the

252 *The Canada Basin is a vast depression in the Arctic Ocean, a world of ice that in the last thirty years has become thinner and thinner because of the greenhouse effect.*

252-253 and 253 bottom *Although it is inhospitable, this wasteland of ice and tundra has been inhabited for 40,000 years by populations of Asian origin. In remote times the Bering* *Strait did not exist, which favored migration between Siberia and Alaska. The Inuit or Eskimos govern their province, Nunavut, which together with the Yukon and Northwest* *Territories overlooks the Arctic Circle from its steep cliffs. This is virgin land with steep mountains, vast areas of which are part of Canada's national parks system.*

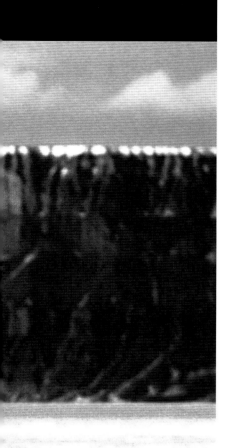

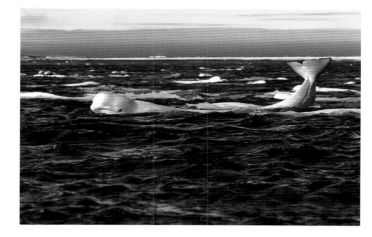

254-255 The Arctic region is the domain of the polar bear or Thalarctos maritimus*, which was an endangered species because it was hunted for its coat. Of the twenty or so species of Arctic mammals, this creature is one of the largest.*

254 bottom The freezing water is the home of many pinnipeds such as walruses (left) and seals (right).

255 top The most impressive whale is the beluga or white whale, which inspired Melville's great novel Moby Dick.

255 bottom Icebergs as large as mountains float in the Northwest Passage.

black-throated diver. The ice cap, which is becoming thinner and retreating every year, is the domain of the polar bear, known as *Thalarctos maritiumus* by scientists and *nanók* among the Inuit. Hunted for its fur, this creature faced extinction. Up to thirty years ago, its habits were a mystery. We only knew that it was huge and quite aggressive. Now we know that it has a very sensitive sense of smell, weak eyesight, lives for about thirty years, weighs as much as 1100 lbs (4950 kg), can swim for about 100 miles (160 km) without stopping, and that four out of ten cubs do not live long enough to complete their weaning stage at the age of three. Then, among the fjords, steep mountains, valleys and expanses of tundra there live about twenty other species of mammals, including wolves, Arctic foxes (*Alopex lagopus*), the musk-ox (*Ovibos muschatus*) and the Peary caribou, named after the famous American explorer. In the Ellesmere Island National Park, at the northernmost tip of the Canadian Arctic at the foot of mountains of ice, there is still the hut he used as a base for his expeditions to the North Pole. In the summer, the valley becomes a huge expanse of white wild cotton balls and crimson rhododendrons that defy the cold.

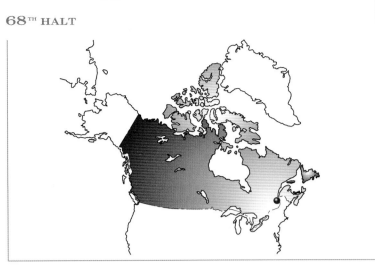

QUÉBEC CITY
CANADA

This is the only fortified city in North America. With its wholly European look, free-minded and holiday spirit, and abundance of cafés, restaurants and art galleries, Québec City is the nerve center of French Canada. The old town lies at the foot of the citadel, which towers over the St. Lawrence River from Cap Diamant (Cape Diamond). A strategic stronghold for over three centuries, the historic section has lovely gardens and imposing buildings with museums concerning its military past. Steps and a funicular connect the Upper Town with the narrow streets and alleys of the old Lower Town. It was at Place Royal that the explorer Samuel de Champlain established a French colony in 1608. In 1660 the town had 500 inhabitants who were engaged in different branches of commerce. The old port, in a strategic position where the St. Charles River flows into the St.

Lawrence River, has a surface area of 81.5 acres (33 hectares) and impressive buildings, bearing witness to centuries of intense maritime activity. The historic town, named a World Heritage Site, comprises about 4 sq. miles (10 sq. km) of low houses with stone walls and sloping slate roofs with skylights as well as streets dominated by impressive 18th- and 19th-century buildings. This area is best seen on foot, or at most in a gig. The massive walls run around the citadel for a total length of 2.85 miles (4.6 km), making it a sort of North American Gibraltar. The star-shaped plan of the fortification, built in 1820-50 and finished 30 years later, was modeled after the forts built in France in the second half of the 17th century by the military engineer Sébastien Vauban. Four gates give access to the citadel, whose interior has a series of imposing edifices, now the home of li-

braries, museums and churches of the various English and French religious orders that were active in the city. Coexistence was by no means easy or peaceful, as can be seen by the military character of the quarter: barracks, an arsenal, a prison and the collections of military uniforms, weapons, decoration and equipment used by both armies for over two centuries. Today this defensive stronghold has a more pleasant atmosphere.

The Place d'Armes, the parade ground, is used by strolling musicians, jugglers and the like, and is also a venue for concerts and spectacles. Nearby is the Terrasse Dufferin, a 770-yd (700-m) promenade the leads to the best viewpoint over the river and its surroundings. Here in 1620 Samuel de Champlain built the first city fort. His successor, Charles Jacques Huault de Montmagny, built a castle that later became the residence of the governor of New France for two cen-

256 left The imposing, 198 ft (60 m) high Château Frontenac dominates the city. Finished in 1893, it became the residence of the governor and was later converted into a hotel.

256 right The elegant government buildings overlooking avenues much like those in Paris, bear witness to the role of strategic stronghold that Québec City played for three centuries.

256-257 The St. Lawrence River offers the best panoramic view of the only fortified city in the Americas. The stairways and a funicular link the upper city with the lower districts.

257 bottom The old town still has its narrow cobblestone streets, churches and 19th-century buildings constructed by the colonists in the style of French towns on the Atlantic.

AMERICA

turies. Destroyed by fire in 1834, the palace was replaced by the promenade, at the entrance of which is the lovely Château Frontenac, 198 ft (60 m) high, overlooking the city. The palace had housed the governor, the Count de Frontenac; the Château was built in 1893 and a tower added in 1924. At present the Château is one of the most popular hotels in Québec City. It was also the venue of historic meetings among heads of state, such as those between Churchill and Roosevelt in 1943 and 1944. Another lovely sight is the Notre Dame des Victoires basilica, the oldest stone church in North America, the result of 350 years of construction. It was built in the late 17th century on the main city street in the prevailing Baroque style. Damaged by bombardments in 1759, it was restored several times. The modern, Neo-Gothic part of the church dates from 1830 and seems to have been constructed to attract people's attention with the statues on the façade, the 225-ft (69-m) tower, and the richly decorated interior, decorated with gilded sculptures, baldachins and one of the largest organs in the world. But basically, the basilica is a tribute to the French heritage of Québec.

260-261 *This aerial view shows both frontiers that face the fantastic falls: the American at left and the Canadian at right. Precisely at the border between* the two countries, the placid Niagara River suddenly plunges 185 ft (56 m). The discharge is among the world's biggest: 7800 cubic yards (6000 cubic m) per second.

260 bottom *The ferry approaches the 2227-ft (675-m) wide Horseshoe Falls (Canadian side); the American Falls are 1056 ft (320 m) wide. The first ferryboats to Table Rock began to operate in 1820.*

261 *Niagara Falls were discovered by a French explorer in 1613. Two centuries later they began to be a tourist attraction, and today over 15,000,000 persons visit them every year.*

NIAGARA FALLS
USA, CANADA

These are the most famous waterfalls in the world - by no means the highest, but among the largest as regards volume of water, 7800 cubic yards (6000 cubic meters) per second. The 185-ft (56-m) drop is due to the 330 ft (100 m) or so difference in height between Lake Erie and Lake Ontario. This is a short but intensely powerful stretch that has made a world-famous spectacle of the Niagara River, a seemingly placid watercourse that suddenly explodes like fireworks right on the Canadian-American border. The falls have two sections: the American Falls are 105 ft (320 m) wide, while the Canadian, known as Horseshoe Falls, extend for 2227 ft (675 m). However, their position has varied with time. According to geologists they have been gradually receding for a long time. In fact, in the last 10,000 years they have eroded almost 7 miles (11 km) of rock. To be more precise, since 1764 Horseshoe

Falls have retreated about 940 ft (285 m), and if they continue to recede at this pace they will reach the city of Buffalo in another 10,000 years.

The falls originated in the prehistoric period, and the bed of the Niagara River has yielded fossils of animals and plants that were deposited in the sediment millions of years ago. Naturally, from a geological standpoint, the falls are a rather young phenomenon. According to the Jesuit Gabriel Lalemant, one of the first persons to describe the rapids, the original name was Onguiaahra, or 'the strait,'

given by the Iroquois Indians, a name later simplified by the white settlers into Niagara. The falls were discovered by the French explorer Samuel de Champlain in 1613. Two centuries later the first sightseers began to arrive. In 1820 steps were built at Table Rock and the first ferry service began to operate. The majestic falls, which resound like thunder for miles and miles, are seen best from a ferryboat. In 50 years, despite the lack of comfortable transportation, the number of visitors increased tenfold, and tourism became the main activity on both sides.

Today Niagara Falls are one of the leading attractions on the American continent, with over 15 million visitor every year, many of whom are American newlyweds who go there for their honeymoon. And for good reason: an intimate dinner on a restaurant terrace with this grandiose natural wonder in the moonlight is an unforgettable experience.

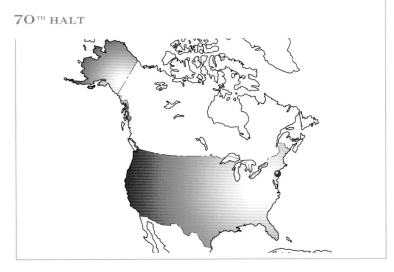

MANHATTAN
NEW YORK CITY, USA

Much of America is to be found in New York City, and today much of this metropolis is condensed in Ground Zero. The huge semi-subterranean site of the former World Trade Center, destroyed during the infamous terrorist attack of 11 September 2001, is the site of much activity. The "footprints" of the Twin Towers themselves will be the site of the primary memorial to those who died, while the 1776 ft (540 m) Freedom Tower will salute the future. As its architect Daniel Libeskind says: "It will be the symbol of our vitality and optimism after the tragedy." And in fact, the Americans' dynamism has remained intact. This is demonstrated in Lower Manhattan, near the tip of the island that no longer has the Twin Towers, as can be seen quite clearly from the Statue of Liberty. The symbol of the United States was a gift from the French (1886) to celebrate American independence. Visitors have to climb 354 steps to get to the crown, 307 ft (93 m), which offers the best panoramic view of Manhattan. Be-

tween the Hudson and East rivers past and future converge, and the colonial churches and historic monuments lie in the shadow of the skyscrapers. New York City was born here, and this is also the place where the nation began to take its first steps. In 1626 the Dutchman Peter Minuit purchased the island of Man-a-hatt-ta from the Algonquian Indians in exchange for a crate of fabrics and trinkets worth $24. Trade flourished at Wall Street, which was named after the wall built to keep the Indians out of the young settlement. The Stock Exchange, the

heart of the Financial District and now the hub of world finance, was founded here in 1817. And the most important banks and trading firms were established all around it. The headquarters building of the Federal Reserve Bank system, considered by many to be the world's most important financial institution, is situated here. It now occupies a Neo-Renaissance building finished in 1924. An equally solemn building is the Federal Hall, where in 1789 the first president of the United States, George Washington, was sworn in. His statue stands on the steps of the entrance to the present-day Neo-Classic successor structure built in 1842. Four years later, almost as if to underscore the contrast, Trinity Church, standing at Broadway and Wall Street, was rebuilt. The result was one of the largest churches of the time and one of the best examples of the American Neo-Gothic style, with spires, pinnacles and richly sculpted brass doors. Until 1860 its 86-ft (26-m) tower was the highest structure in New York City. But it was soon eclipsed by skyscrapers of

262 *The Chrysler Building, built in pure Art Deco style, reminds one of the grill of a radiator and the rays of a nascent star. The skyscraper was erected in 1930 for what was the largest automobile manufacturer of the time.*

262-263 *New York City was born in Lower Manhattan, which is the home of the Financial District and Ground Zero, the gaping hole left by the Twin Towers after the terrorist attack of 11 September 2001.*

263 bottom left *The most exclusive homes in Manhattan face Central Park, which was laid out in 1858. It is a perfect 843-acre (340-hectare) rectangle with hills, pools, meadows and over 500,000 trees.*

263 bottom right *The unmistakable silhouette of the Empire State Building, with its telescopic shape, is crowned by a mast used to anchor dirigibles. Finished in 1931, this famous skyscraper immediately became the symbol of New York City.*

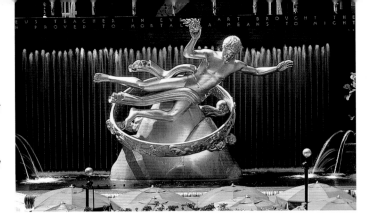

264 top A gilded Prometheus is the symbol of Rockefeller Center, the largest private complex in Manhattan, consisting of nineteen buildings dating from the 1930s to 1973.

264 bottom left The Guggenheim Museum was designed by Frank Lloyd Wright.

264 bottom right The Pan Am Building, designed by Walter Gropius. With the construction of the first skyscrapers in the 1950s, Park Avenue became a prestigious commercial and financial area.

265 Left to right are the bow-fronted Federal Building; the pyramid-roofed Federal Courthouse and the cupola-topped Municipal Building.

AMERICA

every kind. One of the first steel giants built in New York was the Flatiron Building, a wedge-shaped structure on 23rd Street at the crossing of Broadway and Fifth Avenue that in 1902 was the tallest building in the world. Then in 1931 the Empire State Building with its unmistakable mast, took and held the record for many years. Though no longer the world's tallest building, its 102 stories continue to be the symbol of New York City and one of its leading tourist attractions; people flock to it for a striking panoramic view of the city and its surroundings. In fact, the 86th floor observation deck saved the building from going bankrupt: built in record time, only two years, its offices were half-empty for years because of the Depression. The Woolworth Building, on the other hand, the headquarters of the famous department store chain, never changed owners and had no financial problems. In 1913 it was considered the most beautiful office building anywhere: built in Neo-Gothic style with figures of bats and other animals on the exterior, it has a pyramid roof and the interior is decorated with marble, filigree and mosaics. It

was a worthy rival of the AT&T Building, nicknamed Chippendale, which is a forest of columns of Baroque inspiration that make it look like a gigantic wedding cake. Whereas the Chrysler Building, built in Art Deco style in 1930 for the automobile manufacturer, looks like a radiator. Another grandiose example of this architectural style is the General Electric Building with its many spires, the flagship of Rockefeller Center. A short distance away is the best of the 1950s' Modernist buildings, the Seagram Building, designed by Mies van der Rohe. The Pan Am Building (now the MetLife Building), on the other hand, was designed by Walter Gropius, the founder of the Bauhaus, is a symbol of the Mid-Manhattan office-tower zone. Nearby is Lever House (1952), one of the city's first 'glass' building. Another building that caused a sensation in the postwar period is the Guggenheim Museum, designed by Frank Lloyd Wright. This latter, a 'white shell,' is the jewel of the so-called Museum Mile on upper Fifth Avenue, which is home to some of the city's finest museums, architectural masterpieces that house masterpieces of art.

266-267 Lower Manhattan, seen here from the Hudson River, has many striking new buildings. The 'ziggurat'-style structure on the left is the Holocaust Museum on Battery City Esplanade.

267 top Times Square, the heart of the Theater District, never sleeps.

267 center The Manhattan and Brooklyn bridges cross over the East River.

267 bottom The South Street Seaport, the old port, now hosts galleries, museums, shops and restaurants.

268 *The Statue of Liberty, made in France and transported by sea to an islet in New York's Upper Bay, houses a small museum and a terrace viewpoint under the crown.*

269 *The statue, including its a star-shaped platform and inlaid base, is 330 ft (100 m) high. It can be seen at quite a distance and since 1886 has welcomed immigrant-laden ships and has been the symbol of liberty for all peoples.*

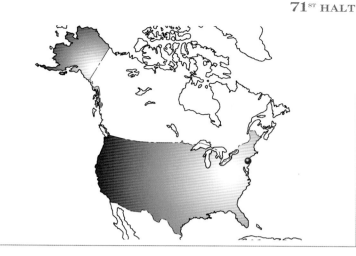

THE STATUE OF LIBERTY
NEW YORK CITY, USA

The Statue of Liberty, conceived in 1865 to celebrate French-American friendship, was designed by Frédéric-Auguste Bartholdi and made possible thanks to the elaborate construction planning of Gustave Eiffel, who devised the scheme for the huge sculpture's inner framework and armature. The statue's components, fabricated in France at a cost of $250,000, were completed in 1884 and then shipped to Liberty Island, New York, where they were set up on a pedestal with a Doric socle, surmounted by a Neo-Classical loggia made of concrete and granite, designed by Richard Morris Hunt. The statue President Grover Cleveland inaugurated on 28 October 1886 was considered a colossus: 148 ft (46 m) high and 225 tons in weight; at the time the largest construction in the United States. It became the classic sign of welcome for thousands of immigrants from all over the world.

The statue, which is built around a steel armature lined with copper plates 1/10th of an inch (2.5 mm) thick, represents the Roman goddess of freedom trampling the chains of slavery. She is wearing a seven-point crown, the symbol of all the seas and all the continents, through which her message of liberty shines, symbolized by the torch she holds in her right hand and by the Declaration of Independence she holds in her left hand. A large elevator takes visitors up ten stories, then there is a 168-step climb to reach the crown, which offers a fine panoramic view of New York City.

The huge base structure contains a small museum with a collection of documents, drawings and photographs that narrate the statue's history from its conception to the inauguration. Miss Liberty, as the Americans call her, has been restored several times. In 1987, on occasion of the 100th anniversary of the inauguration (which was magnificently celebrated), $70 million was spent on special maintenance work, including the replacement of the torch, which is covered in gold leaf.

The Statue of Liberty, a national monument since 1924, towers over a small island of only 12.5 acres (5 hectares) in New York's Upper Bay, about 2.5 miles (4 km) southwest of Battery Park, where ferries leave for the monument. Completion of the statue was made possible through a lottery that raised the necessary funds. However, more money was needed in order to transport the parts from Paris to New York, so Joseph Pulitzer, publisher of the New York World launched a subscription campaign that raised another $100,000: a display of support for what has been for over a century the universal symbol of free men.

270-271 Chichén Itzá was the most important Maya and Toltec city on the Yucatán peninsula. The principal pyramid, which is 79 ft (24 m) high, is the Temple of Kukulcán, known as the Castillo.

270 bottom The archaeological area of 741 acres (300 hectares), known to the Spanish, contains other religious monuments as well as the observatory, called Caracol or "snail shell" because of its shape (right).

271 left The Ball Court is the largest and most richly decorated structure of its kind in Central America. For the Maya, the game, similar to pelota, was really a cosmic ritual that ended with the decapitation of the losing team.

271 right The plumed serpent god, known as Kukulcán to the Maya and Quetzacoatl to the Toltecs, is seen here sculpted in stone. The massive heads delimit the Platform of the Eagles and Jaguars.

CHICHÉN ITZÁ
MEXICO

The most famous archaeological site in Mexico, situated in the middle of the Yucatán peninsula, Chichén Itzá was the leading city of the Maya and Toltec peoples. It owes its fortune to its deep natural wells (*cenotes*). In this semi-desert region, wells were precious sources of drinking water and allowed the population to found new cities. This holy city, whose name means 'mouth of the Itzás' well,' was founded by the Maya around the 5th century A.D. and flourished until about the year 900. The Itzá population then conquered it in about 1000. Later, for about two centuries, it was under the rule of the Toltecs, led by the deified king Quetzalcoatl (whom the Maya called Kukulcán). The new conquerors left their mark on the most prosperous city in the Yucatán and lived there until 1400, when Chichén Itzá was abandoned for some mysterious reason. The archaeological area of 741 acres (300 hectares) was already known to the Spanish. Archaeological excavations have revealed the presence of two distinct urban areas: in the southern section was Chichén Viejo, a typical example of Maya art and architecture of the late classical peri-

od, and Chichén Nuevo, which is larger and bears the Toltec imprint. Among the main structures in the more ancient part of this site is the House of the Nuns complex, so named by the Spanish Conquistadores because it looked like European convents. It is decorated with geometrical patterns, while the Tomb of the High Priest is a small pyramid whose interior had seven tombs. A work of the transition period is the Caracol (snail shell), a cylindrical astronomic observatory. Its top room with seven narrow windows was used to determine the equinoxes and solstices. Chichén Nuevo is dominated by the pyramid of Kukulcán. The Spanish called it the Castillo or castle because of its imposing size. With a square base of 181 ft (55 m) per side, the pyramid is an immense calendar in which every detail is an aid in the perfect measurement of time and the seasons. The four stairways have 90 steps for the days of the year. The last four steps and the top platform, which is at height of 79 ft (24 m), are the so-called five evil days. The pyramid is positioned so that on the days of the spring and autumn equinox there is a complex play of shadows along the main

stairway of the temple down to the ground that creates the image of the god Kukulcán-Quetzalcoatl. In fact, the pyramid houses a temple with a stone altar in the shape of the Jaguar with Jade Eyes. This animal, the symbol of the Toltec soldiers, is also in the nearby Temple of the Warriors, in the splendid Temple of the Jaguars and in the Group of the Thousand Columns, all of which are decorated with bas-reliefs and sculptures of eagles, priests and jaguars devouring human hearts. Chichén Itzá has the largest and most decorated ancient Ball Court in Central America. This is a huge court about 297 ft (90 m) long enclosed by two long side walls almost 26 ft (8 m) high that are decorated with bas-reliefs depicting moments of this Maya game, somewhat similar to pelota, in which players had to throw the ball — using only their hips, elbows and knees — into a stone ring decorated with serpent motifs. However, this was not considered a sport but was rather the climax of a religious ritual, a sort of struggle against the demons to save the people. The game was taken most seriously, and it is thought that the losers were sacrificed to the gods.

272 top This bas-relief decorates the Platform of the Tzompantli. The skeletons were meant to intimidate potential attackers.

273 The statue of Chac-Mool watches over the entrance of the Temple of the Warriors. Worshippers placed offerings on its flat stomach that the idol later took to the gods.

A M E R I C A

272 center left A typical example of Toltec art is the Group of the Thousand Columns, erected sometime between 900 and 1200 AD. The columns, decorated with carvings, represented warriors in armor.

272 center right One of the main structures in the most ancient section is the House of the Nuns complex, which was given this name by the Spanish because it reminded them of a European convent.

272 bottom The Temple of the Warriors was dedicated to the elite of Toltec society and decorated with splendid carvings of the jaguar, the symbol of the military class.

274 top and bottom The giant sea turtle (galàpago) weigh as much as 550 lbs (250 kg). Its name was given to the Galápagos archipelago, the home of the waved albatross (Diomedea irrorata), which now lives only on these islands.

274-275 and 275 Only five of the islands are inhabited. The others, consisting of 19 islands proper and 107 islets of volcanic origin lying off the coast of Ecuador, are the home of 7214 species of unique fauna, including numerous sea iguanas.

GALÁPAGOS ISLANDS
ECUADOR

It was the Bishop of Panama and explorer and navigator, Tomás de Berlanga, who in 1535 discovered this out-of-the-way archipelago in the Pacific Ocean, over 600 miles (970 km) from the coast of Ecuador. But the person who made it famous was Charles Darwin, who landed there in 1835 during his famous voyage aboard the *Beagle*. The English naturalist stayed there for five weeks to study the effect geographic isolation had on the evolution of species. There was a primeval world at his disposal, populated by animals and plants that had evolved in absolute isolation and freedom. In particular, Darwin studied the thirteen species of Galápagos finches and noted how each had different feeding habits in order to avoid competing among themselves. This was one of the arguments that lay at the base of his theory of evolution, described in his classic work *On the Origin of Species*,

published in 1859. The Galápagos Islands lie in a radius of 3200 sq. miles (8000 sq. km) around the Equator and comprise 19 islands and 107 islets and rocks. Only five islands are inhabited, with a total population of about 17,000. The others are the undisputed domain of unique wild life, from the land and sea iguanas to the sea lion, whales, albatross and the gigantic land tortoises, after which the islands were named (*galápago* in Spanish). The *Geochelone elephantopus* tortoise can weigh as much as 550 lbs (250 kg) and reach the age of one hundred. Darwin was struck by both their habits and tasty meat. In the past they were avidly hunted and about 15,000 have survived, including some subspecies that are facing extinction. To date, 7214 species have been classified in the archipelago, almost a third of which are endemic. The Galápagos Islands, consisting of black lava and impenetrable craggy

mountains, have a rather foreboding appearance. They were formed at least 4 million years ago by eruptions of underwater volcanoes and today there are 2000 craters that are still active. For a long time they were the den of English pirates, who took shelter after raiding the Spanish ships laden with gold and silver found in South America. Then they served as a base for whalers (whales are still quite numerous in the open sea here). Later on the archipelago become a penal colony and in recent years was turned into a naturalist's paradise, a reserve visited by more than 80,000 tourists every year. Only a small part of the archipelago is accessible, but this is more than enough to give an idea of its exceptional wild life. As de Berlanga had noted, the animals are quite tame and are not afraid of humans. There are no large predators there and each species controls its own habitat in peace.

AMERICA

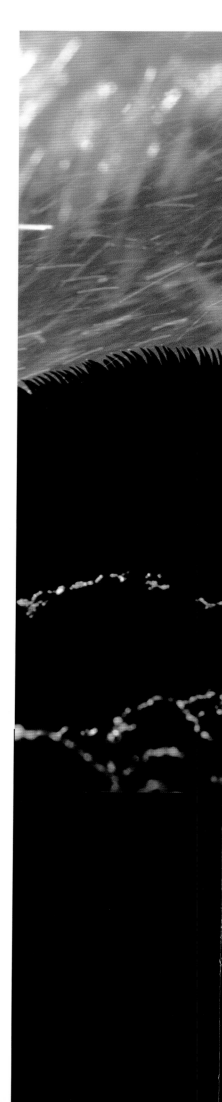

Every island is different. Heading from the northwest, you come upon the Isla Genovesa, the remains of a large crater that is almost wholly under water. Here there is the sweet scent of the *Bursera graveolens* trees, which are barren in the hot season but blossom with the rainfall around Christmas. This lava and basalt island is the home of 50,000 *Sula nebouxii* boobies with their light blue feet, while the mangroves are the nesting ground of the magnificent frigate birds (*Fregata magnificens*), the chicks of which have white feathers like down, while the Galápagos gulls (*Larus fuliginosus*) scurry about next to the sea lions. Cumbre volcano, 4930 ft (1494 m), dominates Isla Fernandina with its dark lava, *Brachycereus nesioticus* cactus, euphorbia, and multicolored lichens. Here you are sure of spotting seals, sea lions and, in particular, sea iguanas (*Amblyrhynchus cristatus*), which look like prehistoric monsters, the only saurians in the world that feed exclusively on algae. The lighthouse of Isla Bartolomé is one of the most panoramic spots in the archipelago, especially at sunset, when the coast takes on fuchsia and deep crimson hues. From there one can admire the pelicans that dive into the sea to catch fish, immediately surrounded by hungry penguins that manage to survive in the equatorial waters thanks to the cold Humboldt Current. The waved albatross (*Diomedea irrorata*), on the other hand, prefers to nest only on Hood Island, where about 10,000 couples, comprising almost the entire world population, live at Gardener Bay.

276-277 *Almost every cliff is home for the sea iguana (Ampblyrhynchus cristatus). This creature looks like a prehistoric monster and is the only saurian in the world that eats plants, or better, algae, which is an unlimited source of food for this animal. The Galápagos Islands were* *the first place to be declared a UNESCO World Heritage Site (1979). The islands were once a retreat for pirates and then became the base for whaling ships, a penal colony, and lastly a naturalist's paradise. Today only three percent of the archipelago is open to the public.* *277 bottom Among the numerous species that live in the Pacific Ocean around the Galápagos Islands there are penguins and hammerhead sharks (right), which can be as much as 6.5 ft (2 m) long.*

278-279 The cone-shaped peak of Huayna Picchu, at 8975 ft (2720 m), dominates the ruins of the fabled city, the last refuge of the Incas from the ineluctable onslaught of Pizarro.

278 bottom left Machu Picchu was built in 1460-70 in a sacred site. The residential complexes, each of which consisted of ten stone houses, were inhabited by about 1200 persons.

278 bottom right The stone block 'puzzle' configuration of the storehouses is like a labyrinth. This building technique was used for the terrace walls and the mountain therefore became an immense stairway on which corn and potatoes were grown.

279 The tower-like Temple of the Sun was an astronomical observatory. Every December 21st, the winter solstice, the dawn sunlight illuminates the central window of the structure.

MACHU PICCHU
PERU

Founded by the Incas in an area they considered magical, at the conjunction of the Andes and Amazon territories, Machu Picchu is to this day a fascinating mystery. Officially it was discovered on 24 July 1911 by the American archaeologist Hiram Bingham, a leading figure in the National Geographic Society and Yale University. Bingham came upon the site by chance after a long period of exploration. The *ciudad perdida* or lost city, the last refuge of the Incas during the Spanish conquest headed by Pizarro, is perched among mountains and rock faces capped with clouds. In 1532 the Spanish arrived at Cuzco and razed it to the ground, but they never found out about the existence of Machu Picchu, which was a secret carefully guarded by the few inhabitants in the valley. The city lies in a saddle between Machu Picchu peak (the old mountain) to the north, and Huayna Picchu (the new mountain) to the south. Below, under a breathtaking precipice of 1320 ft (400 m), is the Urubamba River. The impenetrable vegetation all around the site concealed the city for centuries.

Machu Picchu was laid out at an altitude of 7755 ft (2350 m) at the behest of the ruler Pachacuti in 1460-70. For the Incas, the city was the sacred site of the origin of the world. Moreover, it became an ideal link between the *tierras calientes* or warm lands, and the cold *tierras frias*, a free port through which fruit, tuber vegetables, silver and other goods passed on their way to the mountains and forests. The city, whose ruins reveal the Incas' building skills, had a population of about 1200.

The site is divided into two main sections, agricultural and urban, each with a different configuration. The former is characterized by terraces that are still cultivated, level embankments reached by steps carved on the mountainside, with a network of efficient irrigation canals. The archaeological area has about 200 buildings, mostly two-story houses and storehouses laid out around square courtyards. Access to the city was afforded at the top of the climb through a perfectly rectangular gate made of square stones. The most important religious edifices are laid out around large squares that were used for ceremonies. The monuments include the Great Temple with its finely constructed walls embellished with niches placed at regular intervals. Then there is the Hall of the Three Windows, which is the starting point of a flight of steps leading to the summit, known as Intihuatana, which means 'the place where the sun bound itself.' Here stands the large monolithic stele, sculpted on the spot where on June 24 the solemn sun festival, the Inti Raymi, took place. Lastly is the Temple of the Sun, much like a tower, which was used as an astronomical observatory. Behind this lies the so-called Road of the Fountains, along which there is a series of small basins that may have been used for ritual ablutions. On Huayana Picchu is the Temple of the Moon, standing in a natural grotto and decorated with bas-reliefs.

Little is known about how Machu Picchu was built. Its outstanding features are a constant source of admiration: the perfect union of man and the land; the extremely rational use of space; and the architectural technique and art used in the construction – the blocks fitting into one another seem to be a perfectly planned, intricate puzzle. According to legend, these marvels came about thanks to a magic plant whose leaves had the power to melt the stones so they could be modeled at will. This may not be true, but it is certainly nice to think it is.

EASTER ISLAND
CHILE

Rapa Nui is the real name of this Chilean island, but Westerners have always called it Easter Island because it was discovered by the Dutch admiral Jakob Roggeveen on Easter of 1722. Made quite empty during the second half of the 19th century by Peruvian slavers and by the diseases imported by the Westerners, in 1935 the island of Rapa Nui was eventually declared a national historic monument by the Chilean government. This beautiful and wild island owes its fame above all to its monuments, and the main attraction here are the gigantic stone heads and busts, the so-called Moai, which according to local tradition represent the sacred ancestors who remained on the island to protect the villagers from evil spirits. Ranging from 6.6 to 66 ft (2 to 20 m) in height, these monoliths are made mostly of rich yellow-ocher lava rock that is found almost exclusively in the quarries of the Ranu Raraku volcano. On the top of some of these huge blocks of stone were placed cylindrical masses of red stone, probably symbols of figures with religious powers. The Moai are perhaps the most striking testimony of the development of this population of Poly-nesian origin that according to the latest research settled here around the 3rd century A.D. But they are not the only monuments. Archaeological artifacts are scattered throughout Easter Island. These include the Ahu sanctuaries, consisting of long, narrow platforms on which the Moai were placed, facing the interior, and the sites of the tombs of the most important villagers. The natives' dwelling places are almost all round, with fires around them where the food was cooked for the entire village.

There were ovens with fireplaces, stables, and small enclosures for the animals indispensable for the population's survival. There are also hieroglyphs called *rongo rongo*, which scholars have not yet been able to decipher satisfactorily but which mark the transition of the Moai culture, based on organization in peaceful, sedentary tribes, to that of the Matatoa warriors, who rejected the Moai and ordered their destruction. In order to escape from this peril, the Moai gathered in small villages, creating what could be called reserves with a strong religious matrix in which the cult of the 'bird-man' prevailed. The zenith of the religious rituals, which were held regularly from 1500 to 1878, was the annual sacred feast held in the village of Orongo. It consisted of a competition among all the villagers on the island, who had to swim to a small strip of land opposite Orongo and find the egg of the holy bird, the lovely sooty tern, considered the incarnation of the god Make Make. The first person to bring back the egg had the right to name his village chief 'bird-man of the year,' who was then revered and protected by the gods.

280 The Moai are colossal stone sculptures scattered over the island; they supposedly represent the spirits of the original inhabitants that remained on Easter Island to protect the population from evil.

280-281 Some Moai stand along the coastline and can be seen from quite a distance because of their impressive size (they can be as much as 66 ft/20 m high and weigh 90 tons), thus appearing to warn sailors that this island is well protected.

281 bottom left Here we see some Moai without the typical stone 'hat' that presumably served to increase the height of the sculptures. It still is not certain how the people of Rapa Nui managed to lift and transport these heavy objects.

281 bottom right It is interesting to note the difference in the features of the Moai, which seem to belong to different ethnic groups. Some have elongated ears and pointed noses, while others have high cheekbones and round faces.

CERRO FITZ ROY
ARGENTINA

From its 11,137-ft (3375-m) summit, the Cerro Fitz Roy dominates the frozen expanse of the Los Glaciares National Park in Patagonia. This region at the bottom of South America underwent glacial erosion that gave rise to the dizzying peaks of this mountain. The Andes range is studded with beautiful and impressive mountains, but none is as famous as Fitz Roy, which is also known as Cerro Chaltén. Its perfect tower of light golden rock can be seen from a great distance and, like a vain woman, is mirrored in the cold, crystal-clear waters of the Desierto Lake. At its feet the summer and autumn take on the green and then red hues of the sub-Arctic forest of *Nothofagus pumilio* beech trees. The rest of the year its imposing bulk towers over the snow and ice on this stretch of the immense Campo de Hielo Patagónico, the largest frozen expanse in the world except for the two polar caps. This area also has the famous Perito Moreno, the only glacier in the world that is still expanding, which periodically reaches the opposite side of the Canál de los Timpanos, a narrow passageway that connects the Brazo Rico and the Brazo Sur to the main basin of Lake Argentino. The glacier therefore blocks the water exchange, causing the Brazo Rico to rise and consequently increasing the pressure of the water that infiltrates the blocks of ice. The Perito Moreno then begins to break, making a tremendous noise while doing so.

In this barren terrain the Fitz Roy peak stands out like a sentinel, almost as if it wanted to stop anyone who intends to penetrate this world of rock and ice. Its summit plays hide-and-seek behind the clouds, a phenomenon that has given rise to many legends. In ancient times, the Tehuelche Amerindians took the clouds for smoke and thought the peak concealed the mouth of a volcano, so they named it el Chaltén, the volcano. The first documented encounter between Man and Fitz Roy dates from 1782, when Don Antonio Viedma, after founding Porto di San Julian, ventured into the interior. But it was the expedition of Admiral Robert FitzRoy (1805-1865) that gave the name to this enchanted mountain. The summit was reached by a French team in 1952. Today, despite the many tracks that have been opened, the mountain continues to be one of the most fascinating and popular in the world.

282 Mt. Fitz Roy dominates a broad glacial valley. It is part of the Los Glaciares National Park, a strip of the Campo de Hielo Patagónico, the largest stretch of ice in the world except for the two polar caps.

282-283 The Fitz Roy massif, also known as the Cerro Chaltén, is mirrored in the transparent water of Lake Desierto. Its perfect tower is 11,137 ft (3375 m) high and can be seen from a long distance away.

283 bottom Clouds often cap the peak. In ancient times, the Tehuelche Amerindians thought they were smoke from an active crater and therefore called the mountain el Chaltén, or the volcano.

IGUASSÚ FALLS
ARGENTINA, BRAZIL

The Iguassú River flows slowly and placidly down from the Serra do Mar for 810 miles (1300 km). Then, right on the Argentine-Brazilian border, it swells enormously and plunges into a semicircular basin of basaltic lava. Its color changes from mud to white, and its quiet waters become frothy and turbulent. On the cliff the river is split up into 275 waterfalls that hurl themselves into a huge chasm 238 ft (72 m) high and 8910 ft (2700 m) wide, making a deafening roar in the silence of the luxuriant forest.

These are the Iguassú Falls, the 'great waters' in the Guaranì language. The name has replaced the older one, Santa Maria, used by the Spaniard Alvaro Nuñez Cabez de Vaca, who discovered the falls in 1541, and it is certainly renders the impression one has while walking along the paths that penetrate the *cataratas*. Step by step it is a continuous crescendo among dozens of streams that all together and yet separately drop into the precipice among clouds of mist and a ceaseless, overwhelming rumble. Then you arrive at the footbridge that leads to the top of the Garganta do Diablo or Devil's Gorge, the wildest and most impressive of them all. According to legend, this cascade was created by the river god, who was furious because he had lost his beloved: a drop of 238 ft (72 m), where the rainbows and butterflies stand out against the rock faces covered with plants. The greenery in the background is part of the national parks that protect both sides of the ravine. At night the relative humidity is 90% and during the day the high temperature transforms the zone into a huge subtropical greenhouse. This is a luxuriant forest with over 2000 species of plants, including 80 different species of orchids and various bromeliads, the black lapacho tree that may be as much as 132 ft (40 m) tall, giant ferns, bamboo, guava trees, ficus and many species of palm trees such as the *Euterpe edulis* feather palm. Howler and capuchin monkeys climb up and down the lianas, while in the underbrush there live nine different species of armadillos, giant anteaters, small deer that are a favorite prey of the jaguars, pumas, cougars, foxes and ferrets. The forest is also the home of 450 species of birds, including toucans, hummingbirds, woodpeckers and many varieties of multicolored parrots.

284 The rainbow created by the mist shines on the lush vegetation behind the Iguassú Falls, on the Brazilian-Argentine border.

284-285 A panoramic view from a helicopter of the Garganta do Diablo, or Devil's Gorge, which with its 238-ft (72-m) drop is the highest falls of Iguassú, which means 'the great waters' in the Guarinì language.

285 bottom The banks of the basin constitute an immense natural greenhouse that is under the tutelage of national parks. The jungle, which has over 2000 different plants, is the home of many species of wild animals.

286-287 The Iguassú River suddenly precipitates into a semicircular amphitheater of basalt lava. On the cliff its waters splits up into 275 falls that together have a width of 8910 ft (2700 m).

288-289 *The 3893-mile (6280-km) Amazon River flows parallel to the equator. It forms a 2.8 million sq. mile (7 million sq. km) basin, equaling practically one-third of South America.*

288 bottom left *The river has created an exceptionally rich ecosystem: one hectare (2.47 acres) of its rain forest contains 500 different species of trees. The same surface area in Europe has no more than one hundred.*

288 bottom right *The Amazon River is the largest in the world for discharge and number of tributaries. No fewer than 1100 rivers, fifteen of which are over 1250 miles (2000 km) long, flow into it, often in spectacular fashion.*

289 *The Amazon begins at the confluence of two headstreams from Peru. Its navigable course is the only 'road' in the lush primeval forest. Just before the 130-sq. mile (320-sq. km) basin (left), it takes in the waters of the Rio Jari (right).*

THE AMAZON RIVER BASIN
BRAZIL

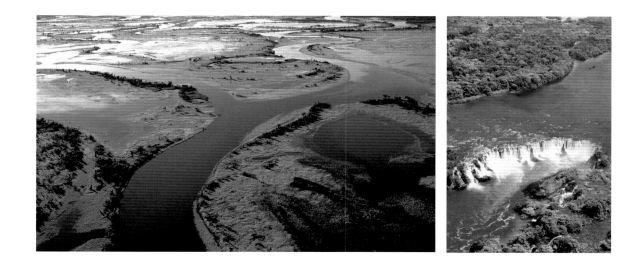

The Amazon River certainly deserves a place in the record books, since it has the greatest number of tributaries (1100), and the largest basin, 2.8 million sq. miles (7 million sq. km), just about the equivalent of one-third of South America. And although it is not as long as the Nile (the world's longest river), it carries more water than any other river, up to 7 million cu ft (200,000 cu. m) per second. But what is really amazing is the ecosystem it has created along its 3893-mile (6280-km) course.

The Amazon is formed by two headstreams from the Peruvian Andes, the Marañon and the Ucayali, which merge near the city of Iquitos, where the river begins its course parallel to the Equator down to the Atlantic Ocean. The natives called it *amacunu*, which literally means 'crash of the water cloud.' The vast basin corresponds to the Amazonia region, most of which is in Brazilian territory.

The Amazon is a navigable waterway penetrating into the rain forest, which is the 'lung' of the Earth and boasts more animal and plant species that any other place in the world. Vice versa, the population is only 1 person per sq. km; or 0.8 persons per square mile.

Up until the late 1970s or so the tropical forest had proved strong enough to resist colonization. However, in the last twenty years about one-third of its vegetation has been destroyed. Efforts made to populate the land, with the promise of fertile land and fine harvests, have failed so far. Paradoxically, Amazonia can reproduce itself in magnificent fashion, but this is not what Man would like to impose on it. The tropical forest terrain is very poor in nutritional substances because the waters of the Amazon are almost totally lacking in minerals. Indeed, its tributaries have hardly anything left to erode in the continental masses north

and south of Amazonia, since they have been doing this for two billion years. The only exceptions are the tributaries from the Andes, which are a mere 70 million years old and thus still young in geological terms. But most of them, whether with clear or muddy water, do not contain nutritional substances. The clear water rivers such as the spectacular Rio Tapajós, can be compared to distilled water. And the dark rivers such as the Rio Negro owe their tea-like color to the particles of humus from the acid earth, and acid environments produce very few forms of life. The contrast between the two types of water is particularly fascinating at Manaus, at the junction of Rio Negro and the Rio Solimoes. For many kilometers the two simply do not merge, creating two strips of water, clear and dark.

Thus, the lush Amazon forest has not developed because of the characteristics of its soil, but rather despite them. The

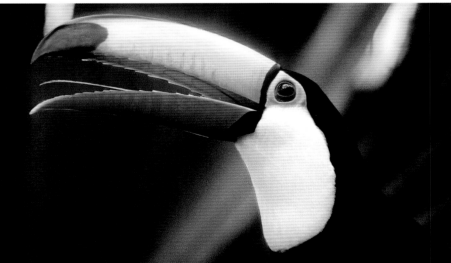

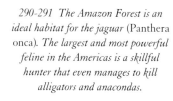

290-291 The Amazon Forest is an
ideal habitat for the jaguar (Panthera
onca). The largest and most powerful
feline in the Americas is a skillful
hunter that even manages to kill
alligators and anacondas.

290 bottom The impressive colored
beak is a feature of the toco
(Ramphastos toco), one of the species
of toucans that live in Amazonia.

291 top In the rain forest there is no
lack of food for the Cacajao calvus
calvus or oukari monkey, one of
numerous species that live in the
labyrinth of lianas.

291 bottom For its daily meal, the
gigantic Phyllomedusa bicolor frog
can choose from among roughly
30,000,000 different insects.

AMERICA

plants have a thick carpet of roots that live in close contact with mycorrhizal fungi, and they live in symbiosis. The fungi absorb nutrients from the earth, some of which they give to the plants in exchange for sugar. The innumerable termites in the area also play a vital role here, since the wood they pulverize soon becomes a nutrient in the ground. The exceptional variety of plant and animal species in Amazonia, whose exact number has yet to be ascertained, is simply amazing: one hectare (2.47 acres) of rain forest contains up to 500 different species of trees, while in Europe the flora has a maximum of one hundred. In the entire Amazon River Basin there are presumably 5000 species of trees, 50,000 species of flowers and something like 30 million species of insects. The Amazonia fauna also includes jaguars, Brazilian tapirs, peccaries, spider monkeys, sloths, armadillos, caymans, alligators, river dolphins, boa constrictors and anacondas. Among the birds, there are toucans, parrots, scarlet macaws, hummingbirds and falcons. In no other place do so many organisms depend on one another for their survival. There is a Brazilian saying that goes: "God is great, but the forest is even greater."

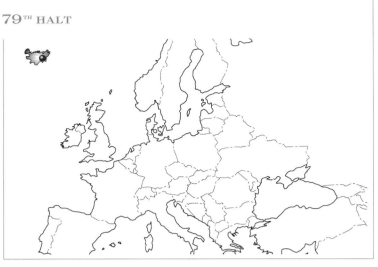

THE VATNAJÖKULL GLACIER
ICELAND

In Icelandic the name 'Island' means 'land of glaciers'; for good reason, since over one-sixth of this island in northwest Europe is occupied by glaciers. The largest and most representative one is called Vatnajökull – 84 miles (135 km) long, 62 miles (100 km) wide, 1980 to 2640 ft (1600 to - 800 m) thick on an average and 3300 ft (1000 m) in its central section: in other words, a colossus. Vatnajökull reaches an altitude of 6357 ft (2119 m), the highest point in Iceland. The most famous slope is the Fjallsjökull, a lateral tongue of the glacier that around the late 1700s totally engulfed the Fjall farmstead, hence its name.

At present the glacier extends as far as a small glacial lake completely enveloped in fog and connected to the sea via a fascinating, small canal. It looks like the entranceway to nothingness, but beyond the curtain of fog is a glacier as large as all the others in Europe put together. However, its shape is not like the typical Alpine glaciers that cover the valley floors like frozen flooding rivers. The Vatnajökull is an ice cap, that is, it stands on the mountain like a skullcap. This configuration is due to the winter snow, which is soft and light because it is full of air; the summer sun melts its surface, the water filters inside the cap and freezes once again. This process is eternal, year after year, lending Vatnajökull its imposing, immutable appearance.

The road from Reykjavik that skirts the glacier for quite a distance is fascinating, since it reveals the ice in all its splendor, with the golden hues of sunset. But this is not all. The northwest part of the glacier rests on an active volcano, Grimsvotn, which in 1996 produced one of the most grandiose geological phenomena in the modern age. A violent quake created a crater more than 330 ft (100 m) long that can be seen in its entirely inside the glacier. A new mountain was formed inside this crater, its peak situated 660 ft (200 m) under the original level of the glacier, like an islet surrounded by boiling water. The overflow of a large amount of water to the south completed the phenomenon, flooding a large barren zone and making it boggy. Now the snow has covered everything, and the only visible trace of the eruption is a lake that is a must for tourists. The Vatnajökull glacier, whose massive stretches of snow, made grey by the volcanic ash, almost reach the Atlantic Ocean, bears witness to the majesty of nature in continuous evolution.

292 A column of smoke rises from an expanse of snow: this is due to the underground volcanic activity that characterizes all Iceland and that every so often creates amazing geothermic phenomena even in the core of the glaciers.

292-293 This lake situated at the foot of the Vatnajökull glacier is one of the many that are formed because of the snow melting, which at times is accelerated by sub-glacial eruptions, such as the one in 1996 that actually cause the flooding of a valley, which to this day is not negotiable.

293 bottom left A panoramic view of the snow-covered expanse of Vatnajökull. There are plains, depressions with frozen falls, marshy zones and enchanting natural terraces with views of the ocean.

293 bottom right The top of Vatnajökull, which is 6357 ft (2119 m) high, conceals a very active volcano, Grimsvotn, which is responsible for the permanent fog that envelops the huge glacier.

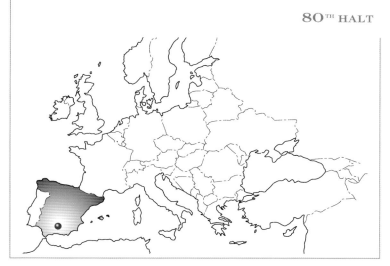

THE ALHAMBRA
GRANADA, SPAIN

294 The construction of the Moorish citadel was commissioned by Muhammad I al-Gahib and began around the mid-13th century. Once the royal palace, it is now a museum made up of a series of courtyards, halls, stairways and fabulous gardens.

295 left The Alcazaba fortress towers over the Sierra Nevada. With its 23 watchtowers, it was the impenetrable headquarters of the Nasrid dynasty for 250 years up to 1492, when the city was conquered by the Spanish Christians.

295 center and right The courtyards and gardens are extremely elegant. The Alhambra was also a fervid cultural center and the court welcomed artists and scholars, including famous botanists, who were responsible for the collection of rare plants.

The name of this monument derives from the Arabic *Qalaat al-Hamra*, or Red Fortress. The Alhambra, an architectural complex built in the Moorish style by the last Muslim princes of Spain (13th to14th century) over the remains of a citadel, stands on a hill that dominates Granada. Seen from outside, it looks like an austere fortress enclosed by walls that conceal a fabulous microcosm worthy of an Arab sultan. The Arabic inscription on the outside part of the wall of the Alhambra is a warning: "Nothing is crueler than being blind to Granada. And once you have entered, you understand the reason quite well."

Amazingly enough, there are still intact parts of the Alcazaba, a fortress built in the 11th century that was enlarged and fortified during the reign of Muhammad I ibn al-Ahmar, the founder of the Nasrid dynasty. Enclosed by a wall, the palace consists of two complexes articulated around two perpendicular courtyards. Muhammad I's successors, Yusuf I and Muhammad V (14th century) were responsible for the construction of the Court of the Myrtles, which was named after the two long bushes that flank the marble porticoes around the pool. This area gave access to the gardens, with over 160 species of plants, loggias for relaxation, fountains and gushing water.

The royal baths were also the work of the later sultans. These are rooms with marble floors and ceilings with star-shaped windows in which politicians and diplomats met. And around the Court of the Lions, a courtyard surrounded by porticoes with small columns in which twelve alabaster lions support the central fountain, were the apartments of the sultan and the area reserved for women. While the Court of the Harem is badly damaged, the Hall of the Kings, divided into five spaces by large, lavishly decorated plaster arches, has preserved its fascination.

The decoration on the walls and vaulted ceilings is simply breathtaking. By combining different treatment (carving, chasing, printing) of materials such as wood, brick, marble, ceramics and stone, the artists reproduced Moorish-style petrified interlace ornament and decorative motifs. Since Islam prohibited figurative art, the decoration has an abstract flavor about it: repeated floral and geometric motifs as well as splendid verses from the Koran beautifully carved in angular but decorative Kufic characters in the stone and stucco. The soft

296-297 *In the Court of the Lions there is a porticoed access to the royal apartments and the central fountain, a typical architectural element of the entire complex. In fact, the water that issues from the fountains symbolizes the purifying Islamic rivers, and the decoration is strongly influenced by the Koran.*

296 bottom *In these two photographs one can see the decoration of the halls. At left is a domed ceiling in the Hall of the Abencerrajes that is completely decorated and covered with majolica tiles. At right is the* muqarna, *the stalactite 'honeycomb' vaulting that decorates the arches and colonnades.*

297 top *The Court of the Myrtles has a long rectangular pool that decorates the palace entrance. The reception room and audience halls are located in the central body, while the two wings, which are lower and more compact, were used for the apartments.*

297 bottom left *Detail of the columns in the Court of the Lions.*

297 bottom right *This building has a typical veranda with a colonnade.*

298-299 *The decoration in the Court of the Lions is the classic type used in Islamic architecture: stylized naturalistic elements, geometric motifs and verses from the Koran.*

monochrome areas of the stucco alternate with painted portions and the bright colors of the *azulejos* (glazed pottery tiles) that decorate the walls of the galleries, halls, and baths. Then the stalactite decoration on some arches and ceilings is simply staggering: while observing it, one has the impression of a honeycomb with its contrasting light and shadow. The Alhambra was damaged after the Spanish *Reconquista* in 1492, and in 1526 Charles V (Emperor of the Holy Roman Empire and King of Spain) added a Renaissance style palace that has a distinctive plan, with a round patio 126 ft (42 m) in diameter, surrounded by massive marble columns set into an imposing square space. In sharp contrast with the *Thousand and One Nights* atmosphere of the former royal residence, this palace is now the home of the Alhambra Museum. After a difficult period when the palace-fortress fell into a state of neglect, its former splendor was restored and its chambers were visited by famous personalities such as Richard Ford and Washington Irving, the latter of whom stayed there for months. About three years later the American author produced one of his most famous works, *The Alhambra*, which in page after page transmits all the magic of Moorish life, combining legends and documented historic events and recreating the fascinating, spellbinding atmosphere he experienced while sojourning in the old fortress.

INDEX

c = caption
bold type = chapter

A
Abbas the Great, 150, 151c
Abd al-Malik, 142
Abu Said Othman, 90
Abu Simbel, **102-107**
Acacus Massif, 94c, 95, 96c
Agra, 156, 158
Aiguille du Midi, 34, 35c
Akrotiri, Santorini, 77
Alaouites, Place des, Fez, 90
Alcazaba, 295, 295c
Al-Dair Monastery, Petra, 147c, 149c
Alexandria, 99, 146
Alhambra Museum, 297
Alhambra, 93, **295-297**
Ali ben Yusuf, 93
Ali Qapu Palace, Isfahan, 150
Allah, 90, 135
Alps, 34, 71
Al-Qarawiyin Mosque, Fez, **90-94**
Alte Nationalgalerie, Berlin, 64c
Altes Museum, Berlin, 64c
Altes Palais, Berlin, 64
Amazon River Delta, **288-291**
Amazonia, 289, 291
Amon, Great Temple of, Luxor, 115c
Amon-Ra, 104, 112c, 113
Ananda Temple, Pagan, 170
Anawrahta, King, 170
Andes Mts., 282, 289
Angkor Thom, 181
Angkor Wat, **178-181**
Angkor, temple of, 178c
Aniruddha, King, 170
Antarctic, 117
Antiochus I of Commagene, 136, 137c
Aqaba Gulf, 130c, 131
Archaeological Museum, Khajuraho, 154
Arctic Circle, 252, 253c
Arctic Ocean, 2c, 3c, 253c
Arezzo, 49c
Argentino, Lake, 282
Arnim, Bettina von, 64
Asam, Kosmas Damian, 67
Aspronissi, isola, 77
Assisi, 7, 49
Assumption Cathedral, Moscow, 87c
Aswan High Dam, 104
AT&T Building, New York, 264
Athens, 74
Atlantic Ocean, 2c, 95, 116c, 117, 257c, 289
Atlantis, 77
Auyuittuq National Park, 252
Avanos, 139
Averroes, 93
Avranches, 13
Ayers Rock, 7, **204-207**

B
Bad el-Mandeb Strait, 131
Badaling, 199c
Bahia Concepción, 227
Baja California, **226-229**
Balmar, Jacques, 34
Baltic Sea, 70c, 71, 81
Banff National Park, **248-251**
Bangkok, 174c, 175
Barcelona, 14, 14c, 16
Bartholdi, Frédéric August, 269

Bastille, Paris, 84
Battery Park, New York, 267c, 269
Bavaria, 58
Bayon temple, 181, 181c
Bebel Platz, 63
Beijing, 192, 199c
Béla IV, 68
Belzoni, Giovanni Battista, 108, 109c
Benguela, corrente del, 117
Bent Muhammad al-Fehì, Lalla Fatma, 93
Bering Sea, 228
Bering Strait, 252, 253c
Berlin, 63, 81
Berliner Dom, 62c
Bernini, Gian Lorenzo, 27
Bingham Hiram, 279
Blois, 31
Bohemia, 67
Bonanno Pisano, 40
Bonaparte, Napoleone, 18, 108
Bora-Bora, 7, **214-217**
Borobudur, **182-184**
Bosphorus, 223
Botticelli, Sandro, 45, 82
Bouteiller, Jean de, 20
Brahe, Tycho, 67
Brahma, 153, 154
Bramante, Donato, 45
Brandeburg Gate, 62c, 63, 64c
Brazo Rico, 282
Brazo Sur, 282
Brecht, Bertold, 63
British Museum, London, 74, 74c
Broadway, 264
Bronze horses of St. Mark's, Venice 55
Brooklyn Bridge, 267c
Brown Castle, Portofino, 39
Brussels, 71
Budapest, 7, 68
Buffalo, 261
Buonarroti, Michelangelo, 44c, 45, 46, 46c
Burckhardt, Johann Ludwig, 146, 149
Byron, Lord, 9

C
Cabo San Lucas, 227c
Caesar's Palace, Las Vegas, 233c
Caillou, Jean-Sylvain, 31
Cairo, 108, 109c, 123, 146
Callicrates, 74
Campo de Hielo Patagónico, 282, 283c
Canada Basin, 253c
Canadian Arctic, 2c, 7, **252-255**
Canál de Los Timpanos, 282
Canova, Antonio, 83c
Cap Diamant, 256
Cape Cross, 116d
Cape Mohammed, 133c
Cape York, 208c
Caravaggio, 82
Carikli Church, 139
Carthagine, 99
Castle of the Pharaoh's Daughter, Petra, 146
Catherine II the Great, empress of Russia, 81, 83c, 87
Caturbhuja Temple, Khajuraho, 154
Caunsat Yogini temple, Khajuraho, 154
Cedros Islands, 228
Central Park, New York, 263c

Ceres, Temple of, Leptis Magna, 99
Chambord Château, **31-33**
Chambord, Museum, 32c
Chamonix, 34
Champs-Elysées, Parigi, 63
Charles V, emmperor, 31, 297
Château Frontenac, 257c, 259
Chaucer, Geoffrey, 9, 10c
Cheops, 5c, 108
Cheops, Pyramid of, 109c, 110, 230, 233c
Chichén Itzá, **270-273**
Chichli (Bo Hai) Gulf, 198
Chrysler Building, New York, 5c, 24, 263c
Churchill, Winston, 259
Cimabue, 50
Clement VII, Pope, 46
Cleveland, Grover, 269
Clinton Castle, New York, 267c
Clutha River, 212
Coast of Skeletons, **116-117**
Col de la Seigne, 34, 35c
Col du Grand Ferret, 34, 35c
Collegium Maius, Kraków, 71, 72c
Colorado River, 227, 230, 234, 235, 304c
Colosseum (Flavian Amphitheater), 7, **42-43**
Colter, John, 243
Columbia Icefield, Yellowstone Park, 248
Commagene, 137c, 138c
Compagnoni, Cesare, 161
Constantinople, 55, 55c, 133
Cook, Mount, 7, **212-213**
Copernicus, Nicholas, 71
Cordova, 93
Corinthian Tomb, Petra, 149c
Cortés, Hernan, 227
Cortés, Sea of, 227, 227c
Corvinus, Matthias, King 68
Cosson River, 31
Courmayeur, 34
Cousteau, Jacques, 131
Cumbre Volcano, 276
Cuzco, 279
Cyclades, 77

D
Damascus, 146, 149
Danube River, 68, 69c
Darwin, Charles, 9, 275
De Berlanga, Tomás, 275
De Custine, Marquis, 84
De Gaulle, Charles, 78
De Saussure, Horace-Bénédict de, 34
De Sully, Maurice, Bishop, 18
Degas, Edgar, 82
Delacroix, Eugène, 29c
Delhi, 156
Dente del Gigante, 34, 35c
Desierto Central, 227
Desierto de los Chinos, 227
Desio, Ardito, 160c, 161
Deutsche National Museum, Berlino, 62c, 64c
Devi Jagadambi temple, 154
Dickens, Charles, 9
Dientzenhofer, Kilian Ignaz, 67
Diocletian, emperor of Rome, 53c
Disney, Walt, 58
Disneyland, 230, 239c
Doge's Palace, Venice, 52, 53c
Dolent, Mt., 34
Dolgoruky, Jurij, prince of Kiev, 84

Dome of the Rock, **142-144**, 142c, 144c
Domenichino, Domenico Zampieri, known as, 27
Domus Aurea, Rome, 42
Donskoi, Dimitry, 84
Duomo, Milan, 84

E
East River, 262, 267d
Easter Island (Rapa Nui), **280-281**
Edward III, 10
Egypt, 103, 108, 113, 131
Eiffel Tower, **24-25**, 231c
Eiffel, Alexandre Gustave, 24, 24c, 227, 269
Einstein, Albert, 62c, 64
Eire, Lake, 261
El Rancho Vegas, Las Vegas, 230
Elias, Friar, 49
Eliot, Thomas Stearns, 9
Elisabeth, empress of Russia, 80c, 81
Elizabeth, empress of Austria, 68
Ellesmere Island National Park, 255
Empire State Building, New York, 5d, 263d, 264
Engels, Friedrich, 63 Henry VI of England, 8d
Everest, Mount, 7, **162-165**
Excalibur, castle of, 230, 233c

F
Faceted Palace, Moscow, 88c
Fairies' Chimneys, 139
Falkenstein Castle, 58
Federal Hall, Manhattan, 262
Federal Reserve Bank, Manhattan, 262
Feuerbach, Ludwig Andreas, 64
Fez al-Bali, 90
Fez al-Jedid, 90
Fez, 90
Financial District, Manhattan, 262, 263c
Fioravanti, Aristotele, 87
Fitz Roy, **282-283**
Fitz Roy, Robert, 282
Flamingo, Las Vegas, 230, 233c
Flatiron Building, Manhattan, 262
Forbidden City, Beijing, **192-197**
Ford, John, 239c, 240
Ford, Richard, 297
Francis I, 30c, 31
Franz Joseph, Emperor, 68
Frederick the Great, 62c
Frederick William I of Prussia, 63
Friday Mosque, Isfahan, 150, 151c
Friss Palot, Budapest, 68

G
Galápagos, Islands, **274-277**
Ganges River, 183
Gansu, 198
Gardner Bay, 276
Gaudí, Antonio, 14, 14c, 17c
General Electric Building, New York, 264
Gerardo di Gerardo, 40
Germany, 58, 63
Geysers, Yellowstone Park, **242-247**
Ghirlandaio, Domenico, 45
Gibraltar, 256
Ginza district, Tokyo, **200-203**
Giorgione, 82

Giotto, 49, 49c, 50, 51c
Giovanni di Simone, 40
Giza plain, 5c, 109c
Giza, 110
Giza, pyramids of, 7, **108-111**
Godwin-Austen, Mt., 161
Golden Gate Bridge, San Francisco, **222-225**
Golden Horn, 135, 135c, 223
Göreme Valley, 137c, **138-141**, 139
Gorky, Maxim, 63
Granada, 93, 295
Grand Canyon, **234-237**
Grand Palace, Moscow, 85c
Grand Trianon, Versailles, 29
Grandes Jorasses, 35d
Great Barrier Reef, 3c, **209-211**
Great Pyramid of Cheops, Giza, 110
Great Temple, Abu Simbel, 103
Great Temple, Machu Picchu, 279
Great Wall of China, 3c, **198-199**
Greece, 74, 77
Gregory IX, Pope, 49
Grimm Brothers (Wilhelm and Jakob), 64
Grismotvn volcano, 292, 293c
Gropius, Walter, 264, 264c
Grotto of the Dragon, Kraków, 71
Ground Zero, Manhattan, 262, 263c
Group of the Thousand Columns, Chichén Itzá, 271, 272c
Guggenheim Museum, New York, 264, 264c
Gunnung Derapi vulcano, 183
Guyot, Laurent, 32c

H
Habeler, Peter, 162
Hagia Sophia, Istanbul, **134-135**
Hall of the Three Windows, Machu Picchu, 279
Hapsburg dynasty, 68
Harmakhis, 104
Hathor, Temple of, Abu Simbel, 104, 107c
Hatshepsut, 112c
Hatshepsut, obelisk of, 115
Hattori Clock Tower, Ginza district, Tokyo, 200
Hauszmann, Alajos, 68
Hawaii Volcanoes National Park, 218
Hawaii, 218
Hegel, Georg Wilhelm Friedrich, 62c, 64
Heine, Heinrich, 63, 64
Hemingway, Ernest, 129
Henry VII, 9
Hermitage, St. Petersburg, 7, **80-83**
Herodotus, 95, 108
Hildebrandt, Franz Anton, 68
Hillary, Edmund, 162
Himalaya Mts., 183
History Museum, Versailles, 27
Hofbauer, Dominic, 31
Honorius, 42
Hood Island, 276
Hoover Dam, 230
Hornemann, Friedrich, 94c, 95
Horthy, Nicholas, 68
House of the Nuns, Chichén Itzá, 271
Huahine Island, 214

Huayna Picchu, 278c, 279
Hudson Bay, 252
Hudson River, 262, 267c
Humboldt Universität, Berlino, 62c, 64c
Humboldt, Wilhelm von, 64, 276
Hungary, 68
Hunt, Richard Morris, 269
Hunting Museum, Versailles, 30d
Huss, Jan, 67
Hvannadalshnukur, 5c

I
Idriss, Mulay, 90
Ieoh Ming Pei, 62c
Iguassú Falls, **284-287**
Iguassú River, 284, 285c
Indian Ocean, 129
Inhe, Ernst von, 64
Innocent IV, Pope, 50
Iran, 150
Irving, Washington, 297
Isfahan, **150-151**
Isfahan, mosque of, 7
Isla Bartolomé, 276
Isla Fernandina, 276
Isla Genovesa, 276
Island of Liberty, New York, 269
Israel, 142
Istanbul, 135, 223
Ivan the Great, emperor of Russia, 87

J
Jackson, Peter, 212
Jahan, Shah, 156c
Jama Mashid Mosque, Delhi, 156
Jank, Christian, 58, 60c
Jardot, Jean-Nicolas, 68
Jari River, 288c
Jasper National Park, **248-251**
Java Island, 183
Jayavarman II, 181, 181c
Jerusalem, 49, 142
John III Sobieski, king of Poland, 73c
John Paul II , Pope 71, 72c
Jonson, Ben, 9
Jordan, 146
Julius II, Pope 45
Jumna River, 156, 158, 158c
Justinian, Emperor, 135c

K
K2, **160-161**
Kabukiza Theater, Tokyo, 200
Kafka, Franz, 67
Kaibab Plateau, 235
Kairouan, 93
Kalahari Desert, 118, 119c
Kandariya Mahadeva, Khajuraho, 154c
Karakorum, 160c, 161
Karnak, Great Temple of, **112-115**
Kazimierz quarter, Kraków, 71
Kenya, 129
Khajuraho, **152-154**
Khajuraho, temple of, 153
Khazna Treasury, Petra, 146, 147
Khephren, 5c, 108
Khephren, Pyramid of, 109c, 110
Khonsu, 115
Khumbu Glacier, 162
Kiev, 84
Kilaeua Volcano, **218-221**
Kilimanjaro National Park, 129, 129c
Kilimanjaro, Mt., **128-129**
Kinsky Palace, Prague, 67
Kipling, Rudyard, 9
Koch, Robert, 64

Kommode, Berlin, 64
Krak, King, 71
Kraków, 70c, 71
Kremlin, **84-89**
Kublai Khan, 170
Kukulcán, 271
Kukulcán, Pyramid of, Chichén Itzá, 271
Kukulcán, Temple of (Castillo), Chichén Itzá, 270c

L
Lacedelli, Lino, 161
Lady Elliot, 208c
Laguna Ojo de Liebre, 228
Lahore, 156
Lakshamana, Temple of, Khajuraho, 154c
Lanfranco, Giovanni, 27
Langhans, Carl Gotthard, 64c
Las Vegas Boulevard South, 230
Las Vegas, **230-233**
Lawrence of Arabia, 146
Le Brun, Charles, 27, 28
Le Nôtre, André, 26c, 29, 29c
Le Roy, Philibert, 27
Le Vau, Louis, 29c
Leaning Tower of Pisa, 7, **40-41**
Lebda River, 99
Leeward Arcipelago, 215c
Lenin, Vladimir Ilyich 63, 71
Leo, Friar, 49
Leonardo da Vinci, 30c, 31, 82
Leptis Magna, **98-101**
Lerai Forest, 124c, 125, 126c
Lever House, New York, 264
Lhasa, 166c
Libya, 95, 99
Livingstone, David, 122c, 123
Loire River, 30c, 31
London, 74, 129
Lorenzetti, Ambrogio, 51c
Lorenzetti, Pietro, 50, 51c
Los Glaciares National Park, 282, 283c
Louis II of Bavaria, 58, 58c, 60c
Louis Philippe, 27
Louis VII, King of France, 18
Louis XI, King of France, 13
Louis XIII, King of France, 26c, 27
Louis XIV, King of France, 26c, 27, 30c
Louis XVI, King of France, 27
Lower Egypt, 102c
Lower Manhattan, 267c
Luigi Amedeo di Savoia, duca degli Abruzzi, 161
Lukla, 162
Luxor, Las Vegas, 233c

M
Machu Picchu, **278-279**
Madhya Pradesh, 153
Maestro di San Francesco, 50
Maevarva, queen of Bora-Bora, 214
Magadi, Lake, 124, 125
Mahabodi temple, Pagan, 170
Maidan-i Imam (Maidan-i Naghsh-i Jahan), Isfahan, 150, 151c
Makrana quarries, 158
Maligne, Lake, 249
Mall, Washington D.C., 63
Mammoth Hot Springs, Yellowstone, 242c
Manaus, 289
Manhattan, **262-263**
Manhattan Bridge, New York, 267c
Mann, Thomas, 63
Mao Tzedong, 192
Maria Theresa, castle of, Budapest, 68

Marie Antoniette, queen of France, 27
Marin County, 223
Marseilles, port of, 51c
Martini, Simone, 50
Marx, Karl, 63
Matejco, Jan, 73
Maupassant, Guy de, 38c, 39
Mayer, Hans, 129
Mecca, 150
Mediterranean Sea, 99, 149
Mekong River, 178c
Meloria, Battle of, 40
Memory Foundation, Manhattan, 262
Mer de Glace, 34
Meru, Mt., 170
Messner, Reinhold, 162
Mexico, Gulf of, 238
Middle East, 150
Milosz, Czeslaw, 71
Mithradate, 136
Monet, Claude, 82
Mont Blanc, **33-37**
Mont Fréti, Pavillon du, 34
Montgolfier Brothers (Joseph Michel and Jacques Etienne), 27
Mont-Saint-Michel, 5c, **12-13**
Montu, 115
Monument Valley Navajo Tribal Park, 238, 240c
Monument Valley, **238-241**
Moremi Reserve, 121c
Mori, Fabrizio, 95, 96c
Morocco, 90
Moscow River, 85c
Moscow, 63, 84, 85c, 87, 87c
Mouhot, Henri, 179
Moulin Rouge, Las Vegas, 230
Muhammad I al-Gahib, 295c
Muhammad I ibn al-Ahmar, 295
Muhammad V, 295
Muhammad, 90, 135, 142, 144c
Museum Mile, New York, 264
Mussolini, Benito, 63
Mut, 115
Mycerinus, 108
Mycerinus, Pyramid of, 109c

N
Nagybànya and Szolnok schools, Budapest, 68
Namib Desert, 116c, 117
Namibia, 117
Nan-K'ou, 199c
Napoleon Bonaparte, 55
Nasser, Lake, 103
National Geographic Society, 279
National Science Museum, Tokyo, 200
Navajo Indian Reservation, Monument Valley, 238
Nefertari, 102c, 104
Nefertari, Temple of, Abu Simbel, 107c
Nemrut Dagh, **136-137**
Nero, 42
Neuschwanstein, **58-61**
Neva River, 81
Nevsehir, 139
New York City, 5c, 24, 231c, 262, 269
Newton, Isaac, 9
Ngorongoro Conservation Area, 125
Ngorongoro, **124-126**
Niagara Falls, **260-261**
Niagara River, 260c, 261
Nicholas I, emperor of Russia, 63
Nikolskay Tower, Moscow, 87
Nile River, 233c, 289
Nile Valley, 102c
Norgay, Tenzing, 162

North Atlantic, 5c
North Pole, 252, 255
North Rim, Grand Canyon, 234c, 235
Northwest Territories, 252, 253c
Nôtre-Dame Cathedral, Paris, **18-23**
Nôtre-Dame-des-Victoires Basilica, Quebec, 259
Nubia, 102d
Nunavut Province, 252, 253c

O
Oia, Santorin, 77
Okawango Delta, 118-121
Okawango River, 119c
Old Town Square, Prague, **66-67**
Old Town, Kraków, **70-73**
Olgas hill system, 5c, **204-207**
Omar, Mosque of, 142
Ontario, Lake, 261
Opéra Royale, Versailles, 27
Opern Café, Berlin, 64
Oregtoronyo (Old Tower), Budapest, 68
Osiris, 104c
Our Lady of the Assumption Church, Kraków,70c, 73

P
Paccard, Michel Gabriel, 34
Pacific Ocean, 2c, 214, 218, 223, 226c, 227, 228, 275, 277c
Pagan Archaeological Park, 171c
Pagan Valley, 5c
Pagan, **170-173**
Pala d'Oro, Venice, 55, 55c
Palace Tomb, Petra, 149c
Pan Am Building, New York, 264, 264c
Panama, 275
Papeete, 215c
Paris, 18, 27, 55, 63, 231c, 269
Park Avenue, New York, 264, 264c
Parsvanatha Temple, Khajuraho, 152c
Parthenon, Athens, **74-75**
Patagonia, 282
Paul III, Pope, 46
People's Republic of China, 192
Pergamum Museum, Berlin, 64c
Perito Moreno, 282
Perugino, 45
Pest, 68, 69
Peter I the Great, emperor of Russia, 81, 87
Peter III, emperor of Russia, 81
Petit Trianon, Versailles, 29c
Petra, **145-149**
Petrarch, 39
Peyto, Lake, 251c
Phantom Ranch, 235
Phidias, 74
Philharmonic Hall, Berlin, 64c
Philip Auguste, king of France, 12c
Phnom Bareng, Angkor, 181
Phnom Penh, 179
Phra Mondop, Bangkok, 176
Phra Si Satana Chedi, Bangkok, 174c, 176
Picasso, Pablo, 82
Pinturicchio, 45
Pisa, Baptistery, 40
Pisa, Campo dei Miracoli, 40, 40c
Pisa, Duomo, 40, 40c
Pius IV, Pope, 46
Pius VII, Pope,42,
Pizarro, Francisco, 278c
Place d'Armes, Québec, 256
Place Royal, Québec, 256
Platform of the Tzompantli, Chichén Itzá, 272c
Pliny the Elder, 39

Pöllath rapids, 58
Pompeii, 77
Portofino, **38-39**
Portofino, Bay of, 38c, 39
Portofino, Monte di, 39
Potala Palace, **166-169**
Poussin, Nicolas, 82
Prague, 67
Prasad Phra Thep Bidom, Bangkok, 176
Preah Kahn, Angkor, 181
Profitis Ilias massif, Santorin, 77
Propylaea, Athens, 63
Ptah, 104, 115
Pu Yi, emperor of China, 192
Pulitzer, Joseph, 269
Puni of Faanui, king, 214
Punta Helbronner, 34
Purcell, Henry, 9
Purtscheller, Ludwig, 129
Pushkin, Aleksandr, 81

Q
Qadesh, Battle of, 102c, 103c
Qin Shihuangdi, emperor of China, 187, 188, 198
Qin Shihuangdi, tomb of, 187, 188c
Quebec City, **256-259**
Quetzalcoatl, 271
Quinhuangdao, 198

R
Raffles, Sir Thomas, 183
Rama I, 175
Rama IV, 176
Ramesses II, 103c, 104, 104c, 112c, 113, 115
Ramesses II, Temple of, Luxor, 113
Ranu Raraku, vulcano, 280
Raphael, 45
Ras Mohammed National Park, **130-133**
Rastrelli, Francesco Bartolomeo, 80c, 81, 83
Ravy, Jean, 20
Rebmann, Johann, 129
Red Hill (Martori), Lhasa, 166c, 167
Red Sea, 95, 130c, 131
Red Square, Moscow, 84
Rembrandt, 82
Reni, Guido, 27, 82
Reykjavik, 292
Richard I Lion Heart, king of England, 20
Rift Valley, 125, 129
Rio Negro, 289
Riviera, Las Vegas, 230
Robson, Mt., 248c
Rockefeller Center, New York, 264, 264c
Rocky Mountains, 235, 243, 248c, 249, 251c
Rome, 7, 42c, 98c, 230, 233c
Roosevelt, Franklin D., 259
Rossi, Carlo, 83c
Royal Geographical Society, 129
Royal Palace (Dar el-Makhzen), Fez, **90-93**
Royal Palace (Zamek), Kraków, 71
Royal Palace, Bangkok, 175, 176c
Royal Palace, Budapest, **68-69**
Royal Street, Kraków, 71
Rubens, Peter Paul, 82
Russia, 81, 84
Rynek Glówny Square, Kraków, 70c, 73

S
Sagrada Familia, Barcelona, **14-17**
Sahara Desert, 7, **94-96**, 99

Saint Malo, Gulf of, 12c
Saint-Denis Abbey, 18
Samarkand, 156
San Benito Islands, 228
San Francesco Basilica, Assisi, 7, **48-51**
San Francisco Bay, 222c
San Francisco, 7
San Francisco, Sierra de, 227
San Giorgio Church, Portofino, 39
San Ignacio, 227
San Martino Church, Portofino, 38c, 39
San Pedro Martín Mts., 228c
San Pietro al Castello, Venice, 52
San Telmo, 227
Santa Rosalía, 227
Santorin, **76-79**
Saussure Botanic Garden, 34
Schadow, Gottfried, 64
Schinkel, Karl Friedrich, 63
Seagram Building, New York, 264
Seine River, 19c, 20c
Septimius Severus, Roman emperor, 98c, 99
Serengeti National Park, 125
Serra do Mar, 284
Seti I, 115c
Seti II, Temple of, Luxor, 113
Severus Basilica, Leptis Magna, 100c
Severus Forum, Leptis Magna, 99, 100c
Shalimar Park, Lahore, 156
Shanxi, 199c
Shelley, Mary, 9
Shitamachi History Museum, Tokyo, 200
Shiva, 15
Shwezigon, 170
Siberia, 82, 194c
Sierra Nevada range, 295c
Sigismund of Luxemburg, King, 68
Sigismund the Elder, 71
Simone di Pucciarello, 49
Sinai Peninsula, 130c, 131
Sistine Chapel, **44-47**

Sixtus IV, Pope, 45
Solari, Pietro Antonio, 84
Solimoes River, 289
Songtsen Gampo, Lhasa, 167
South Rim, Grand Canyon, 234c, 235
South Street Seaport, New York, 267
Sparta, 74
Spasskay Tower, Moscow, 87
Sphinx, Giza, 5c, 110, 110c, 233c
St. Adalbert Church, Kraków, 70c
St. Aubert, bishop of Avranches, 13
St. Barbara Church, Cappadocia, 139
St. Charles River, 256, 259c
St. Lawrence River, 256, 257c, 259c
St. Mark's Basilica, Venice, **52-57**
St. Marks' Basilica, Museum of, 55
St. Mary of the Graces Abbey, Eastminster, 9
St. Nicholas Church, Prague, 67
St. Peter, Collegiate Church of, Westminster, 9
St. Peter's Basilica, Rome, 42c, 53c
St. Petersburg, 7, 81
St. Wenceslaus Cathedral, Kraków, 71
Staatsbibliotek, Berlin, 64
Statue of Liberty, 262, **267-269**
Stepanovsky Palace, Prague, 67
Stoss, Veit, 73
Strauss, Joseph B., 223
Strip, Las Vegas, 233c
Subasio, Mt., 49
Subirachs, Josep Maria, 14
Suez, Gulf of, 131
Sukienice Market, Kraków, 70c, 73
Sunwapta River, 251c
Suryavarman II, 179
Suryavarman II, mausoleum of, 178c
Swakopmund, 116c
Synagogue of Kraków, 71

Szinnyei-Merse, Pál, 68
Szymborska, Wislawa, 71

T
Ta Keo monastery, Angkor, 181
Ta Prohm monastery, Angkor, 181
Table Rock, 260c, 261
Tahiti, 214
Taj Mahal, 7, **156-159**
Tana, Lake, 7
Taurus Mts., 136
Taynitskaya Tower, Moscow, 84
Temple of Fire, Isfahan, 150
Temple of the Jaguars, Chichén Itzá, 271
Temple of the Moon, Machu Picchu, 279
Temple of the Sun, Machu Picchu, 278c, 279
Temple of the Warriors, Chichén Itzá, 271, 272c
Tennyson, Lord Alfred, 9
Terem Palace, Moscow, 88c
Terracotta army, Xi'an, **186-191**
Thaton, 170
Theater District, New York, 267c
Thebes, 113
Thera, 77
Thor, Mount, 252
Tianjin, 198
Tiberius, emperor of Rome, 98c
Tibet, 162, 167
Tiepolo, Giovanni Battista, 82
Tigullio Gulf, 38c, 39
Tijuana, 227
Times Square, New York, 267c
Tintoretto, 52
Titian, 52, 82
Titus, Roman emperor, 42
Tokali Church (Church of the Buckle), 139
Tokyo National Museum, 200
Tokyo, 200, 201c, 203c
Tomb of the High Priest, Chichén Itzá, 271
Tomb of the Obelisks, Petra, 149c
Tomb of the Roman Soldier, Petra, 149c

Tomb of the Royal Urn, Petra, 146
Tommaso Pisano, 40
Topakapi Saray, Istanbul, 135
Tower of the Redeemer, Moscow, 84, 85c
Town Hall Tower, Kraków, 73
Town Hall, Prague, 66c, 67
Trajan, Arch of, Leptis Magna, 98c
Treasure Island Hotel, Las Vegas, 231c
Trinity Church, Manhattan, 262
Tripolitania, 99
Tropic of Capricorn, 209
Turkey, 136, 139
Tyn Cathedral, Prague, 66c, 67

U
Ueno-koen Park, Tokyo, 200
Uhuru Peak, 129
University of Budapest, 68
Unter Den Linden, Berlin, **62-65**
Upali-Thein Temple, Pagan, 170
Upper Bay, New York, 269, 269c
Upper Egypt, 102c
Ural Mts., 82
Urubamba River, 279

V
Vaitape, 215c
Val Ferret, 34, 35c
Vallée Blanche, 34
Valley temple, Giza, 110
Van der Rohe, Mies, 264
Van Dyck, Anthony, 27
Van Gogh, Vincent, 82
Van Orley, Bernand, 32c
Vasari, Giorgio, 45
Vatican, 44
Vatnajokull glacier, 5c, **292-293**
Venice, 52, 55
Veny Valley, 34
Verne, Jules, 7, 7c
Veronese, Paolo Caliari, known as, 52
Versailles, **26-29**
Vespasian, emperor of Rome, 42, 42c
Victoria Falls, **122-123**

Vienna, 73c
Villa Beatrice, Portofino, 38c
Viollet-le-Duc, Eugène, 23c
Vishnu, 153, 154
Vistola River, 71, 72c

W
Wagner, Richard, 58, 58c, 60c, 64
Wall Street, Manhattan, 262
Washington D.C., 63
Wat Phra Kaew, Bangkok, 7, **174-177**
Wawel hill, 71, 72c
Wayne, John, 239c, 240
Western Cym, 162
Westminster Abbey, 9
Westminster Museum, 10
Westminster, **8-11**
William II, emperor of Germany, 129
William the Conqueror, 9
Winter Palace Square, St. Petersburg, 80c
Winter Palace, St. Petersburg, 80c, 81, 83c
Woolworth Building, New York, 264
World Trade Center, Manhattan, 262
Wright, Frank Lloyd, 264, 264c

X
Xi'An, 188, 190c
Xinjiang Uygur, 198

Y
Yale University, 279
Ybl, Miklos, 68
Yellowstone National Park, 7, 243, 249
Yukon, 252, 253c
Yusuf I, 295

Z
Zambesi River, 122c, 123
Zanettin, Bruno, 161
Zayandeh River, 150
Zeghidour, Slimane, 90

PHOTO CREDITS

right, 216-217, 227 center left and destra, 228 top left and right, 240 bottom, 241 bottom left, 252 bottom, 252-253, 253 bottom left and right

Anders Blomqvist/Lonely Planet Images: pages 148 bottom left, 243 center

Massimo Borchi/Archivio White Star: pages 135 center right, 136 center left and right, 136-137, 137 bottom left and right, 138-139, 138 bottom, 139 center left and right, 140 top, 140 center left and right, 140-141, 141 bottom, 147 bottom right, 152-153, 152 bottom left and right, 153 center, 154 top, center and bottom, 158 center, 159 bottom right, 231 bottom left and right, 232-233, 232 bottom, 233 top left and right, 233 center, 270 bottom left and right, 271 center left and right, 272 top, 272 center left and right, 272 bottom, 273

Livio Bourbon/Archivio White Star: pages 18 center left, 19 bottom right, 20 top left, 20 center, 21 bottom, 24 center, 74 center left and right, 174 bottom left and right, 175 center left, 178 bottom left, 179 center left and right, 180-181, 180 bottom, 181 top and center

A. Bracchetti/P.Zigrossi-Musei Civici Vaticani: pages 44-45

Jose Caldas Gouveia/Agefotostock/Marka: pages 288-289

CameraPhoto: pages 52-53, 54, 55 top, 55 center left and right, 56-57

Claudio Cangini/Archivio White Star: pages 132-133, 132 bottom left, 133 top left, 133 top right

John Carnemolla/Corbis/Contrasto: pages 204-205

Pablo Castagnola/Anzenberger/Contrasto: pages 64-65

Matthieu Colin/Hemispheres-Images: page 26 bottom right

Dean Conger/Corbis/Contrasto: pages 88 top, 182 bottom left

Anne Conway/Archivio White Star: pages 38-39, 38 bottom left and right, 39 center left and right

W. Perry Conway/Corbis/Contrasto: page 126 bottom

Pablo Corral Vega/Corbis/Contrasto: page 282 bottom

Christophe Courteau/Nature Picture Library: pages 118-119, 119 bottom left, 120-121, 120 bottom left

Giovanni Dagli Orti: pages 30 bottom left, 32 top left, 32 top right, 32 center, 32-33, 61 top left and right

Giovanni Dagli Orti/San Francesco Assisi/The Art Archive: page 51 bottom right

Carlo De Fabianis/Archivio White Star: page 144 bottom

Araldo De Luca/Archivio White Star: pages 98-99, 98 bottom right, 99 center left and right, 100-101, 100 center right, 104 top left, 104 top right, 104 center left and right, 105, 106 bottom, 107 top, 107 bottom, 186-187, 187 top left, center and right, 188 top and center, 189, 190 top left and right, 190-191

Nigel J. Dennis;Gallo Images/Corbis/Contrasto: pages 117 center, 122-123

Michael & Christine Denis-Huot: page 129 center

Tui De Roy/Auscape: page 255 center

Stefan Diller/Photoservice Electa/Akg: pages 50 top, 60 bottom left

Doc White/Ardea: pages 254-255

Double/ICP: pages 28-29, 28 bottom left

Patrick Durand/Corbis/Contrasto: page 19 bottom left

Mick Elmore/Lonely Planet Images: pages 182-183

Estock/Sime/Sie: pages 242-243

Fantuz Olimpio/Sime/Sie: page 12 left

Jean-Paul Ferrero/Ardea: pages 208 bottom right, 209 center left

Jean-Paul Ferrero/Auscape: page 204 center

Free Agents Limited/Corbis/Contrasto: pages 59, 183 center left

Michael Freeman/Corbis/Contrasto: pages 184-185, 185 bottom

Christer Fredriksson/Lonely Planet Images: page 249 center

Josè Fuste Raga/Agefotostock/Contrasto: pages 80-81, 261 bottom

Hedgehoghouse: page 161 center

Patrick Frilet/Hemispheres-Images: pages 258-259

John Frumm/Hemispheres-Images: pages 13 center left, 27 center right

Bertrand Gardel/Hemispheres-Images: pages 26-27, 157

Alfio Garozzo/Archivio White Star: pages 76-77, 77 bottom left and right, 76 center left and right, 78-79, 91 bottom, 92-93, 102 bottom right, 103 center right, 112 top, 112 bottom, 284 center left and right, 284-285, 285 bottom left and right, 286-287

Cesare Gerolimetto/Archivio White Star: page 262 bottom

Fausto Giaccone/Anzerberger/Contrasto: pages 62 top, 63 center

Todd Gipstein/Corbis/Contrasto: page 23 center

Christopher Groenhout/Lonely Planet Images: pages 206-207, 210-211

Franck Guiziou/Hemispheres-Images: pages 18 center right, 170 center, 171 bottom left, 171 bottom right, 172-173

Nick Gordon/Nature Picture Library: pages 290-291, 291 top

Chris Harvey/Ardea: page 120 bottom right

Jason Hawkes: pages 8-9, 12 right

J.D. Heaton/Agefotostock/Marka: pages 158-159

Brent Hedges/Nature Picture Library: page 210 bottom left

Hemispheres Collection: page 71 center

Thomas Hoepker/Magnum Photos/Contrasto: page 242 bottom left

Robert Holmes/Corbis/Contrasto: page 203 top

Ralph Lee Hopkins/Lonely Planet Images: pages 274-275

Jeremy Horner/Corbis/Contrasto: page 90 center

Manfred Horvath/Anzerberger/Contrasto: pages 68-69

ICP: pages 61 bottom, 72-73, 242 top, 166-167, 200 center left, 200 center right

Richard I'Anson/Lonely Planet Images: pages 205 bottom right, 274 bottom left, 275 center left

Rich Iwasaki/Corbis/Contrasto: pages 200-201

John/Elk II/Lonely Planet Images: pages 244-245

Peter Johnson/Corbis/Contrasto: pages 116-117, 116 bottom left, 116 bottom right

Dennis Jones/Lonely Planet Images: page 123 center left

Ray Juno/Corbis/Contrasto: page 260 bottom

Wolfgang Kaehler/Corbis/Contrasto: pages 184 center and bottom, 280 center

Richard Klune/Corbis/Contrasto: pages 230-231

Javier Larrea/Agefotostock/Marka: page 47

Tom & Pat Leeson/Ardea: page 250 bottom

Danny Lehman/Corbis/Contrasto: page 134

Charles & Josette Lenars/Corbis/Contrasto: page 182 bottom center

Christophe Lepetti/Hemispheres-Images: pages 170-171

George D. Lepp/Corbis/Contrasto: pages 226 top, 228 center, 229

Erich Lessing/Contrasto: page 49 center right

Diego Lezama Orezzoli/Corbis/Contrasto: pages 88 center left, 88 center right, 88-89, 205 bottom left

Marcello Libra/Archivio White Star: pages 66-67, 66 bottom right, 67 center left, center and right

Massimo Listri/Corbis/Contrasto: pages 28 bottom right, 29 top right, 29 center, 64 top

Christophe Lovini/Archivio White Star: pages 178-179

Jonio Machado/Agefotostock/Marka: page 289 center left

Maecke/Gaff/Laif/Contrasto: pages 62-63

Marka: page 69

Nigel Marven/Nature Picture Library: page 274 bottom right

Chris Mattison/Corbis/Contrasto: pages 226-227

Steve McCurry/Magnum/Contrasto: page 267 center

Gail Mooney/Masterfile/Sie: page 26 top

Bruno Morandi/Agefotostock/Marka: page 150 center left

Marco Moretti: page 151 bottom

Warren Morgan/Corbis/Contrasto: pages 162-163

Pat Morris/Ardea: page 291 bottom

David Muench/Corbis Contrasto: page 251 center

David Noton/Nature Picture Library: page 248 bottom right

Richard T. Nowitz/Corbis/Contrasto: page 258 bottom right

Pete Oxford/Nature Picture Library: page 277 bottom left

Vincenzo Paolillo: pages 132 top, 132 bottom right, 133 center

Partner fur Berlin/FTB-Werbefotografie: page 62 bottom left

Douglas Peeble/Corbis/Contrasto: pages 220-221

Doug Perrine/Nature Picture Library: pages 211 bottom, 277 bottom right

Pierre Pitrou/Photo12: page 6

Carmen Redondo/Corbis/Contrasto: pages 148-149

Frederic Reglain/Gamma/Contrasto: pages 30-31

Philippe Renault/Hemispherea-Images: pages 27 center left, 256 center left, 259 center

Roger Ressmeyer/Corbis/Contrasto: page 220 center

Bertrand Rieger/Hemispheres-Images: pages 22-23

Massimo Ripani/Sime/Sie: pages 15, 90-91

David Samuel Robbins/Corbis/Contrasto: page 184 center right

Royalty-Free/Corbis/Contrasto: page 13 center right

Jeff Rotman: pages 276 top, 276 center, 276-277

Galen Rowell/Corbis/Contrasto: pages 126 center, 156 center, 160 center, 248-249

Galen Rowell/Mountain Light: pages 160-161, 282-283, 283 bottom

Stephen Saks/Lonely Planet Images: page 212 center

Pete Salouتos/Corbis/Contrasto: pages 246-247

Kevin Schafer: pages 121 top, 290 bottom

Kevin Schafer/Corbis/Contrasto: pages 212-213, 281 bottom left

Alan Schein/Corbis Contrasto: page 267 bottom

Jose Schell/Nature Picture Library: page 251 top

Doug Scott/Agefotostock/Marka: page 202 bottom right

Sea Pics.com: pages 208 bottom left, 209 center right, 210 bottom right, 211 top, 218 center left, 221 bottom, 226 bottom left and right, 254 bottom left, 255 top

Ragnar Th. Sigurosson/Artic-Images: page 293 bottom left

Giovanni Simeone/Sime/Sie: pages 4, 12-13, 25, 82 top, 82 center, 82-83, 292-293

Henri and Anne Stierlin: pages 144 center, 155

SuperStock/Agefotostock/Marka: pages 202-203

Torleif Svensson/Corbis/Contrasto: page 292 bottom

Focus Team: pages 164-165

Luca I. Tettoni/Corbis/Contrasto: pages 174-175

The Bridgeman Art Library/Archivio Alinari: pages 30 bottom right, 49 center

Throstur Thordarson/Agefotostock/Marka: page 293 bottom right

Stefano Torrione/Hemispheres-Images: page 70 bottom left

Alessandro Vannini/Corbis/Contrasto: page 14 center left

Sandro Vannini/Corbis/Contrasto: pages 16 top left, 16 top right, 17 right

Giulio Veggi/Archivio White Star: pages 8 left and right, 9 center, 40 center, 41, 66 bottom left, 68 center, 81 center, 84 center left, 84-85, 85 bottom right, 86 bottom, 103 center left, 106-107, 110 center, 115 top right, 149 center

Vidler/Agefotostock/Marka: page 193 bottom left

Patrick Ward/Corbis/Contrasto: pages 16 center, 16-17

Jim Wark: pages 260-261, 262-263

Nik Wheeler/Corbis/Contrasto: page 257 bottom

Staffan Widstrand/Nature Picture Library: page 288 bottom left

Peter M. Wilson/Corbis/Contrasto: page 62 bottom right

Francesco Zanchi/Archivio White Star: pages 80 top, 83 bottom right

Angelo Colombo/Archivio White Star: pages 2-3, 9 top, 13 top, 14 top, 18 top, 24 top, 27 top, 31 top, 34 top, 39 top, 40 top, 42 top, 44 top, 49 top, 52 top, 58 top, 63 top, 67 top, 68 top, 71 top, 74 top, 77 top, 81 top, 84 top, 90, 95 top, 99 top, 103 top, 108 top, 113 top, 117 top, 118 top, 123 top, 125 top, 129 top, 131 top, 135 top, 136 top, 139 top, 142 top, 146 top, 150 top, 153 top, 156 top, 161 top, 162 top, 167 top, 170 top, 175 top, 179 top, 183 top, 186 top, 192 top, 198 top, 200 top, 204 top, 212 top, 214 top, 218 top, 223 top, 227 top, 230 top, 235 top, 238 top, 243 top, 249 top, 252 top, 256 top, 261 top, 262 top, 269 top, 271 top, 275 top, 279 top, 280 top, 282 top, 284 top, 289 top, 292 top, 295 top

*304 The shadows on the slopes of
the most spectacular section of
the Grand Canyon highlight the
extremely craggy configuration of*
*the land. The network of gorges created
by the Colorado River is so complex
that there are considerable climatic
differences at the various altitudes.*

© 2005 by White Star S.p.A.

This 2006 edition published by Barnes & Noble, Inc., by arrangement with
White Star S.p.A.

ISBN-13: 978-0-7607-8316-0
ISBN-10: 0-7607-8316-0

Library of Congress
Cataloging-in-Publication
Data available

Printed and bound in Thailand

1 3 5 7 9 10 8 6 4 2